AF622038

Bibliotheca Indo-Buddhica Series No. - 186

The Bodhisattva Doctrine in Buddhism

edited and introduced
by Leslie S. Kawamura

Bibliotheca Indo-Buddhica Series No. - 186

The Bodhisattva Doctrine in Buddhism

edited and introduced
by Leslie S. Kawamura

Sri Satguru Publications
A Division of
Indian Books Centre
Delhi, India

Published by :
Sri Satguru Publications
A Division of :
Indian Books Centre
Indological and Oriental Publishers
40/5, Shakti Nagar,
Delhi-110007
(INDIA)

© 1981 Corporation Canadienne des Sciences Religieuses/
Canadian Corporation for Studies in Religion

All rights reserved. No part of this work covered by the Copyrights hereon may be reproduced or copied in any form or by any means–Graphics, Electronics or Mechanical including photocopying, microfiche reading without written permission from the publishers.

ISBN 81-7030-563-2

First Indian Edition : Delhi, 1997

The publication of this book in India is made by permission of Wilfrid Laurier University Press.

Published by Sunil Gupta for Sri Satguru Publications a division of Indian Books Centre, 40/5, Shakti Nagar, Delhi-110 007, India and printed at Mudran Bharti, Delhi-110007

TABLE OF CONTENTS

PREFACE v

THE CONTRIBUTORS vii

INTRODUCTION xi

INAUGURAL ADDRESS

The Relevance of the Bodhisattva Concept for Today

Peter Slater 1

INDIA

The Evolution of the Concept of the Bodhisattva

Arthur L. Basham 19

The Bodhisattva Returns to This World

Gadjin M. Nagao 61

TIBET

Influence of the Bodhisattva Doctrine on Tibetan Political History

Turrell V. Wylie 81

The View of Bodhicitta in Tibetan Buddhism

Lobsang Dargyay 95

Bodhisattva - The Ethical Phase in Evolution

Herbert V. Guenther 111

CHINA

The Bodhisattva Idea in Chinese Literature: Typology and Significance

Yün-hua Jan 125

The Bodhisattva Concept: A Study of the Chinese Buddhist Canon

Lewis R. Lancaster 153

JAPAN

The Bodhisattva Doctrine as Conceived and Developed by the Founders of the New Sects in the Heian and Kamakura Periods

Hisao Inagaki 165

Japan's New Religions (1945-65): Secularization or Spiritualization?

Minoru Kiyota 193

The Myōkōnin: Japan's Representation of the Bodhisattva

Leslie S. Kawamura 223

INDEX 238

PREFACE

Despite a threatening Air Canada strike, nearly seventy registrants from places as far away as Australia, Hawaii, Japan, Austria, Thailand, and England gathered at The University of Calgary from September 18 to September 21, 1978. The occasion was the Calgary Buddhism Conference sponsored by the Religious Studies Department, Faculty of Humanities, The University of Calgary.

The purpose of the conference was to investigate the evolution of the Bodhisattva doctrine in the country of its origin and within countries to which Mahāyāna Buddhism has spread. The papers making up this volume were presented and discussed at the conference.

In addition to those who contributed to this volume, the conference benefitted from the presence of the following scholars who acted either as respondents or as chairpersons: Bernard Cooke, Holy Cross College, Worcester, Massachusetts (formerly of The University of Calgary); Narayan H. Samtani, Benares Hindu University (formerly of Chieng Mai University, Thailand); Keith Scott (formerly of the University of Saskatchewan, Saskatoon); Earl Waugh, University of Alberta; Kennard Lipman (presently studying under Lama Norbu, Formia, Italy); Harold Coward, Peter Craigie, Wayne McCready, Ronald Neufeldt, and Terrence Penelhum, University of Calgary.

The cost of hosting the conference was met through financial aid from the following agents and grants: Shastri Indo-Canadian Institute; Special Project Fund of the Vice-President (Academic), University of Calgary; University of Calgary Research Fund; ACAD Research Fund, University of Calgary; Canada Council Grant; Alberta Government Services; and the Office of the Dean of Humanities, University of Calgary.

The typing of the camera-ready copy of this manuscript was made possible through a grant from the Office of the Dean of Humanities. The publication of the volume has been made possible, in part, by a grant from the Endowment Fund of the University of Calgary.

As the co-ordinator and chairperson of the Conference and the editor of this volume, I would like to take this opportunity to thank the scholars who presented papers at the Conference and then prepared them for publication here; those who served as respondents and chairpersons; those who gave financial assistance for hosting the Conference and for publication of this volume; those who took the time and effort to travel great distances to attend the conference as registered participants; the Canadian Corporation for the Study of Religions for accepting this manuscript for publication in the SR Supplement Series; and, finally, the Wilfrid Laurier University Press for undertaking the work of copy editing and publication.

A special word of thanks is due to Joan Barton and Valerie Matwick, secretaries in the office of the Dean of Humanities, for their patience and dedication in typing the final camera-ready copy of this manuscript and to Kay Wong, a student in Buddhist Studies, for her long hours of dedicated hard work in compiling the index.

Time moves quickly and already more than two years have passed since the Conference. I am pleased to be able to present this volume, late as it is, to all whose interest may carry them to the Bodhisattva Doctrine in Buddhism.

Leslie S. Kawamura
Religious Studies Department
Faculty of Humanities
The University of Calgary
Calgary, Alberta

January 1981.

THE CONTRIBUTORS

ARTHUR LLEWELLYN BASHAM, now retired, was until the end of 1979 Professor and Head of the Department of Asian Civilizations, The Australian National University, Canberra. He has received such honours as the Biennial Dr. B.C. Law Gold Medal for Indology from the Asiatic Society, Calcutta (1975) and the D. Litt. degree (London) in the History of South Asia (1966) and honorary doctorates from the University of Kurakshetra and the Nava Nalanda Mahavihara, India (1977). He is the author of *History and Doctrine of the Ajivikas* (1952), *The Wonder that was India* (1954), some fifty articles and many reviews in numerous periodicals, and Forewords/Introductions to many books. He has been a visiting professor of many universities in England, Ceylon, the U.S.A, Mexico, India, Argentina, and Canada. He received his Ph.D. from the University of London, England in 1951 in Indian History.

LOBSANG DARGYAY is presently a University Assistant at the Institute of Tibetology and Buddhist Studies, University of Vienna (Austria), and a Lecturer for Tibetan Language. He earned his Geshay with first-class honours (1958) and his doctor philosophiae cum laude from the Ludwig-Maximilian University, Munich, in 1974. He has lectured at Punjab University, Pattiala, for the Kalmuk community of Western Germany, and has been research fellow at the Institute of Indology, Munich University.

HERBERT V. GUENTHER is Professor and Head, Far Eastern Studies Department, University of Saskatchewan, Saskatoon. He studied in Munich, Vienna, India, and Tibet and has taught at Vienna University, Lucknow University, the Sanskrit University, and the International School of America. He has authored some 20 books among which are *Das Seelenproblem im älteren Buddhismus*, *The Royal Song of Saraha*, *The Life and Teaching of Naropa*, *The Jewel Ornament of Liberation*, *The Tantric View of Life*, and *Kindly Bent to Ease Us*, Parts I, II, and III. He has written some seventy articles and many reviews in various journals. He holds the Ph.D. (Munich, 1939) and the Dr. Phil. Habil. (Vienna, 1943).

HISAO INAGAKI is Lecturer in Far Eastern Buddhism at the School of Oriental and African Studies, University of London, England. He was awarded the British Council Scholarship for post-graduate studies (1966-68) after completing his course work in the doctorate programme in Shin Buddhism at Ryukoku University, Kyoto (1960). Among his publications are "Sokushinjōbutsugi, translation and annotations," *Asia Major* (1972) and *An Index to the Tibetan Version of the Larger Sukhāvatīvyūha Sūtra* (1978). He received his Ph.D. from the University of London, England, in 1968.

YÜN-HUA JAN is Professor of Religion, Department of Religious Studies, McMaster University, Hamilton. He has received a Canada Council Fellowship (1973-74) and has lectured in Chinese Studies at Visva-Bharati University, India. He has been a visiting researcher at the Institute of Oriental Culture, University of Tokyo (1974). He is the author of *A Chronicle of Buddhism in China 581-906 A.D.* (1967) and has ready for publication *The Autobiography of Ch'i Pai-shih*. He has contributed many articles written in Chinese and English to various journals. He received his Ph.D. from the Visva-Bharati University, India.

LESLIE S. KAWAMURA is Associate Professor, Religious Studies Department, University of Calgary, Alberta. He has authored, co-authored or edited six books among which are *Golden Zephyr* (1975), *Mind in Buddhist Psychology* (1975), and *Buddhist Thought and Asian Civilization: Essays in Honor of Herbert V. Guenther on His Sixtieth Birthday* (1977). He has contributed articles to several books and journals, has been a recipient of several scholarships and grants, and was awarded the Calgary Institute for the Humanities Fellowship (1977-78). He received his Ph.D. from the University of Saskatchewan, Saskatoon, in 1976.

MINORU KIYOTA is Professor, Department of South Asian Studies and the Department of East Asian Languages and Literature, University of Wisconsin-Madison. Among his publications are "Yogācāra Impact on Pure Land" (1974), "Buddhism and Social Change in Southeast Asia" (1978), *Shingon Buddhism: Theory and Practice* (1978). He received his Ph.D. from Tokyo University, Japan, in 1963.

LEWIS R. LANCASTER is Chairman of the Department of Oriental Languages, University of California, Berkeley. Among his publications are "Story of a Buddhist Hero," *Tsung-hua Journal of Chinese Studies*, X:2 (July, 1974), "An Early Mahāyāna Sermon about the Body of the Buddha and the Making of Images," *Artibus Asiae*, Vol. 36 (Switzerland, 1974), "The Oldest Mahāyāna Sūtra: Its Significance for the Study of Buddhist Development," *The Eastern Buddhist*, New Series, Vol. VIII, No. 1 (May, 1975). "The Editing of Buddhist Texts," L.S. Kawamura and Keith Scott (ed.), *Buddhist Thought and Asian Civilization* (1977). He is the editor of *Prajñāpāramitā and Related Systems: Studies in Honor of Edward Conze*, Berkeley Buddhist Series, Vol. 1 (1978) and is the compiler of *The Korean Buddhist Canon: A Descriptive Catalog* (1978). He received his Ph.D. from the University of Wisconsin-Madison.

GADJIN M. NAGAO is Professor Emeritus, Kyoto University. He has been awarded the Japan Academy Prize (1959) for research contribution to Chu-yung-kuan. He is the author of various books including *Mōko Gakumonji*, *Chibetto Bukkyō Kenkyū*, *Chūkan to Yuishiki*, *The Ancient Buddhist Community and its Cultural Activities*, *Index to the Mahāyānasūtralamkāra* (2 vols.), has edited the Sanskrit manuscript of Vasubandhu's *Madhyāntavibhāga-Bhāṣya*, served as editor for many works such as *Daijō Butten* (in 15 vols. 1973-76) and has written many articles on the Mādhyamika and Yogācāra schools of Buddhism. He has taught in many universities throughout Japan and has been a Brittingham Professor, University of Wisconsin-Madison (1965-66) and will be a Killam Visiting Scholar to the University of Calgary (1982). He has travelled extensively throughout India, Ceylon, Nepal, Burma, Thailand, and China. His D. Litt. degree was conferred upon him by Kyoto Imperial University in 1950.

PETER SLATER is Professor of Religion and Chairman of the Department, Carleton University, Ottawa. He has served as Chairperson of the Philosophy of Religion and Theology Section of the American Academy of Religion and as President of the Canadian Society for the Study of Religion/La Société Canadienne pour l'Étude de la Religion. He has edited *Religion and Culture in Canada/Religion et Culture au Canada* (1977), and is the author of *The Dynamics of Religion: Meaning and Change in Religious Traditions* (1978). He received his Ph.D. from Harvard University in 1964 with distinctions in Buddhism and Philosophy of Religion.

TURRELL V. WYLIE is Professor, Department of Asian Languages and Literature, University of Washington, Seattle. He has been awarded a Ford Foundation Fellowship (1955-57) for study in Italy and India and an ACLS Fellowship, Rome, Italy (1973-74). He is the author of *The Geography of Tibet According to the 'Dzam-gling-rgyas-bshad* (Serie Orientale Roma, 1962) and devised the Turrell Wylie system of romanizing the Tibetan alphabet. He has contributed many articles to numerous journals including "Tibet: A Study in Chinese Chauvinism" (1976), "The Tibetan Tradition of Geography" (1965), "Tibetan Passports: Their Function and Significance" (1968) and others. He received his Ph.D. from the University of Washington in 1958.

INTRODUCTION

Har Dayal's *The Bodhisattva Doctrine in Buddhist Sanskrit Literature* published in 1931 was the first extensive study in English of the Bodhisattva doctrine. Dayal discussed the Bodhisattva doctrine as it was expounded in the Buddhist Sanskrit texts, and it remains a question whether anything more can be added to his excellent study. However, no other book on the doctrine has appeared in English subsequent to Dayal's study, and Buddhist scholarship, having expanded beyond the boundaries of the Sanskrit language, must now take into account information found not only in the Sanskrit language but also in other languages fundamental to Buddhist studies. In order to investigate what current research in Sanskrit, Tibetan, Chinese, and Japanese materials could contribute to the study of the Bodhisattva doctrine, the Department of Religious Studies at the University of Calgary planned a conference around the theme of the Bodhisattva. The papers presented in this volume were first read and discussed at the conference.

With the exception of the opening address by Peter Slater, the papers have been arranged here according to the country represented by the major language in which the research was done. Thus the division India, for example, pre-supposes that Sanskrit is the language fundamental to the study of the Bodhisattva doctrine in that country. Though convenient, such groupings of the essays, it should be noted, are somewhat arbitrary since Buddhist studies in general and a study of the Bodhisattva doctrine in particular cannot be accomplished without the use of another (or other) language(s).

The papers speak best for themselves; however, some introductory remarks may be in order to highlight some of the issues raised in the essays. In his "The Relevance of the Bodhisattva Concept for Today," Peter Slater draws our attention to the importance of recognizing that, in the study of religion, meaning and value in life are not communicated by abstract creeds and philosophical speculations, but are typically expressed through stories which may be viewed from several different perspectives. These perspectives allow the reader to seek out the underlying intention of a story. Story in Buddhism, Slater suggests, is intended to quicken progress along the path of ultimate joy. The Bodhisattva's vow, the Buddha's compassion and wisdom which the vow exemplifies, and the conviction that a Buddha is not merely a figure of the past but is one who is actively involved with humanity now are all foci of the intention behind stories found in Buddhist literature. Slater's suggestion that the Bodhisattva doctrine may function as a possible corrective for the current Western religious preoccupation with individual striving as the ultimate foundation for philosophy and religion holds true, it seems, just as much for the study of religions in the East.

In his paper, "The Evolution of the Concept of the Bodhisattva," A.L. Basham traces the development of the Bodhisattva ideal and the vows or resolves accompanying it.

Whereas for the Theravāda tradition, the term *bodhisatta* applies to the previous lives of Siddhattha Gotama as recorded in the *Jātakas*, for the Mahāyānic tradition the term *bodhisattva* refers to those who are constantly active in the service of all beings.

According to Basham, the Theravāda Bodhisatta, in its inception, was probably developed within a purely Buddhist framework, without influence from outside. However, where similarities to Hinduism and Zoroastrianism are too numerous and too close to be fortuitous, he suggests that, in most cases, the similarities are due to a common source in the Middle East.

The Mahāyāna Bodhisattva derives from belief in future Buddhas, the foremost of whom is Metteyya as prophesied by the Buddha himself. The Mahāyāna Bodhisattva, whose goal is full enlightenment, not nirvāṇa, had been forecast in the Rock Edicts of Asoka several centuries before the accepted period of Mahāyāna developments in India. In any event, once the doctrine of future Buddhas became accepted,

Basham argues, the way was open for faith in Bodhisattvas.

On the basis of such materials as the images of princely beings found in Gandharan and Mathuran art, the inscriptions of the Taxila silver scroll and on images from Sarnath, the longer *Sukhāvatīvyūha*, and the twenty-fourth chapter of the *Saddharmapuṇḍarīka*, Basham suggests that the Bodhisattva doctrine was in full force in at least some Buddhist circles by the first century of the Christian era at the latest. He also shows how the development of the heavenly Bodhisattva influenced changes in the view of the transfer of merits which was widespread as early as the beginning of the Christian era. A thorough investigation of various dedicatory inscriptions of North-western India and the Ganga Valley, the Mathura lion capital, and Taxila Copper plate, and an inscription on a Buddha image from Mathura suggests a northern origin for the belief in heavenly Bodhisattvas, the transfer of merit, and for Mahāyāna Buddhism in general.

In "The Bodhisattva Returns to This World," G.M. Nagao focuses his discussion on two kinds of Bodhisattva activities: the Bodhisattva's ascent from the world of sentient beings to the world of enlightened ones owing to *prajñā*, and the Bodhisattva's descent from the state of Buddhahood to the world of sentient beings owing to *karuṇā*. In support of his thesis, Nagao discusses the difference between the Nirvāṇa of an Arhat and the Nirvāṇa of the Bodhisattva. He points out that a Bodhisattva's Nirvāṇa is distinguished from that of an Arhat in that the former one is *apratiṣṭhita* (non-dwelling) nirvāṇa. This means that a Bodhisattva descends to the level of sentient beings because he is compassionate and does not cling to nirvāṇa (i.e., he does not dwell in nirvāṇa). Moreover, this means that a Bodhisattva, because of his wisdom, is not afflicted by the faults of saṁsāra (i.e., he does not dwell in saṁsāra).

Being neither attached to Nirvāṇa nor afflicted by the faults of saṁsāra, a Bodhisattva willingly returns to this world. This willingness to return is technically termed *saṁcintya-bhavopapatti*, a term that is encountered most frequently in the *Mahāyāna-sūtrālaṁkāra*. The Bodhisattva's willingness to return to this world is contextually related to the four kinds of causes for birth, and because a Bodhisattva's birth into saṁsāra is voluntary, it is both miraculous and paradoxical. Saṁsāra is no longer a burden, but birth therein is like taking a stroll through a joyful garden.

In the early introduction of Buddhism into Tibet, the Bodhisattva doctrine helped to transform the religious culture of Tibet from Shamanism to Buddhism. In his paper, "Influence of the Bodhisattva Doctrine on Tibetan Political History," Turrell Wylie notes that when Buddhism was introduced into Tibet, it did not spread widely to the people nor was accepted by the court without conflict. Wylie argues that in view of the political implications inherent in the iconoclastic Ch'an Buddhism (re: bSam-yas debate), it is not surprising that the Indian school received royal sanction. There occurs a hiatus in the information concerning central Tibet where Buddhism died out and Wylie attributes that to having its basis in the biased *chos-'byung* literature that ignores central Tibet.

The Bodhisattva doctrine encouraged the unique concept of "reincarnation" (*yang-srid*) that served to transform Tibetan politics from a hierocracy (charisma of person) into a theocracy (charisma of office). Not long after the concept of "reincarnation" surfaced in Tibet, the reformation movement of Tsong-kha-pa (Yellow-hat sect) patronized by Phag-mo-gru surfaced. Its opponents, the Lords of Gtsang, were patronized by the Karma-pa hierarchs (Red-hat sect). Thus, Tibet, hitherto politically united, moved toward a viable separation of church and state.

The third Dalai Lama, facing harassment from his Gtsang adversaries, travelled to Mongolia where he died. His "reincarnation" was discovered in the great-grandson of Altan Khan who was then installed in Lhasa as the hierarch of the Yellow-hat sect. The sect continued to grow in strength until, with the aid of the Mongols, the fifth Dalai Lama defeated his enemies and was made both spiritual and temporal head of Tibet. Wylie argues that one of the factors responsible for the continuous unity of church and state in the hands of successive Dalai Lamas was the Bodhisattva doctrine.

However, the Bodhisattva doctrine in Tibet was not only politically oriented. In "The View of Bodhicitta in Tibetan Buddhism," L. Dargyay demonstrates the range of the discussion on *bodhicitta* found in both Indian and Tibetan traditions. According to Dargyay, both *bodhi-praṇidhi-citta* and *bodhi-prasthāna-citta* underlie the structure of *bodhi-citta*. Citing passages from the Tibetan commentaries on the *Abhisamayālaṃkāra* by Tsong-kha-pa and Mi-pham, Dargyay explains their distinction as follows:

a) *bodhi-praṇidhi-citta* is the wishful aspiration for enlightenment;

b) *bodhi-prasthāna-citta* is the active realization of this aspiration for enlightenment.

In discussing *bodhi-citta* as it prevails in Tantric literature, Dargyay points out that the problem there is one of determining whether *bodhi-citta* is *citta* (mind as such) or *caitta* (a mental attitude or wish). There have been two opposing views on this problem held by Tibetan scholars, and Dargyay concludes that the valid view is based upon the thought of Haribhadra and his disciples -- *viz.*, the lucid, motionless, merely perceiving mind (*citta*) becomes elevated owing to a wish (*caitta*) that brings about a change in the Bodhisattva's personality.

This change in personality is a specific spiritual operation which, in his paper "Bodhisattva - The Ethical Phase in Evolution," H.G. Guenther argues to be what the Tibetans meant to express when they rendered the Indian term *bodhisattva* into the Tibetan *byang-chub sems-dpa'*. Thus, *bodhisattva* being a descriptive term for a qualitative process, it does not designate a static or concrete person. In defence of this thesis, Guenther introduces various indigenous Tibetan works from among which he concludes that Vairocana's version of the *bDe-ba chen-po byang-chub-kyi rmad-du byuṅg-ba'i le'u* is the earliest source for the term. As a stage in the evolutionary process, *byang-chub sems-dpa'* establishes a feedback line by which communication between the "I" and the "other" is established. In such communicative systems, Guenther argues, individual ethics gives way to ethics of whole systems - i.e., to ethics grounded in and leading to freedom.

It is perhaps in China that the Bodhisattva doctrine played a much larger and more important role than its narrow philosophical discussions may imply. Proceeding from this assumption, Y-h. Jan discusses "The Bodhisattva Idea in Chinese Literature: Typology and Significance." Jan introduces three typologies, the first of which is made up of the Chinese translations of the Buddha's birth stories (*jātaka*). These stories depict the Bodhisattva as a perfect Being of wisdom and compassion whose virtue is cosmological in dimension. Here the Bodhisattva is powerful and ready to sacrifice his own life for the benefit of others. In comparing the images of such a bodhisattva depicted in the birth stories with the ancient Chinese characterizations of the early sage kings, such as Emperor Yao and Shun, Jan argues that despite the great contributions that these sage kings made to Chinese civilization, theirs were not seen as lively, concrete, cosmological, and personal as the acts of the Bodhisattva described in the Chinese translations of the birth stories.

In typology two, the Bodhisattva ideal is described in terms of a spiritual goal attainable by any serious religious person, provided that the precept of spiritual cultivation is taken seriously. From a soteriological viewpoint, this spirit of attainability is most meaningful to a person who is suffering and wishes release from it. Jan regards the *Shih-ti ching* (十地經) as the most systematic account of the idea of attainability through religious practices and shows how the systems of the spiritual stages have undergone evolution not only in the manner in which they were understood by the Chinese but also in the way they developed in India. Although the various Chinese renderings of the *Shih-ti ching* may differ, Jan convincingly shows that the intentions are the same: i.e., the religious goal is attainable by religious practices. This presentation of a concrete, detailed spiritual map to the Chinese was an influential factor in converting the Chinese to Buddhism and in forcing other Chinese philosophies to redirect, rediscover, and revitalize their tradition.

It was, however, the literature of the third type that had the greatest impact on the Chinese masses. In this literature that influenced the establishing of festivals, rites, and places of worship for the celestial Bodhisattvas, the Bodhisattva is described as a celestial being who is compassionate, powerful, and responsive to personal requests. Foremost among these Bodhisattvas was Küan-yin (觀音) whose position of high honour among the Chinese is documented by such materials as Chinese Buddhist sūtras, statements of testimony, gazeteers of the places of pilgrimage in honour of the Bodhisattva, and scroll literature. This third type which gave Chinese society a clearcut concept of a personal deity for the first time offered the Chinese masses real hope for salvation. It offered compassion to those who were distressed and it showed a great willingness on the part of the Bodhisattva to help people. So strong was the influence of the Küan-yin worship on the Chinese that the image of the helpful and compassionate being is depicted in popular operas performed in the present century.

But how did the Bodhisattva concept change from the model found in the birth stories to the celestial beings who were prepared to help those in need? L. Lancaster assumes that the Chinese Buddhist canon reflects Buddhist developments in India and also provides information on how the Chinese handled the development of ideas. In his paper, "The Bodhisattva Concept: A Study of the Chinese Buddhist Canon," Lancaster focuses on four major models of the Bodhisattva concept. According to him, it was the *Jātaka* Bodhisattva model to which the Chinese were first introduced, but as they received other texts from India, these *Jātaka* Bodhisattvas were gradually transformed into "Phantasma Bodhisattvas" who were removed from the ordinary process of birth and death and manifested a pattern of existence comparable to the docetic tradition of religions in West Asia.

In addition to the "Phantasma Bodhisattvas," early Māhāyana texts included numerous names of Bodhisattvas who were listed as members of an audience gathered to hear the sermon of the Buddha. These "Audience Bodhisattvas," about which not much more is known, are derived from names of meditations. The tantric texts, which had less of an effect on Chinese Buddhism than on Tibetan Buddhism, account for "Meditation Bodhisattvas," so-called because they appear only in the mind of a meditator. Finally, there are those that Lancaster designates as "Living Bodhisattvas." Originating in Chinese Buddhism but later adopted by Japanese Buddhism, these "Living Bodhisattvas" are beings that future generations recognized as Bodhisattvas.

These numerous models of the Bodhisattva brought controversy into Chinese society, but what stands out in the discussion of the Bodhisattva ideal in China is that the Bodhisattva doctrine did not split the Chinese Buddhists into camps based upon docetistic attitudes.

It was monks such as Kūkai and Saichō who ventured to China and brought back to Japan the forms of Mahayana Buddhism that were prevalent at the time. However, the lofty Bodhisattva ideal held by them faced collapse in the Kamakura period.

In his paper, "The Bodhisattva Doctrine as Conceived and Developed by the Founders of the New Sects in the Heian and Kamakura Periods," H. Inagaki discusses how the degenerating *mappō* era, the *ekayāna* idea, and the *hongaku* theory influenced the development of the Bodhisattva concept in the Zen sects of Eisai and Dōgen, in the Pure Land sect of Hōnen and Shinran, and in the Nichiren sect of Nichiren.

Although Saichō believed that the degenerate *mappō* era made it difficult for priests and nuns to observe the precepts, Kūkai thought that people could and should abide by them nonetheless. Of the new sects that developed, the Pure Land masters of the Kamakura period abandoned any hope of attaining enlightenment through the practice of the Bodhisattva precepts and showed that only the Pure Land teaching was practicable. Zen masters were strict in observing the precepts themselves and urged all people to do the same. Nichiren considered the degenerate era an ideal time to recite the *Daimoku*.

For the Japanese Mahāyāna sects established after the Heian period, it was the *ekayāna* idea rather than the Bodhisattva ideal that was emphasized. The emphasis of *ekayāna* was the quick attainment of Buddahood. Although the *Saddharmapuṇḍarīkasūtra* is the most popular scripture that expounds the *ekayāna* idea, it was the *ekayāna* idea upheld by the Kegon school that gave birth to the two *ekayāna* schools of the Heian period. However, the drastic transforming agent of the traditional Bodhisattva theory was the *hongaku* theory, because according to the *hongaku* theory a being is enlightened from the very beginning and Buddahood is not a final goal but a reality to be experienced here and now. Inagaki concludes that the Bodhisattva path that employed the *mappō*, *ekayāna*, and *hongaku* theory and was followed by the founders of the new sects reflected a vibrant, living form of Buddhism.

The Pure Land sects, the Zen sects, and the Nichiren sects continued their influence into the modern period, but it was what Kiyota refers to as the "New Religions" that posed a challenge to the established schools of Buddhism. In his paper, "Japan's New Religions (1945-65): Secularization or Spiritualization?" Kiyota discusses how the new religions that articulated the traditional Bodhisattva principle represent a mass movement directed against the established religions. At issue, he says, is not whether the Bodhisattva doctrine underlies the new religions, but rather, whether the doctrine has secularized the *sangha* or spiritualized the laity.

The new religions originated in the confusion following the surrender in 1945. Some of the seeds of violent revolution that were brewing sprouted into the new religious movements. They achieved political power in the context of the left-wing activity that was a reaction to Communist and Socialist doctrine. Among the "new religions," those derived from the Nichiren sect made remarkable progress both in numbers and in political power. The followers of these sects came to number about the same as adherents of the traditional Buddhist sects. Soka Gakkai, for example, grew from 439,000 adherents in 1950 to 15,234,136 in 1964.

Kiyota gives the background on the origins and development of Sōka Gakkai, explains key Sōka Gakkai terms such as *daimoku* and *shakubuku*, and elucidates how the Sōka Gakkai is structured along military lines. Kōmeitō, the political arm of Sōka Gakkai, won twenty-five seats in the Upper House of the Diet in the 1967 election and thus became the third power in the political arena of Japan.

Alongside these developments, established schools of Buddhism lost their attraction, especially among the younger people, because Buddhist parish temples were not implanting spiritual experiences into the religious behavior of the average Japanese. They continued to be very formal and ritualized. Kiyota suggests that, although the new religions pose a challenge to established schools of Buddhism, they do not intend to replace them.

Although the traditional Pure Land masters of the Kamakura period abandoned any hope of attaining enlightenment through the practice of the Bodhisattva precepts, the highly developed *Nembutsu* practitioners of the Pure Land sect displayed activities that could be classified as activities of a "living Bodhisattva." L. Kawamura, in his paper "The Myōkōnin, Japan's Representation of the Bodhisattva," sketches the historical problems involved in compiling the *Myōkōninden* or the biography of wonderful *Nembutsu* practitioners. He traces the term *"myōkōnin"* back to Shan Tao's commentary on the *Meditation Sūtra* and then discusses how the *myōkōnin* Seikuro's life characterized by a feeling of joy, gratitude, and unworthiness conveys the Bodhisattva's attitude of wisdom and compassion. By explaining various incidents in this rare and wonderful *Nembutsu* practitioner's life, Kawamura shows how Seikuro's life reflects a life in which the Bodhisattva's six perfections are put into practice. Thus, in spite of the fact that, traditionally, the Pure Land sect does not claim that its adherents can attain enlightenment by the practice of precepts, the fully developed *Nembutsu* practitioner in going through life with a feeling of joy, gratitude, and unworthiness strolls through saṁsāra as if strolling through a joyful garden and thereby displays a life of putting the Bodhisattva's six perfections into practice.

The papers presented at this conference show the extent and depth of the Bodhisattva concept. Although it is impossible to cover all of the issues involved in this concept, the papers here have given a picture of the Bodhisattva doctrine as it evolved from the birth stories in early Buddhism to living Bodhisattvas in later periods within the countries in which it flourished. There are, I am certain, many aspects of the doctrine that have been overlooked, but it is the hope of the present editor that this volume will inspire further studies and conferences on the Bodhisattva doctrine in Buddhism.

THE RELEVANCE OF THE BODHISATTVA CONCEPT FOR TODAY

Peter Slater

Not long ago I met a Catholic nun whose name is Sister Irma. It's not a name that I would have chosen for anyone and I gathered that she herself had originally proposed three different names. But the Sister Irma in her convent had recently died and her Mother Superior felt that "it was time we had another one." When it was discovered that the new sister had had an aunt called Sister Irma, the matter was settled. By the time we talked the new Sister Irma clearly had accepted her name and the tradition that went with it. Her appearance was far from traditional. I am old enough to remember nuns as creatures dressed mostly in black. They used always to travel in pairs and, as boys, we used to make a game of darting between them as they walked down the street. But this sister wears ordinary street clothes and is at ease when alone in the workaday world. She is not what might be expected if we knew only her predecessors. Yet as superintendent of a Catholic school system she too is on the path to sainthood. If she were a Buddhist, we might say that she is on the way to becoming a bodhisattva.

The concept of the bodhisattva has to do with the finest title and noblest role to which any Buddhist can aspire. Just what 'bodhisattva' means in the various languages of Buddhist cultures is something that we shall learn as our discussions proceed. But essential to the concept is the state of being enlightened. This state is the condition of our release from a seemingly endless spiral of fears, cravings, immature attachments and distorted perceptions of who we really are and where our true happiness lies. More particularly, one is called a bodhisattva whose existence is permeated with the power of ultimate truth, but who postpones the freedom from suffering that this entails, in order to help others to realize the same state of unqualified joy. A bodhisattva is one who will certainly become a Buddha — an Enlightened One — and as such will enter whatever state follows from the cessation of our need-driven conflicts. But, before this, he or she turns back to help all who are still caught in more repressive patterns of behaviour.

The Buddhist conviction is that, as long as there is suffering in this world, we may look for a succession of bodhisattvas coming to the aid of their fellow-creatures.

The idea of successive Sister Irmas, or of a series of bodhisattvas, is one which may seem strange to those of us who are Protestants. But if we look to our own roots in the villages and towns from which we came, we find similar patterns. The roles of preacher, storekeeper, farmer, schoolmistress and the rest were passed from uncle to nephew, from mother to daughter, as each new generation's needs were met by each new generation's active citizens. Many of us today were met by each new generation's active citizens. Many of us today are living examples of this process. So also it has been in the countries where the group of traditions called Buddhism has flourished. Whether in India, where the present movement began 2500 years ago, with Gautama's Enlightenment under the Bodhi Tree, or in Thailand or Japan, or now in North America, among followers of the Buddha's "Middle" Path, families and roles have come together to sustain a vision of life beyond suffering, life free from ignorance, that is truly enlightened or "Buddhist."

The sense of family here is an extended one, not just from immediate relatives to a whole village, but from the blood-ties of present kin to spiritual ties embracing all creatures. In Buddhism, "family" loyalty embraces every mammal, bird, fish and insect with which we share this world. The object of the Buddha's concern is every living thing in every phase of its existence. The scope of the Buddha's community is truly universal.

When we think of patterns of behaviour carried over from one generation to the next, with far-reaching consequences, we most easily think of diseases and wars, not of lasting bliss. We can think, for instance, of Arabs and Israelis on the borders of Lebanon, Catholics and Protestants in the suburbs of Belfast, Vietnamese and Chinese in the cantons around Hanoi, Muslims and Christians in Nigeria or Uganda, Quebecois and Anglophones in the Ottawa valley, or our own native peoples and European immigrants in the West and North of Canada. Wherever we look, the natural scenery is marvelous. But the social prospect is grim. In this context, the Buddhist vision of ultimate wisdom and joy in all creatures gives us a rare opportunity to hear good news. It is a religious vision in that it sees not only the extent of our present misery but also the prospect of our eventual wellbeing. It is a missionary vision in that it actively reaches out to all who know that misery but have yet to hear the promise found in ultimate wisdom. It is a true vision in that it has stood the tests of time and transfer across major civilizations. We shall do well to heed what the experts have to tell us of this good news, in the papers which are to follow.

Central to the Buddhist vision of the end to suffering is the concept of the bodhisattva. This is not always obvious. When they read some of the legends of bodhisattvas handed on by earlier generations, even traditional Buddhist scholars say that these contain more fancy than fact. But in religious studies today we recognize that meaning and value in life are not generally communicated by abstract creeds and philosophical speculations. They are typically expressed through stories which may be viewed from several different perspectives. Some of the greatest stories concern the exploits of bodhisattvas. Instead of asking what language-games ancient sages played with such stories, we look for their religious point, their saving truth, as told in context.[2] We do not suppose that there is some single, ideal picture of what a Buddha or future Buddha is "really" like, for example, and then rank Buddhist stories according to which one gives us the most "accurate" portrait. Rather we recognize that each story has its point and that what it points us to goes beyond anything that we can capture in a single word-picture.

Consider, for example, the opening chapter of the *Vimalakīrti Nirdeśa Sūtra*, the famous Mahāyāna account of a lay bodhisattva.[3] It portrays the Buddha addressing his followers in a park at Vaiśālī. But instead of a handful of monks, these number over eight thousand. Also in attendance is a heavenly gallery of thirty-two thousand resplendent bodhisattvas, comparable to choruses of angels in Western literature. The talk is of the purity of the Buddha's domain, where saving truth is always heard and immediately understood. Śāriputra, one of the earliest disciples, wonders about the relationship between this apparition of a heavenly preacher and the historical Gautama, who won through to enlightenment despite the distractions of our everyday world. How could Gautama have inhabited such an "impure" spot, when these bodhisattvas enjoyed such a pure land? As a future Buddha, was he not also a bodhisattva?

The Buddha replies that whether a place is pure or impure depends upon the one who sees it as such, not on the place itself. From one point of view, we are, this very minute, sitting in heaven hearing of saving truth in words which reverberate across the mountains like a lion's roar. But to ordinary eyes, clouded by other concerns, we are in no such setting. How we see the Buddha at any given time depends on our need and the Buddha's skill in communication. This is as various as his audience. In any case, the crux of his teaching does not lie in the fabulous settings provided for him by medieval missionary authors.

What are we to make of this Sūtra today? On one level, we can read it as an internal Buddhist argument over who the "real" Buddha is. The Mahāyāna author is rebutting criticism by Theravāda or traditional followers of the historical Buddha, to the effect that later stories of the Buddha's "Pure Land" are fabricated by people too lazy to work out their own salvation.[4] He counterattacks by putting superior wisdom in the mouth of a layman, to the discomfort of both monks and heavenly bodhisattvas. But, on another level, what we perceive is the "halo" effect, so to speak, resulting from interaction between the same Buddha and his audience in a different epoch. Just as some who heard Jesus saw in him the Messiah, so some who heard Gautama saw in him the Buddha. Just as some who sang the praises of the Messiah pictured him as a heavenly king, despite his crucifixion, so some who sang the praises of the Buddha pictured him as a heavenly teacher, despite his earthly death near Benares. The point, in either case, is not to dwell on the details of some heaven to which we may go after death. It is to underline the cosmic scope of the saving power which even now touches our imaginations. Whether the setting is supernatural and extravagant or mundane and prosaic, the underlying intention of each version of the Buddha story is to quicken our progress along the path to ultimate joy.

If the impact of the Buddha's preaching depends not only on his enlightening presence but also on the nature of his audience, then we must understand that preaching for ourselves partly by considering our readiness to receive it. With reference to the stories of earthly and heavenly bodhisattvas, we have to ask what in these speaks to our condition. In the remainder of this paper I want briefly to draw attention to four facets of the bodhisattva conception, of which we shall be receiving detailed analysis in the papers to follow. These are the bodhisattva's vow to save all suffering creatures, the compassion and wisdom of the Buddha which this vow exemplifies, and the conviction, in all schools of Buddhist thought, that the Buddha is not just a figure from the past but also one who is coming towards us, as part of our future, in the form of the bodhisattva Maitreya.

Consider first a bodhisattva's original "vow." The immense task of coping with all the suffering in this universe calls for an equally immense countereffort. We as individuals caught in the web of worldly feuding are incapable of such effort. Our will is sapped by the seeming futility of even our best work. But over the centuries, according to Buddhist tradition, different bodhisattvas have formed the resolve to outweigh by their good deeds all the evils which depress the scales of life's fortunes for the rest of us. The scope of this aspiration is expressed by the following statement from Śāntideva (*Bodhicaryāvatara*, iii, 6-19):

> May I be the protector of the helpless!
> May I be the guide of wayfarers! May I be like a boat, a bridge, a causeway for all who wish to cross [a stream]! May I be a lamp for all who need a lamp! May I be a slave for all who want

> a slave! May I be for all creatures a philosopher's stone (*cintāmaṇi*) and a pot of fortune (*bhadraghata*), even like unto an efficacious rite of worship and a potent medicinal herb! May I be for them a *kalpa-vṛkṣa* (a wish-fulfilling tree) and a *kāma-dhenu* (cow yielding all that one desires)![5]

To achieve their aims bodhisattva-animals hurled themselves from cliffs, in order to become meat for starving tigers below. Bodhisattva-husbands gave even their wives and children to complete strangers. Bodhisattva-spirits appeared to travelers lost in the dark. And so the stories go.

The tone of these stories is devotional. The setting is often bizarre. But the characters are consistently humane and the plot is directed towards the welfare of others. Collectively, they bring to our attention something which modern commentators on human behaviour tend to neglect. Ethicists, for example, talk of abstract moral laws and individual actions, for the most part, in isolation. They debate whether it is ever right to lie, to have an abortion and so on. They do not look at *patterns* of behaviour, at *habits* of thought developed over long periods, which condition our immediate responses in moments of crisis. Yet what our society needs is not a set of rules, formed without regard for changing circumstances, or a series of *ad hoc* decisions, taken without regard for lasting consequences. What is needed is precisely that constantly reinforced impulse towards saving ourselves and others which defines the transformation of an ordinary moral agent into a bodhisattva.

According to all the Buddhist stories, people do not become bodhisattvas overnight. Enlightening teachers do not become such without prior preparation. The concept of those becoming Buddhas is one of sustained, consistent moral development, based on steadfast commitment. It pertains neither to a reactionary insistence on always doing the "done-thing" nor to blind groping after "doing your own thing." It refers rather to that universal family of living beings which we mentioned earlier. It depicts a force for good in human conduct which we have neglected to our cost, that is the force of a whole stream of moral resolutions flowing from one generation to the next, through the entire range of our role changes and cultural revolutions. By showing us the eventual outcome of this movement, it gives us hope for social improvement which our shortrun experience might otherwise undermine.

The importance of vows in religious ways of life is not much noticed by students of the world religions. Yet they are crucial to any story of humanizing characteristics and how we may acquire them. Among the most famous of the bodhisattva vows is the eighteenth one attributed to Dharmākara, the future Buddha Amitābha/Amida. In it he declares, "May I not attain the highest enlightenment" except on one condition. This is that, with few exceptions, whoever sincerely thinks of him up to ten times shall be reborn into his Pure Land.[6] Since tradition tells us that he attained his goal, the conclusion is that his condition has been met. Consequently, even the dullest and most irresolute among us has some hope. We may not share the full Buddhist vision now. But we have only to *aspire* to share in this Buddha's glorious illumination and we shall be sure of success. The basic character of resolving to offset evil has already been acted on and has become part of our spiritual environment. We have only to make the much less demanding decision to transpose ourselves into the Buddha's domain, and we shall eventually be free. Such is the success of Dharmākara's mission.

Critics have claimed that what is called Pure Land Buddhism substituted the mechanical chanting of Amitābha's name for the sustained exercise of enlightening power associated with Gautama. But commentators on Shinran, the most radical exponent of Pure Land teaching, insist that there is nothing mechanical about such faith. At issue is how we channel our passions. The earlier Buddhist tradition seems to say, "Meditate day and night as Gautama did and you will eventually root out all the passions which tie you to your worldly illusions." Shinran instead directed attention away from self and self-effort towards the infinite promise and compassion of the heavenly Amitābha.[7] In the process, he enlisted all our hopes and fears in the cause of the world's enlightenment. He made our passions work for us instead of against us. Despair over our own worthlessness and inability to help others now become motives for positive devotion to one who acts through us to lift the burden of misery in this impure world. Not we ourselves as such, but the Buddha Nature working in us, acts on the bodhisattva vow.

Again the story can be read on two levels. Taken literally, the extravagant version seems to be just another example of "pie in the sky" religion. But we have already noted that the Pure Land and the impure world are the same place, differently regarded. What is proposed is a *spiritual* rebirth in which our power to love and hate is transformed. Instead of inflating our isolated egos, it now unites us in a common front against disease, destruction and loss of the ability to relate as creature to creature through the ebb and flow of personal life. In practice, this vision has indeed been used to distract attention from social wrongs which require more than pious aspirations on our part to overcome. Like anything else, it has been open to abuse. But in principle it is as revolutionary a call for social justice, true *dharma*, as any that we hear from our secular contemporaries. It unites us with every other living thing, plant and animal as well as fellow-human, against the pressures of factional exclusiveness and private pleasure-seeking. It promotes, not class warfare, but the mutual interest of all species.

This brings us to the topic of the Buddha's universal compassion. The theme runs through all schools of Buddhism. Instead of immediately becoming absorbed in permanent bliss, Gautama turned in compassion to teach the Way to others. At the outset of his career, as we have just seen, Amitābha vowed not to become a Buddha unless his becoming so would lead to cosmic joy. On all Buddhist lists, two of the most important bodhisattvas are Mañjuśrī and Avalokiteśvara. They epitomize, respectively, Wisdom and Compassion. They are not remote figures in some exotic heaven, to which we might go in the next life, if there is one. They are named forces active now. They are intermediate links between the Buddha Nature of the philosophers and the Buddha Body of the priests, on the one hand, and the daily trials and tribulations of ordinary people, on the other hand. They are positive grounds for hope in this changing world.

Among the Chinese, Avalokiteśvara typically appears in female form. Many are the tales of her interventions on behalf of simple devotees. Her compassion arises out of the fact that she shares our experience of life. In several versions, for example, the tale is told of a provincial governor who had no sons. He was determined to make an outstanding match for his beautiful daughter. But she was fascinated by the mystery of a nearby monastery. Whenever she asked about it, people changed the subject. Early one morning she eluded her attendants and ventured alone into the forbidden precincts. Alas for her, the monks there had long since abandoned celibacy in favour of sexual promiscuity. Using their temple gongs to drown out her cries for help, they proceeded to rape her. Meanwhile her father, the governor, had discovered her whereabouts but was convinced that she was keeping a tryst with a secret lover. Ordering his guards to shoot any who escaped, he had the place surrounded and burnt to the ground. Moved by her undeserved fate, Heaven then promoted her to the rank of a goddess assigned to rescue all who are in peril. Appearing in a vision to her father, she tells him that henceforth her name will be *Kuan Shih Yin*, Hearer of the Cries of the World.[8]

In other versions, she seems to have been identified with the Princess Miao Shan. Instead of perishing in the flames she is rescued by a gigantic tiger. She descends to hell and obtains the release of its inmates. Amitābha then appears to her and directs her to take up residence on an island in the Eastern Sea of the Dragon King. By the merit of compassionate deeds, performed between periods of cleansing meditation, she attains to bodhisattvahood. She saves the Dragon King's third son from a fisherman's net. In thanks he sends her a marvelous pearl, by the light of which she is able to read sacred books far into the night. The pearl is delivered by the son's niece, who is so entranced by Kuan Yin that she stays to become one of her attendants. And so the stories go.[9] In them we have a conflation of images from the whole range of Chinese mythology. We could discourse here on the Mother Goddess, the Lord of Death, the Tiger, the Dragon, the Fisherman's Friend, the Eastern Isles of the Blessed and much more. Through it all, we should keep in mind that, according to the story, this heavenly saviour once suffered as a mortal. She does not rest in otherworldly bliss but constantly appears to all who call on her for help. Until the modern revolutionary era, her image was to be seen in thousands of shrines throughout the country.

If we would contemplate the recent loss of Kuan Yin's shrines and devotees from a Buddhist point of view, we must draw on the tradition of Buddhist Wisdom. The books which that princess read between missions would have taught her the ultimate emptiness of all things. As a compassionate bodhisattva, she naturally took the forms which her fisher-folk followers expected her to take. Thus she was present to them as a living, vibrant individual. But in her wisdom she knew that none of her selves or roles is absolute. Each is simply a way of relationship with her followers. It is not always needed and does not last forever. Here we touch on the doctrine of "No Self" at the heart of the Buddhist concept of wisdom, which is always a corollary to, not a contradiction of, the concept of compassion.

In Buddhist cultures, it is important to acknowledge a relative place for momentary physical pleasures and local attachments. Otherwise we shall never understand how a religion of world-renunciation generates such April fooling and *joie de vivre* as the festivals of water and light celebrated in Sri Lanka, Burma, Thailand and the rest of the Buddhist world. The Buddha in his previous lives, while still a bodhisattva, is portrayed as, among other things, a majestic beast, a virtuous ruler and a devoted mistress. He is never just an emaciated ascetic. Through the *Jātakas*, stories of his previous lives, countless Buddhists have found models for their own situations and warrants for enjoying good fortune and good deeds. But these are all bracketed by the question: can we honestly say that any of these is of *permanent* value? Granted its relative worth, is whatever to which we are attached, in any sense, absolute?

That to which most of us are absolutely attached are ourselves, our egos. We can be quite sophisticated about this. We can dissociate ourselves from our bodies: they may not be prisons, but neither are they palaces. We may become detached from our children, our publications, our future plans and so forth. But not to want to be remembered in some way, not to want to put our own mark on history or achieve some kind of private immortality, if not by personal effort then by courtesy of some heavenly saviour — that takes more ego-loss than most of us are willing to accept. Just for this reason, the Buddha taught, and the Bodhisattva of Wisdom reemphasizes, the doctrine of "No Self," no absolute individual or corporate identity, as the presupposition to the end of all suffering. If you ask what is absolute or permanent or ultimately reliable in all that we see or touch, the answer is "No thing."[10]

The paradox in the Buddha story is that, when the Buddha finally renounced all passionate attachments, fully realizing the "No Self" of himself, he alone truly had compassion towards all living beings. Somehow, what is consciously denied returns of its own accord with a power that conscious effort could never have achieved. Give up seeking personal happiness and you find it. Give up fixation on the question whether anyone loves you and you find yourself loved. Give up asserting your own opinion at every turn and people start asking your opinion. Let go the drive to achieve perfect freedom and you become free. Renounce the world for *Nirvāṇa* and you, at last, live at peace with the world.

So it is for each of us. We do not have to "go" anywhere in order to enter *Nirvāṇa*. We do not have to "do" anything in order to discover who we really are. The basis for worldly/otherworldly and self/non-self talk, according to Buddhism, turns out to be like a grand illusion. It is in the letting go of all aspirations to permanence, including finally the aspiration to be a Buddha, that ultimate truth is known. This is the secret of the bodhisattvas' wisdom and compassion. Not by asserting that each of us is infinitely valuable, but by sharing in and knowing that all claims to infinity are empty, the bodhisattvas show us what we really are and what is the only realistic basis for love or true relationship. Since Gautama gave up, first his life of luxury as a prince, then his life of self-laceration as a solitary monk, to teach the Middle Path, this has been at the core of Buddhist concepts of wisdom and compassion.

Following Jewish and Christian teaching concerning the importance of each individual in the eyes of God, contemporary Western philosophies have increasingly focused on the individual human being as the principal bearer of meaning and value in life. On its positive side, this emphasis has heightened our concern for human rights and led to notable advances in attitudes towards child development. As an example of perfect love, we are not likely today to cite the story of handing over wife and children to a stranger. No person, we believe, is the possession of another, to be given in such a way. Yet our recognition of intrinsic individual worth has not led to any great outpouring of wisdom and compassion. The Nobel Prize least often awarded in our society is still the Peace Prize. Indeed, Marxist critics of prevailing worldviews see our stress on individuality as a sign of increasing alienation.

Is it altogether coincidental that the decade which saw, in Germany, the publication of Martin Buber's *I and Thou* and Sigmund Freud's *The Ego and the Id*, also saw the rise to power of Adolf Hitler? Buber's "I-You" is still grounded in a relationship to God, the "Always You." But for Freud each ego should become its own Moses, its own Jesus, its own saviour. Such excessive egotism not surprisingly collapses into a death wish. By contrast, the Buddhist juxtaposition of wisdom and compassion forestalls both utter individualism and utter totalitarianism. In Kuan Yin's concern for each creature, each individual is given his due, while in the perfection of wisdom the final emptiness of all talk of "me" and "mine" is realized.

Whereas Western religious stories tend to emphasize the element of plot, depicting life as a struggle between good and evil, Buddhist stories accentuate the element of character. We can exaggerate the differences, of course. In any cycle of stories we find both elements. But the question of emphasis is important. Without going further into the matter here, we can, I think, appreciate how the Buddhist traditions concerning wisdom and compassion serve as a corrective to our current preoccupation with individual striving as the ultimate foundation for philosophy and religion.

Finally, and very briefly, I want simply to note the presence in Buddhist traditions of the Bodhisattva Maitreya. Besides Gautama in his previous lives, Maitreya is the one bodhisattva who certainly appears in both Theravāda and Mahāyāna Buddhism.[11] He is pictured waiting in his heaven for the day when all hope for this world is lost. When saving truth is no longer heard and suffering becomes unbearable, he, the future Buddha, the next in the line of enlightening presences, will restore the Buddha character to pre-eminence in our society. We hear more of the conditions leading to his coming than of his distinctive characteristics.[12] As a future Buddha, his portrait conforms to type. What is important is simply the fact of his coming. For by his presence on the horizon he sets a limit to all present experiences of evil. Decline of faith, destruction of sanctuaries, moral and physical decay, these are not the last word in the Buddha story. Beyond this is Maitreya, ready and able to cope with the task of reversing the negative consequences of our common actions.

Once again we must know how to interpret the imagery. No one knows how this world may end. The point of apocalyptic visions is not to reveal in detail what will happen but to undermine any assumption that our present situation is permanent.[13] The function of the fabulous stories of heavenly Buddhas and Bodhisattvas is to loosen the hold of one-dimensional thinking on our imagination and enlarge our expectations for the future. We can leave to metaphysicians discussions concerning how one possible mode of existence ties in with another. The religious purpose is served simply with the reminder that there *are* such possibilities and assurance concerning their realization. The grounds for such assurance lie in the continuity of character between the transfiguring Presence which gives us strength to persevere now and the revolutionary prospect of a future Buddha who will confirm our final freedom. It is the same compassion and wisdom which characterize the expectations of Maitreya that we know already from the stories of Gautama and Amitābha. Enlightenment dispels not only ignorance concerning who we really are but also delusions concerning what our ultimate prospects might be. However these may be described, Buddhist traditions affirm that they will be congruent with the bodhisattvas' continuing aspirations to release us from all misery.

The future orientation of almost all religious ways of life is seldom sufficiently noticed by those who think of religious traditions. It is the combination of tradition and hope that constitutes a living faith. The traditions themselves, if we listen to them, speak not of the past for the past's sake, but of the promise from the past for the future. This is what Maitreya symbolizes in Buddhism. In Ceylon (Sri Lanka), for example, Buddhist monks typically conclude their work by saying, "With the aid of these acts of *puñña* (merit) may you see Metteya and attain Nibbana."[14] (The spelling is Pāli.) Often this may be no more than a parting formula, like wishing someone "all the best" or Jews saying to each other, "Next year in Jerusalem." But the constant reminder of this potential future keeps fresh the vision of an end to all our patterns of stimulus and response. Maitreya is the Buddhist assurance that the story of this end will be good news rather than bad.

In summary, the figure of the bodhisattva spans the range of our experience. Through the prehistory of this present world we follow the stories of Gautama's previous lives. Among the archetypes of our spiritual environment are Mañjuśrī and Avalokiteśvara. In the end comes Maitreya. Insofar as we always need wisdom, compassion and hope, their stories are timelessly relevant. For our own society in particular, their pattern of service to others provides a counterexample to prevailing egocentricity. Their concern, not just for human beings, but for all living things, enlarges the dimensions of our moral outlook. Their prevalence over the course of centuries prevents us from lapsing into shallow cynicism or despair. And, besides all this, their stories are good fun. They are a part of our universal cultural heritage which we in Canada do well to celebrate.

FOOTNOTES

[1] See e.g. H. Saddhatissa, *The Birth Stories of the Ten Bodhisattas and the Dasabodhisattuppattikathā*, The Pali Text Society (London and Boston: Routledge & Kegan Paul, 1975) p. 26-27:

> "...one factor which may have stimulated the growth of the Buddha-legend (is) the ability, possessed by some people, of seeing visions when they are meditating. When such people have good teachers they will be guided away from believing in the reality of these visions... Where there is no guidance, visions of Buddhas and Bodhisattas and their lives could be taken, not as fictions manufactured by the mind, but as events that have happened already, or are sure to happen in the future."

The religious point, however, is not how we come by such visions but what their consequences are for our ways of life.

[2] On this subject see James B. Wiggins (ed.), *Religion As Story* (New York: Harper Forum pb, 1975). Concerning Buddhism especially see Frederick J. Streng, *Emptiness: A Study in Religious Meaning* (Nashville: Abingdon, 1967) Ch. 1.

[3] See Robert A.F. Thurman (tr.), *The Holy Teaching of Vimalakirti*, (Pennsylvania State University Press, 1976).

[4] Saddhatissa, *op. cit.* p. 13. See also p. 33.

[5] Quoted in Har Dayal, *The Bodhisattva Doctrine in Buddhist Sanskrit Literature* (London: Kegan, Paul, Trench, Trubner, 1932) p. 58.

[6] Quoted in Alfred Bloom, *Shinran's Gospel of Pure Grace*, Association for Asian Studies, Monographs & Papers No. XX (Tucson: University of Arizona Press, 1965) p. 2-3.

[7] See Bloom, *op. cit.* p. 24-34.

[8] See John Blofeld, *Bodhisattva of Compassion: The Mystical Tradition of Kuan Yin* (Boulder, Colorado: Shambala Publications and London: George Allen & Unwin, 1977) p. 68-69.

[9] *Ibid.* p. 69-71.

[10] Specifically concerning a bodhisattva's meditations see Frederick J. Streng, "Mystical Awareness or·How To Be In The World But Not Of It," in Peter Slater (comp.), *Philosophy of Religion and Theology: 1976 Proceedings* (Missoula, Montana: Scholars Press for the American Academy of Religion, 1976) p. 222-239.

[11] Saddhatissa's list of ten bodhisattas, as he shows, is from a late period in Theravāda and probably reflects the influence of Mahāyāna.

[12] See Henry Clarke Warren, *Buddhism in Translations* (Cambridge, Mass.: Harvard University Press, 1953) para. 102.

[13] On the role of apocalyptic imagery in Christian thinking see e.g., Jacques Ellul, *Apocalypse: The Book of Revelation*, tr. George W. Schreiner (New York: Seabury, 1977).

[14] Saddhatissa, *op. cit.* p. 32.

THE EVOLUTION OF THE CONCEPT OF THE BODHISATTVA

A.L. Basham

Preliminary

For the purpose of this paper the word Bodhisattva or Bodhisatta means a being who has attained a very high level of spiritual or supernatural knowledge and power and is close to the achievement of the highest wisdom, which will result in his attaining Buddhahood. It is well known that the interpretation of the concept of the Bodhisattva differs as between the Mahāyāna and Hīnayāna branches of Buddhism. In the former the Bodhisattva has resolved to use his great powers for the benefit of all living beings in lower stages of development. He has to all intents and purposes reached the highest wisdom already, but he voluntarily postpones indefinitely his achievement of Nirvāṇa or Buddhahood. In the Hīnayāna sects he does not do this, but aims at full enlightenment as quickly and directly as possible.

As far as the Theravāda is concerned, the Bodhisatta is virtually a historical figure, and the term is generally applied to the previous lives of Siddhattha Gotama as recorded in the *Jātaka* book. In the Māhāyana, on the other hand, the heavens are peopled by innumerable Bodhisattvas who work for the welfare of all beings. They are constantly active in the service of all things living and not only provide the ideals on which the believer, monastic or lay, should model himself, but also serve as potent sources of help in trouble.

In this paper I assume that in general the Theravāda system is closer to the sort of Buddhism patronized by Aśoka and taught long before his death than are any of the other systems.[1] By this I do not imply that Theravāda has undergone no change or development since Aśoka, and far less do I suggest that it is 'what the Buddha really taught.' I do suggest, however, that we are more likely to find traces of 'primitive' Buddhism in the Pāli scriptures than in any other Buddhist texts. This in no way excludes the possibility that genuine traditions may have been transmitted in the scriptures of other sects, but merely implies that the earlier strata of Buddhism are more likely to be revealed in the Pāli texts than in those in Buddhist Sanskrit.

By this criterion the Pāli Bodhisatta is likely to be earlier than the Bodhisattva of Mahāyāna — a probability strengthened by the intrinsic nature of the two concepts. It is possible to suggest stages whereby the Theravāda Bodhisatta, influenced by popular theistic and soteriological ideas, developed into the finished Bodhisattva of Mahāyāna. A reverse process, on the other hand, is hard to conceive.

Together with the actual concept of the Bodhisattva we have to consider the vow or resolve with which he begins his career, especially in its developed Mahāyāna form. At a very remote period in the cyclic past of the universe, the contemporary stage of the chain of being which produced any given Bodhisattva, Avalokiteśvara for instance, while still an ordinary man, made a solemn resolve that he would strive towards supreme wisdom (*saṃbodhi*) and become a Bodhisattva, in order to devote his mighty superhuman powers to relieving the suffering of others and furthering their spiritual progress. Ultimately, after numerous rebirths, he achieved that aim and now he pours down grace and blessing from the almost immeasurable store of merit he has accumulated. He will not abandon his task while any struggling being remains tossed in the sea of *saṃsāra* below him. The resolve of the Bodhisattva forms one of the focal points of Mahāyāna ethics, and must have had an incalculable but very real effect in encouraging altruism in every country where Mahāyāna has been preached, for the believing Mahāyāna Buddhist is encouraged to make a firm and earnest resolve to become a Bodhisattva himself.

Many Mahāyāna texts give versions of the Bodhisattva's vow[2] and many also pour scorn on the selfish Hīnayānists, who do not make such a vow, but aim at achieving Nirvāṇa as *arhats*, by the shortest possible route and in the shortest possible time.[3] This latter aim is characterized as egotistic, a slightly higher form of selfishness than are the more obvious manifestations of that all-embracing vice. The Mahāyānists, in their polemics against the *śrāvakas*, seem to overlook the fact that in order to achieve his goal of becoming an *arhat* the Hīnayānist must perform immense acts of self-sacrifice for the welfare of others, as a perusal of the *Jātaka* stories will soon show.

In the remainder of this paper an attempt is made to trace some of the stages of the evolution of the Bodhisattva ideal and the vows or resolves accompanying it. I owe much to the work of earlier scholars, in particular Dr. Har Dayal[4] and Dr. Marie Thérèse de Mallmann,[5] and I cannot add much to the conclusions of their excellent studies, except in attempting, from the historian's angle, to give a little further precision to the chronology of the subject.

The Theravāda Bodhisatta

No word such as *Bodhisattva*, or any word composed of similar elements, occurs in the voluminous Vedic literature, to the best of our knowledge, and the same is true of the literature of early Hinduism and Jainism. This leads to the tentative, though unprovable conclusion, that the concept in its original form arose in a purely Buddhist framework, without influence from outside in its inception, whatever influences may have been felt in the development of the idea of the Bodhisattva in its later Mahāyāna form.

Since the Pāli canon contains a tremendous amount of material, including all the *Abhidhamma Piṭaka* nearly all the *Vinaya Piṭaka*, and most of the *Sutta Piṭaka*, which could not possibly have been composed by the historical founder of Buddhism, we hesitate to ascribe the invention of the term to Gotama Buddha himself, but the fact remains that its earliest occurrences appear in words attributed to him, in reference to his own career before his enlightenment.[6] In the *Kathāvatthu* of the *Abhidhamma Piṭaka*, ascribed to the period of Aśoka, the Bodhisatta is equipped with symbolism and an incipient theology,[7] but the passages in question may still refer only to the historical Buddha before his enlightenment, though this is by no means certain.

The Pāli term *Bodhisatta* is commonly translated by 'a being whose essence is enlightenment' or some such phrase, on the assumption that it is equivalent to Buddhist Sanskrit *Bodhisattva*. The equivalence seems fairly obvious, and might be taken as virtually certain, were it not for the ambiguity of the Pāli language and the inappropriateness of the conventional interpretation, for since the Bodhisatta, according to the Theravāda usage, has not yet achieved full enlightenment it seems hardly reasonable to describe him as the very essence (*sattva*) of perfect enlightenment (*bodhi*). We must admit the possibility that the Sanskrit form is a false 'back formation,' and that the latter component of the Pāli term originally represented something other than *sattva*. An alternative derivation is Sanskrit *-sakta* 'attached to,' 'devoted to,'[8] which would give the term the meaning 'One who is intent on (achieving) enlightenment.' A further possible etymology, put forward by Har Dayal,[9] would relate the Pāli *satta* in this context to Vedic *satvan*, 'hero, warrior.' Har Dayal bases his interpretation chiefly on the Tibetan equivalent of Bodhisattva, *byang-chub sems-dpa'*, of which compound *byang-chub* is the common equivalent of *bodhi* and *sems-dpa'* means 'mind-hero.' While Tibetan translations may be useful in clarifying many Buddhist Sanskrit terms, not much can be gathered from this example, however, since no hint of this etymology of *-sattva* is to be found in any Buddhist Sanskrit sources and the Tibetan translation of the term must have been made well over a thousand years after it first became current in India.

In the *Jātaka* book of the *Khuddaka Nikāya*, as is well known, the word *Bodhisatta* figures at least once in each of the 547 stories, and a fully elaborated doctrine of the Bodhisatta, according to the Theravāda system, has already developed. The *Jātaka* collection, especially the prose commentary but also to a lesser extent the verse portions, in the form in which we have it is by no means as ancient as the four main *Nikāyas* of the *Sutta Piṭaka*,[10] but we may be sure that *Jātakas*, and with them the doctrine of the Bodhisatta, were important elements in popular Buddhism by the time of the carving of the reliefs of the Bharhut *stūpa* railings, which depict about thirty *Jātaka* tales. These, from an inscription on one of the pillars,[11] can be definitely dated to the Śuṅga period, and thus we can say with confidence that by about 100 B.C. at the latest the Theravāda concept of the Bodhisatta was widely popular. The fact that this concept was particularly associated with the *Jātaka* stories suggests a way in which it may have developed and gained wider currency.

The *Vinaya Piṭaka*[12] contains specific instructions that a monk should not enter a village to participate in story-telling on themes of love, war, crime and adventure. The list is fairly comprehensive and, if taken seriously, would include almost every popular tale of India's rich folk-lore. For this rule to have been promulgated in the first place presupposes the fact that some monks had been listening to and repeating such tales, probably using them, as they were used in later Buddhism, to stimulate the moral fervour and piety of the lay-folk. The Buddha himself is said to have enlivened many of his sermons with tales of one kind and another, and we have no reason to believe that he did not do so. It would be surprising if his successors did not follow his example.

It is clear that the regulations of the *Vinaya Piṭaka* are not, except perhaps in a very few cases, authentic rules laid down by the Master himself. Many of them presuppose a fully developed monastic system, with monks permanently settled in well established monasteries. It may be, however, that this regulation relating to the telling of stories was a comparatively early one, promulgated by certain senior monks who were worried about the secularization of their movement, and the introduction of popular elements in what began as an austere system of self-discipline for an intellectual élite, whose members felt few obligations to the laity and had little contact with them.

The ban on the telling of stories could only be evaded through giving the tales told by the monks the seal of authenticity by attributing them to the Master himself. Being omniscient (*sabbaññu*) he had known all his previous births in fullest detail. Obviously in those previous births, at least in the more recent of them, he had performed deeds of unexampled altruism and wisdom. We suggest that the collection of *Jātakas* was compiled, partly on the basis of existing stories and partly with new stories devised for the purpose, to legitimize the practice of the monks telling edifying legends and fables in order to gain and maintain the support of the simpler laity. Hence the concept of the Bodhisatta, in its Hīnayāna sense, was born.

Thus we conclude that the doctrine of the Bodhisatta, as it appears in Theravāda literature, was an internal development of early Buddhism and appeared some time after the Buddha's death. It may be that the Master himself did claim to know his earlier births, as many Indian mystics have done since, but we have no reason, other than the unreliable tradition of the prose *Jātaka*, to believe that he devised the fully fledged doctrine of the Bodhisatta personally. For the reasons already given, it appears to be the product of a developed Buddhist church, when many of the monks were already settled in permanent monasteries and took pastoral care of a significant body of lay adherents.

The Bharhut evidence proves that at least some of the *Jātaka* stories were a well established and popular aspect of Buddhism by about 100 B.C., and the doctrine of the Bodhisattva, in its Theravāda form, must have been well known and generally accepted by this time. There is some reason to believe, however, that it was already current by the third century B.C., from the evidence of the inscriptions of Aśoka.

That the cult of the earlier Buddhas was practised at this time is quite certain from Aśoka's enlargement of the *stūpa* of Buddha Konāgamana at Nigliva.[13] However critical we may be of the Buddhist historical tradition, this gives definite proof that a developed Buddhology had arisen by the mid-third century B.C. and indeed earlier, for when Aśoka visited Nigliva a small *stūpa* must already have been in existence which was revered by local Buddhists as that of an earlier Buddha. It has been pointed out that in his inscriptions Aśoka makes no specific mention of several basic Buddhist categories, for instance Nirvāṇa, the Four Noble Truths, The Noble Eightfold Path, and the Chain of Dependent Causation (*pratītya-samutpāda*); but the concept of Complete Enlightenment (*saṃbodhi*)[14] is mentioned, as is the formula of the three Jewels (*triratna*),[15] and the location of Aśoka's pillars shows that the sites of the Buddha's birth, enlightenment, first preaching and death were already revered as sacred places. From the appearance in force of *Jātaka* illustrations at Bharhut, admittedly somewhat later than Aśoka, it is reasonable to infer, though without absolute certainty, that edifying stories about the Bodhisatta's earlier lives were already being told. Several such stories, put into the Buddha's own mouth, are given in the *Sutta Piṭaka*, later to be reproduced in the *Jātaka* collection.[16] This gives reason to believe that some of the *Jātakas* are quite ancient, and were known in Buddhist circles long before Bharhut.

According to the developed Buddhology of both Hīnayāna and Mahāyāna sects the chain of life leading up to Gotama, then in the form of a young ascetic named Sumedha, at an almost unimaginably distant time, when Dīpaṅkara Buddha was preaching, took a solemn vow to work onwards to Buddhahood.[17] He went through a course of 547 rebirths on earth, in various forms of life, punctuated by long intervals spent in the heavens, as the Bodhisatta, until he became Siddhattha Gotama, and achieved enlightenment as Buddha. Even if this doctrine was not fully elaborated by the time of Aśoka it must have existed in some form, to account for the Bharhut evidence of a century or so later. And if Gotama Buddha developed from a Bodhisatta, the same must have been true of Konāgamana and all the previous Buddhas.

An interesting piece of evidence on the development of the Bodhisattva ideal may be contained in Aśoka's Eighth Rock Edict. Here we are told:

> In the past kings set out (*nikkhamisu*) on pleasure trips (*vihārayāttā*)..., but when king Devānampiya Piyadassi had been anointed ten years he set out for *Saṃbodhi*.[18]

The former pleasure trips are then contrasted with the more recent *Dhamma*-trips, when holy men are honoured, alms are distributed, and the *Dhamma* is preached. The reference to Aśoka's going to *Saṃbodhi* is generally taken to refer to a pilgrimage to the Bodhi tree at Gayā. The alternative explanation that Aśoka resolved to achieve full enlightenment as quickly as possible is generally rejected.[19] Nevertheless, the alternative deserves reconsideration.

Of the readings given by Bloch, the Girnar version differs slightly, having in this context *ayāya saṃbodhiṃ*, in which the verb is connected with the Sanskrit root *yā*, 'go.' The others (Kalsi, Dhauli, Shahbazgarhi, Maski and the Sopara fragment) all have forms linked with Sanskrit *niṣkram* 'set out,' 'depart.' The same verb appears everywhere except at Girnar, which also replaces it by *ñayāsu* (* *ni-ayāsu* from Sanskrit *nir+yā*)[20] in connection with the pleasure trips earlier referred to in the same inscription. This makes it practically certain that the original text, as written or dictated by Aśoka himself, employed a verb based on *niṣkram*, rather than *yā*, in relation to *Saṃbodhi*.

Semantically *niṣkram* has overtones of departure rather than arrival at a precise destination. The most famous Buddhist usage of the root is in the compound *Mahābhiniṣkramaṇa*, the 'Great Going Forth' of Siddhārtha Gautama in search of *Saṃbodhi* or full enlightenment. The word would be quite appropriate in respect of 'pleasure-trips,' since in such cases their destination is normally not very significant as compared with the pleasure they yield. The root *yā*, on the other hand, suggests ultimate arrival at a definite destination, especially without the prefix *niṣ-*; it seems on the face of it that Aśoka intended to tell his subjects that he had set out for *Saṃbodhi*, but had not yet arrived there. Thus it is probably a spiritual journey that he refers to, not a physical one. This theory is strengthened by reference to the topography of South Bihar.

The distance from Patna to Bodh Gaya is about 60 miles by road and there are no serious geographical obstacles to be faced. In the time of Aśoka the journey would have been no harder or more tedious than it was at any time before the invention of mechanical means of transport. By the standards of those days it was an easy journey, especially for a mighty ruler, for whom the way would be cleared and changes of horses or elephants provided whenever needed. A trip to Gaya would have required only one night away from the capital. Aśoka 'set out for *Saṃbodhi*' when he had been anointed ten years; his conversion to Buddhism, according to the general interpretation of the thirteenth Rock Edict, took place when he had been anointed for eight years.[21] Thus, if we are to accept the conventional interpretation of *Saṃbodhi*, a period of some two years elapsed before the newly converted emperor found time to visit one of the most famous sacred sites of Buddhism, which was situated almost on his doorstep. This is, on the face of it, unlikely.[22]

The implications of this alternative interpretation of Aśoka's trip to *Saṃbodhi* are quite clear. He had made some solemn vow or resolve that he would strive to achieve full enlightenment. Bloch seems to take this interpretation as invalid from a chronological point of view:

> Dans ce cas il faut supposer admise a l'époque une doctrine que nous ne trouvons enseignée formellement que dans les livres du Grand Véhicule.[23]

But even if our tentative interpretation is accepted, this does not imply a fully developed doctrine of the Mahāyāna Bodhisattva type. If the legends of the previous births of the Buddha were already popular, it would not be surprising if some pious souls made vows similar to those made by Sumedha before Dīpaṅkara Buddha in the long distant past. The aim of Aśoka's resolve, however, if our interpretation is correct, is not *Nirvāṇa*, a concept nowhere occurring in the Aśokan inscriptions, but *Saṃbodhi*, or enlightenment. In this it corresponds to the vow of the Mahāyāna Bodhisattva, who did not strive directly from *Nirvāṇa* but rather for *Saṃbodhi*, employing the merit, wisdom and power he had accumulated from the welfare of other beings.

The Evolution of the Mahāyāna Bodhisattva

It seems that the Mahāyāna doctrine of the Bodhisattvas may be derived logically from belief in future Buddhas. If earlier Buddhas had existed there must be other Buddhas yet to come. There is every reason to believe that by Aśoka's day the typical Indian doctrine of unending cycles to time was already prevalent, since Aśoka expresses the hope that his reforms will endure until the end of the *kalpa*.[24] The earliest account of the future Buddha Metteyya occurs at the end of the *Cakkavatti-sīhanāda Sutta*,[25] a lengthy text which bears all the marks of lateness. The account of the *cakkavatti* King Daḷhanemi, who conquers the world without bloodshed by the power of his magic wheel, suggests that its author knew of the *Dhammavijaya* of Aśoka. It may be suggested that the *sutta* was composed either during or immediately after Aśoka's reign, in order to provide justification for his new policy and to warn his successors against reversing it.

The reference to Metteyya occurs in the form of a prophecy made by the Buddha himself after his description of the gradual brutalization of life from the death of king Daḷhanemi onwards. We are told that the future Buddha will be the first one of the forthcoming ascending phase of cosmic development, and will be born as a man after the 'Seven Days of the Sword,' when the period of decline comes to an end with the decimation of human life, and when the remnants of mankind begin to improve their ways and strive to live in peace one with another. The message of hope contained in the account of Metteyya, after an apocalyptic description of future horrors, suggests a later addition to the *sutta*, but this is not by any means certain, and in any case the passage describing Metteyya may not have been added much later than the composition of the main body of the text. On this basis we may suggest that the future Buddha Metteyya was believed in in some circles by about 200 B.C. or earlier, soon after Aśoka's death, if not during his reign. Belief in future Buddhas is, in any case, an obvious logical corollary of belief in former ones, which certainly existed by about 250 B.C.

Once the doctrine of future Buddhas, especially Metteyya, became accepted, the way was open for faith in Boddhisattvas active in the contemporary world. Each earthly birth of the Bodhisattva of the *Jātaka* stories was divided by very long periods of residence in the heavens. Thus the chain of being which would ultimately lead up to Metteyya Buddha must already be in existence, in all probability in the form of a heavenly being. This far at least, the evolution of the Bodhisattva ideal of the Mahāyāna might be deduced from the earlier Theravāda Buddhology.

The latest date by which belief in heavenly Bodhisattvas and their worship could have begun is indicated by the presence of images of princely beings, often with moustaches and wearing jewellery, found in Buddhist contexts in Gandhara and Mathura. Some of these have been identified as representing Maitreya, (Pāli, Metteyya), the future Buddha, and others as Avalokiteśvara, the most famous of the Bodhisattvas of later Mahāyāna mythology. As Marie-Thérèse de Mallmann points out,[26] these identifications are in most cases tentative and in some cases they may be false but it is fairly certain that the figures are intended to represent Bodhisattvas, for they are certainly not Buddhas, and they can hardly be either Hindu gods or stylized images of donors or lay patrons. They indicate that the cult of Bodhisattvas existed in something like its finished Mahāyāna sense in Western India fairly early in the Christian Era. Unfortunately they give us no greater precision than this, since the chronology of the two schools of sculpture is still vague and uncertain, depending as it does on the perennial chronological problem of the date of Kaniṣka.

A more definite date can be established from the inscription of the Taxila silver scroll,[27] which is dated in the year 136 and which mentions an unnamed Kuṣāṇa king as at present reigning. This refers to a private *Bosisatvagaha* (*sic*), or Bodhisattva chapel. Again the date is uncertain, depending on the uncertain base date of the era used, but the inscription can hardly be later than the second half of the 1st century A.D. and the kind referred to is certainly a predecessor of Kaniṣka. It proves quite conclusively that by now heavenly Bodhisattvas were not only believed in but also worshipped by some of the Buddhists of Taxila.

Three images from Sarnath bear inscriptions referring to the setting up by a certain monk named Bala of a Bodhisattva and a ritual umbrella (*Bodhisatvo chatrayaṣṭi pratiṣṭhāpito* - sic).[28] A similar figure, also dedicated by Bala, was found at Śrāvastī and another at Kosambī, the latter bearing an inscription recording its installation by a learned nun Buddhamitrā. The same lady is singled out to be referred to by name in one of the monk Bala's inscriptions, among the numerous people whom he mentions as associated with him in the gift — his parents, teachers, fellow monks, pupils and the two local satraps of Kaniṣka. These images bear dates in the year 3 of Kaniṣka's reckoning, the Kosambī one of the 8th of the second month of Hemanta (i.e. Pauṣa) and the Sarnath ones all on the same day, the 22nd of the third Hemanta month (i.e. Māgha). The images belong to the Mathura school of sculpture and are made of the typical Mathura sandstone. The evidence suggests that the Monk Bala and the Nun Buddhamitrā were propagandists for a new cult, and that they collected large sums of money, paid for and supervised the carving of the statues in the workshops of Mathura, and then accompanied them in slow-moving bullock carts to their destinations further East. About 44 days elapsed between the setting up of the image at Kosambī and that at Sarnath, which would agree very well with this theory.

It is suggested, and widely believed, that these figures are in fact the earliest Mathura Buddhas, though they are called Bodhisattvas 'out of deference to old scruples against the figurations of the Master.'[29] Certain other early images, which appear to be Buddhas, also bear inscriptions stating that they are Bodhisattvas. By the time of Huviṣka, however, in the year 51 of Kaniṣka's era, a Mathura image appears explicitly mentioned in the inscription as being that of the Buddha (*Bhagavataḥ Śākyamuneḥ pratimā*).[30] Thus, according to the general theory, for a period of about 50 years it was considered legitimate to represent the Buddha, but it was not permissible to mention the fact. This seems to us intrinsically very improbable. If the images were intended to represent the Buddha it would be most unlikely that the Monk Bala and his friends would have circumvented the ban on representing him by such a lame pretext. We believe that the images erected by Bala and those that followed were what they claimed to be — images of a Bodhisattva. But probably the Bodhisattva in question was none other than Siddhārtha Gautama up to the time of his enlightenment, and these images really give us little or no further information on the date of the inception of the cult of the heavenly Bodhisattvas, who must, from much other evidence, have been believed in already by the time of Kaniṣka, whenever we place his date.

The latest possible date for the beginning of belief in heavenly Bodhisattvas can be reached from the longer *Sukhāvatīvyūha*, which was first translated into Chinese by Lokakṣema, who lived from AD 147 to 186.[31] Here[32] innumerable Bodhisattvas are described as coming from many worlds to wait on Amitābha Buddha in the Sukhāvatī heaven. They outshine the *śrāvakas* (here probably the Hīnayāna monks) in splendour as a hundred thousand *koṭis* of *yojanas* exceeds a fathom; and among them two mighty Bodhisattvas outshine the rest and illumine the whole cosmos. These are Avalokiteśvara and Mahāsthāmaprāpta. By the time this text was composed, probably well before it appeared in China, something like the full Mahāyāna mythology, including belief in the heavenly Bodhisattvas, must have been in existence. The prose part of the 24th chapter of the *Saddharmapuṇḍarīka Sūtra*, but not the verses at the end, which seem to be a later addition, was included in Dharmarakṣa's Chinese translation of the text, made in 286.[33] This forms the *locus classicus* on the saving power of Avalokiteśvara. He frees those who call on his name from fire, flood and shipwreck. He can save the victim condemned to death who calls to him on the scaffold. He delivers caravans from robbers. He removes evil passions, such as hatred, from those who call upon him. He provides children for childless wives. Moreover, most surprising of all, from one act of reverence to Avalokiteśvara a worshipper can acquire as much merit as from acts of reverence and gifts to all the Buddhas, whose number is 62 times the grains of sand in the Gaṅgā. Avalokiteśvara takes the forms of Buddhas, *pratyeka-buddhas śrāvakas*, Hindu gods, demons, *cakravartī* kings and other Bodhisattvas, in order to teach the law more effectively.[34]

By this time a form of Buddhism had emerged, in which one Bodhisattva at least, Avalokiteśvara, transcended even Amitābha himself, both in splendour and efficacy. And we must rid ourselves of the idea that this was just a popular Buddhism for the consumption of semi-literate lay Buddhists who needed a saviour. Many scholars and intellectual

Buddhists in Japan and elsewhere seem to believe that the philosophical doctrine of śūnyatā is the essence of Mahāyāna Buddhism. This may be so on the philosophical plane, but even on this plane the Bodhisattvas have at least as much 'reality' as the beings and things of the material world. On the plane of religion, as distinct from philosophy, the Bodhisattvas, and Avalokiteśvara in particular, have become the objects of an intense faith and trust which was certainly not confined to the ignorant or worldly. If we are to believe his biographer,[35] Hsüan Tsang, one of the most learned and intelligent Buddhists of his day, in the course of his perilous journey across Central Asia, constantly invoked the Bodhisattva Kwan-yin in the face of robbers, storms or demons, and was invariably preserved from danger. Since his invention, Avalokiteśvara, and his Far Eastern *alter ego* Kwan-yin or Kwannon, have been among the most potent sources of hope and comfort in the religion of any part of the world, and it would be wrong to dismiss Avalokiteśvara as a mere popular excrescence on a profound mystico-philosophical system. Rather the reverse is the case.

With the development of the new mythology of heavenly Buddhas and Bodhisattvas the shifting of aim from the *arhat* to the Bodhisattva is but logical. If these great spirits result from men who in the past made a solemn resolve to achieve the highest wisdom and then devote the immense merit, knowledge and power they had attained to the service of others, it is but natural that the sincere Buddhist, whether monk or layman, man or woman, should strive to follow in their footsteps.

The doctrine of the transfer of merit is not absolutely necessary to the doctrine of heavenly Bodhisattvas, but it is highly appropriate to it. In his finished form the Bodhisattva not only helps and guides men in obvious and practical ways, but also devotes the immense store of *puṇya*, which he has gathered over countless ages, to their welfare.[36]

There are passages in the Pāli texts which declare that the transfer of merit is quite impossible, and this remains the official doctrine of Theravāda Buddhism, though many compromises have been made in the more popular expressions of Buddhism in Sri Lanka, Burma and Thailand and, as Har Dayal points out, traces of the idea of transfer of merit can be found even in later Pāli texts.[37] Nevertheless in general, for the Theravāda, merit or good *karma* is a 'treasure that cannot be given to others,'[38] and even an *arhat* can only affect the spiritual, as distinct from the physical, condition of another being through his example, preaching and advice. Possibly this doctrine was found unsatisfactory by many gentler spirits quite early in the history of Buddhism. The quality of *karuṇā*, thus interpreted, could offer little more than first aid to the suffering of others. By the transfer of merit in sufficient quantity, on the other hand, the effects of *karma* could be mitigated, or perhaps even avoided altogether.

Positive evidence that the doctrine of the transfer of merit was widespread in Buddhism as early as the beginning of the Christian Era may be derived from the numerous dedicatory inscriptions of Northwestern India and the Ganga Valley, most of which end in the pious hope that the donation may be for the welfare of various groups of persons.[39] Parents are nearly always mentioned; the local ruler and his overlord occur frequently; often other recipients of the blessings of the gift are the monks and nuns of the four quarters, with whom laymen and laywomen are sometimes associated; and generally 'all beings' are included after the main list of recipients. The monk Bala concluded his dedications with a formula like this,[40] forgetting (like many other Buddhist monks before and since) that theoretically he had abandoned all his family ties, and that therefore his seeking to benefit his parents before others was an admission of his failure to 'give up the world' completely. Pious aspirations such as this can be traced back almost as far as Indian epigraphy goes, to the Sixth Rock Edict of Aśoka, where he states that he has issued his *Dhamma-lipi* 'that it may long remain, and that my sons, grandsons and great grandsons may follow it for the welfare of all the world' (or of all worlds, *sarva-loka-hitāya*).[41] But there is no need to postulate transfer of merit here; probably Aśoka intends to imply only that the world will prosper materially and spiritually if his policy is maintained after his death. More significant is the inscription of the Meridarch Theodoros (*Theüdora*) on the Swat relic casket, stating that the remains of the Buddha are deposited 'for the welfare of many people' (*bahu-jana-hitāya*).[42] The inscription is undated, but the palaeography and the Greek name and title suggest a date around 100 B.C., or perhaps a little later. Clearly the Meridarch intends to transfer some or all of the spiritual benefit of his good deed to the world at large.

The same seems probably implied by the inscriptions on the Mathura lion capital. Here the chief queen of the Great Satrap Rajula establishes a *stūpa* containing a relic of the Buddha and a monastery for the community of Sarvāstivādin monks. The thirteenth line of the inscription is very doubtful, but Sircar reads the words *mukti-hitāya*, 'for the salvation and welfare' not only of the queen herself but also of her mother, her grandmother, her brother, her daughter and the residents of the Great Satrap's *antaḥpura* or harem.[43] On the same capital is a further inscription made while Rajula's son Śudaṣa (*Śoḍāsa*) was reigning, which is a record of another gift made by the latter's three sons to the same Sarvāstivādin monks, 'for the worship of all the Buddhas, for the worship of the Dharma, for the worship of all Sakastan (*sarvasa Sakrastanasa puyae*).' Here we have evidence not only of an important Sarvāstivāda monastery at Mathura, but also of a widespread worship of a plurality of Buddhas. In the light of the probable date of this inscription it is very likely that these are heavenly Buddhas of the type of Amitābha. The *pūjā* offered to the Buddhas, as well as to the other two elements of the *Triratna*, suggests that it was believed at the time that Buddhas still existed as distinct personalties.

In another inscription of the same family, the Taxila Copper plate of the year 78,[44] Patika, son of the Satrap of Cukhsa, Liaka Kusulaka, who is given the title "Great Lord of Gifts' (*mahādānapati*), uses a similar formula in respect of establishing a monastery at Taxila with a reliquary of the Buddha 'for the worship of all the Buddhas, worshipping his mother and father, for the increase of the age and strength of the satrap with his sons and wives, and worshipping his relatives and neighbours.'[45] Here again the term *pūjā* is used, but the formula is significantly altered with regard to the satrap and his family, in whose case 'worship' is replaced by devout wishes for their health and longevity. This also suggests the transfer of merit to the Satrap. The important but very badly damaged Takht-i-Bahi inscription of the 26th year of Gondophares, dated in the year 104, also employs the term *puae* (=Sanskrit *pūjāyai*).[46]

The implications of the word *pūjā* and its Prakrit equivalents in their contexts are not altogether clear. *Pūjā* may imply a wide range of relationships from intense awe-inspired worship and devotion to the honour and respect felt for an elder or superior. It does not, however, normally suggest any intense desire for the welfare of its object; rather it indicates a feeling of humility before a being more powerful and more holy than oneself. A devotee who believed in the transfer of merit would hardly choose a term such as this to imply that he voluntarily passed on the *puṇya* acquired by his good deeds to the persons mentioned. Significant in this respect is the Taxila scroll of the year 136, already mentioned, where the donor, a certain Bahalia, makes his gift, 'for the bestowal of health upon the great king, the king above kings, the son of the gods, the Khuṣaṇa (*sic*), for the worship (*puya=pūjā*) of all the Buddhas, for the worship of all the *pratyeka-buddhas*, for the worship of the *arhats*, for the worship of all beings, for the worship of mother and father, for the worship of friends, colleagues (*amaca=amātya*), kinsfolk and blood relations, and for his own blessing of health and Nirvāṇa.'[47] Bahalia mentions the perfected beings of Hīnayāna sects, the *pacceka-buddhas* and *arhats* of the Pāli scriptures, but only with reverence and respect. Though he possesses a *Bodhisattva-gṛha* of his own, he is not interested, apparently, in becoming a *Bodhisattva* himself. Among the recipients of his *pūjā* the *Bodhisattva* are not mentioned, and he aspires, not for *Bodhi* of the *Bodhisattva* but for the *Nirvāṇa* of the *arhat*. Yet he appears to believe that some portion of the merit of his gift can be transferred to the

Kuṣāṇa king, in order to improve his health. This one phrase suggesting transfer of merit is perhaps little more than a respectful and formal compliment to the contemporary ruler, but it is significant nevertheless.

The situation changes with the inscription on one of the images of the monk Bala, referred to already, set up early in Kaniṣka's reign. Here, in place of the long formulae introducing the word *pūjā*, appears at the end of the dedicatory inscription the simple phrase: 'For the purpose of the welfare and happiness of all beings' (*sarva-satvanaṃ hitā-sukhārtthaṃ* -sic).[48] While in the area now Pakistan *pūjā* is still occasionally mentioned among the motives of Buddhist donations,[49] phrases of this latter type become usual from Kaniṣka's time onwards in Buddhist inscriptions from Swat to Varanasi.

A completely theistic Mahāyāna is reflected in an inscription on a Buddha image from Mathura, dated in the year 14 of Kaniṣka's reign.[50] In this a lady named Saṅghilā 'sets up the image for the purpose of the worship (*pūjā*) of the Lord, the grand father (*pitamahā*-sic), the Well-Englightened (*samya-saṃbuddha* -sic) ..., the God (*deva*).' The final motive of the gift is mentioned succinctly at the end of the inscription. Its purpose is 'the destruction of all sorrow' (*sarva-dukkha-pahānārttham* -sic). Here Buddha receives the title commonly applied to the old Vedic high god, Prajāpati — the *Pitāmaha*, the first progenitor of all things. The term seems to presuppose something like the *trikāya* doctrine, imperfectly understood by the lady donor (*Pitāmaha* suggests the *Dharmakāya*, *deva* the *Saṃbhogakāya*, and *samyak-saṃbuddha* the *Nirmāṇakāya*), and the final phrase must involve belief in the transfer of merit. The fashion of replacing *pūjā* by *puṇya* also affected the Hindus. A Mathura inscription of the year 28 of Kaniṣka's era refers to the endowment of a *puṇyaśālā* for feeding brahmans, and for the benefit of 'the orphans, the hungry and the thirsty.' The inscription concludes with the pious wish:

> Whatever merit may be in this (gift), may it belong to the Son of the Gods, the Ṣāhi Huviṣka, and may the merit belong to those to whom the Son of the Gods is dear (*priya*). May the merit belong to the whole earth.'[51]

It seems that outside the area controlled by the Kuṣāṇas the new formula spread among Buddhists considerably later. The Buddhist inscriptions of the Western Deccan use neither the *pūjā* formula nor the *puṇya* one. Beyond the Kuṣāṇa empire inscriptions in which the merit of the gift is transferred appear first, it seems, at Nagarjunakonda, where, in making a Buddhist donation, a royal lady, Śāntiśrī aunt of the Ikṣvāku king Vīrapuruṣaddatta, desires 'the bringing of welfare and joy to both families (*ubhaya-loka-hita-sukhāvaha*), the achievement of *Nirvāṇa* for herself (*atano ca nirvāṇa saṃpati*) and bringing welfare and joy to the whole universe (*sarva-loka-hita-sukhāvaha*).'[52] The passage shows an interesting mixture of Mahāyāna and Hīnayāna concepts. The lady Śāntiśrī evidently believes in the transfer of merit, but her sights are aimed at *Nirvāṇa*, not *Bodhi*. This inscription, however, cannot be earlier than A.D. 250 and is probably to be dated nearer 300. Hence it throws no light on the chronology of the doctrine of the transfer of merit.

Thus the doctrine was in full force in at least some Buddhist circles by the first century of the Christian Era at the latest. It appears to have been part of a widespread reaction, evident also in Hinduism at the time, against belief in the rigid operation of *karma*.[53] We have no evidence of a rejection of *karma* and transmigration altogether, but the *Bhagavad Gītā* contains passages which teach that the grace of Kṛṣṇa cancel the effects of past sins, so that through faith even *śūdras* on death can go straight to God.[54] Nowhere in India was this doctrine of salvation by faith so strongly emphasized as among some groups of Buddhists, whose beliefs are represented by the *Sukhāvatīvyūha* in its different recensions, and who were the ancestors of the 'Pure Land' schools of China and Japan.

The inscriptional evidence points very clearly to a northern origin for the belief in heavenly *Bodhisattvas* and the transfer of merit, and indeed for Mahāyāna Buddhism generally. Basing their views on textual evidence, some scholars maintain that Mahāyāna originated in South India.[55] Whether or not this is true of Mahāyāna philosophy, it is not supported by inscriptional or iconographic evidence in respect of the new mythology of Mahāyāna, which, in our view, had a much greater impact on the civilization of the world than any Mahāyāna philosophical system and was the ground out of which Mahāyāna philosophy grew.

Influences

The growth of the *Bodhisattva* doctrine has been attributed to a variety of causes, some of which may be dismissed out of hand. For instance the evidence shows that these concepts were well established in the north of India long before Christianity could have had any appreciable influence in that area. We should not, however, completely reject on this account the possibility of the common influence on both Buddhism and Christianity of proto-gnostic ideas emanating from the Middle East. We think of a passage famous in Judaism and Christianity alike, attributed to the pre-exilic prophet Isaiah, but evidently composed by a captive Jew in Mesopotamia in the early days of the Achaemenid empire. The famous passage describing the 'Suffering Servant,' interpreted by Jews to refer to the People of Israel collectively and by Christians to be a prophecy of the passion of Jesus, may in fact refer to some unnamed Jewish victim of the oppression of the Babylonians. Despite obvious differences, this passage clearly reflects a doctrine similar to the Mahāyāna one of transfer of merit, and seems to look forward not only to the suffering Christ, but also to the later Mahāyāna Bodhisattva, who voluntarily undertakes to share the suffering of the world in order to save it:

> He was despised, he shrank from the sight
> of men, tormented and humbled by suffering....
> Yet on himself he bore our sufferings, our
> torments he endured....
> The chastisement he bore is health for us and
> by his scourging we are healed....
> So shall he, my servant, vindicate many,
> himself bearing the penalty of their guilt.[56]

Parallels between Christianity and Buddhism have often been pointed out, and some of them are vivid and striking. Most of them relate however, to the legend and mythology of the Buddhist Sanskrit texts, rather than to the Buddhism of the Pāli sources. Examples are the parable of a prodigal son in both St. Luke's Gospel and the *Saddharma-puṇḍarīka*, the vision of the New Jerusalem in *Revelation* and the description of the glorious city of Nirvāṇa in the *Milinda-pañha*, the Song of Simeon in Luke and the account of the visit of the hermit Asita to the infant Siddhārtha, found in both Pāli and Buddhist Sanskrit sources, and a number of legends of the childhood of Siddhārtha which are parallelled in the apocryphal gospels.

Some of these legends may be due to direct Buddhist influence on Christianity, as the Eastern Christian legend of St. Josaphat certainly is, but many of the parallels cannot possibly, for chronological reasons, be due to direct borrowing by one religion from another. The similarities are due either to the chance of minds thinking alike or to the influence of a common source.

Among common themes which cannot be due to the direct inspiration of one religion on another are the Prodigal Son, the Heavenly City, and the *Nunc Dimittis* motif, mentioned above. Other beliefs of Mahāyāna Buddhism may be compared with ideas not strongly emphasized in Christianity, but current in certain circles of the Pre-Christian Middle East. Sometimes referred to in this connection is the resemblance between the Buddhist personification of *Prajñā-pāramitā* and the *Hagia Sophia*, the Divine Wisdom of later Judaism.[57] The common Indian doctrines of transmigration and *karma* can be traced back to the early *Upaniṣads*. Similar doctrines in Greece can be traced almost as far, at least back to the 6th century B.C. when Pythagoras taught them at a time before the Achaemenians had provided a bridge between India and the eastern Mediterranean. Beast fables, many of them nearly identical, appear in both civilizations at almost the same time.

We can either attribute these similarities to chance, or we can refuse to do so, finding them too numerous to be coincidental. No calculus hitherto discovered can estimate the inherent probabilities of influence in coincidences such as this, and we are compelled to turn to generalized judgements, into which subjective factors enter. If we believe that the similarities are too numerous and close to be fortuitous the only conclusion must be that in most cases they are due to a common source in the Middle East. Iranian dualism has been generally postulated as this common source.[58] The mythology of the various cults of early Iran, such as Zoroastrianism, Zurvanism and Mithraism, provide probable sources of inspiration for much of the mythology of Mahāyāna Buddhism on the one hand and post-exilic Judaism and Christianity on the other. The later apocalyptic Messianism of the Jews, which culminated in that of Christianity, can be related to that of Maitreya Buddha through a postulated common origin in the Zoroastrian Shaoshyant. The belief in angels and Bodhisattvas alike can be traced to the *fravashis* and *amesha spentas* of Zoroastrianism.[59]

In fact many of the facets of the whole Bodhisattva concept, in its developed Mahāyāna form, do bear this Iranian tinge, and few would be so incredulous as to reject the possibility of influence out of hand, especially as the concept appears to have begun in that part of India which came under the dominance of Central Asians long in contact with Iran and speaking Iranian languages. Moreover it appears around the time of their dominance.

The chronology of Zoroastrianism and of the various strata of the *Avesta* is so contentious that often when we find parallels with Buddhist ideas we cannot be absolutely certain whether, if there was borrowing, it was made by Buddhism from Zoroastrianism or the reverse. But the oldest stratum of the *Avesta*, the *Gāthās*, is generally accepted as the authentic work of Zarathushtra himself, composed before Cyrus consolidated his empire.[60] Several aspects of the attitude reflected in these obscure hymns suggest that primitive Zoroastrianism, as well as the finished Zoroastrian religion of later times, may have prepared the ground for the great change which came over popular Buddhism around the time of Christ.

First, early Zoroastrianism postulated an all-Wise (*Mazdāh*, c.f. *Saṃbuddha*) Lord (*Ahura*, c.f. *Bhagavān*) striving from his throne in the heavens for the triumph of light and righteousness (*Asha*, c.f. *Dharma*) against the Lie (*Druj*, c.f. *Māra*, *Māyā*). He is attended and aided by faithful henchmen or ministers, of whom six personified virtues and natural entities are particularly prominent. The Wise Lord of Zarathushtra suggests, up to a point, a prototype of the Heavenly Buddhas of the Mahāyāna, surrounded by innumerable Bodhisattvas, of whom two, Avalokiteśvara and Mahāsthāmaprāpta, are outstanding. Of these three divine beings Amitābha, the Buddha of Immeasurable Radiance, shares with Ahura Mazdāh an association with light, as has been pointed out by several scholars already.[61] One cannot closely relate the two great Bodhisattvas to the two major *Amesha Spentas*, but the idea of a trinity of very powerful and beneficient heavenly beings was certainly present in both early Zoroastrianism and Mahāyāna Buddhism.

An important feature of early Zoroastrianism, which sharply differentiates it from most Indian religion, is its practical down-to-earth nature. Zarathushtra is concerned with the state of the world and the people around him. His aims are partly political — the establishment of a just society in which the pastoralists and peasants will be able to live out their lives in peace, free from the oppression of those who have chosen the Lie. Like the Buddha, he is concerned at the suffering, human and animal, in the world around him. But Zarathushtra's concern is practical and immediate, rather than metaphysical. He attributes suffering to the wickedness of those who have made the wrong choice, rather than to any fundamental defects in human nature. Appearing as he did in a more violent, unstable society than that of early Buddhism, Zarathushtra sees human misery typified not in the pains of birth, disease, old age and death, but in hunger, rapine and slaughter, the oppression of the proud and evil, the cruel butchering of cattle by the devotees of the old sacrificial religion.[62] His analysis of the human predicament is far less subtle than that attributed to the Buddha, but it is also far more down-to-earth.

This positive, realistic attitude seems to be reflected in the cult of the Mahāyāna Bodhisattvas, especially of Avalokiteśvara. In the face of suffering of the grosser kind, the Theravāda has little practical help to offer, beyond recommending the acceptance of evil as part of the very nature of embodied life, feeling benevolence towards the evil-doer, and striving to emancipate oneself from all personal cravings. The counsels of Theravāda are counsels of perfection, and probably made little appeal to the simple soul, such as the peasant whose cattle has been seized and slaughtered by marauding barbarians and whose family was dying of hunger as a result. Zoroastrianism, on the other hand, promised him divine help of a practical kind. Heavenly helpers are at hand to defend the toiling husbandman, and the ox led to the slaughter. They are not almighty at present, and they need the help of men in their struggle against the Lie; but they are there to help and protect the simple man who tries to live righteously. As the religion developed, the role of the divine intermediary and helper of men was increasingly taken over by Shraosha, not one of the Bounteous Immortals but a spirit theoretically on a somewhat lower level than they, and more readily available to men.[63] Marie-Thérèse de Mallmann has pointed out striking parallels between passages in the liturgy of Shraosha in the *Yast* section of the *Avesta*, and those in the prose part of the 24th chapter of the *Saddharma-puṇḍarīka*.[64] Both divinities are depicted as capable of almost unlimited help on the material plane, protecting the believer from floods, bandits and demons.

A further salient feature of early Zoroastrianism is its emphasis on choice and personal decision. Ahura Mazdāh himself decided once and for all at the beginning of time to maintain righteousness, truth and light, and the believer must do the same. The prophecy that a thousand years after Zarathushtra the Shaoshyant or Saviour will finally expel evil, and all beings will pass through the Ordeal of Molten Metal to the New Creation, when the spirits of darkness and sin are finally defeated and Mazdāh and the Bounteous Immortals reign supreme, is comparatively late, but traces of something like it can be found in the *Gāthās*.[65] It appears that in its earliest form the myth envisaged the total destruction of the wicked, rather than their regeneration in righteousness. The ethics of the Zoroastrian concept of choice seem to imply that, once the right choice is made, in favour of Ahura Mazdāh and the powers of light and truth, the effects of previous sins are removed, though this is nowhere specifically stated, as far as we know, in the earlier parts of the *Avesta*.

The opinion that the doctrine of the future Buddha, Metteyya or Maitreya, owes much to the Shaoshyant of Zoroastrianism is a commonplace, and there is no doubt that Zoroastrianism has influenced soteriological and eschatological doctrines both East and West. But we have shown that both the doctrine of the future Buddha and that of the heavenly Bodhisattvas can be deduced logically from the teachings of primitive Buddhism as far as they can be reconstructed, given an implicit belief in cyclic time. Thus it would be wrong to look on either doctrine as deliberately borrowed from Zoroastrianism or any other branch of Iranian religion. A more feasible interpretation of the data would be that the spread of Iranian influence in the northwestern part of the subcontinent prepared the ground for these doctrines by encouraging among the people at large certain attitudes, for instance: (i) The expectation of a heavenly helper in practical difficulties; (ii) the importance of making a right and firm decision to strive for righteousness; (iii) the hope for a great day in the future when a divine saviour would be instrumental in purifying the world; and (iv) the ultimate salvation of all things living. Buddhism met these needs as it spread in the Northwest, Afghanistan and Central Asia by evolving, for the first need, the doctrine of the heavenly Bodhisattvas; for the second, the earnest resolve of the Bodhisattva, repeated by many earnest Buddhists of the Mahāyāna sects; for the third, faith in the beneficent work of the Bodhisattvas in promoting the spiritual progress of the universe, and in the future Buddha Maitreya with other unnamed Buddhas after him; and for the fourth, the belief that ultimately the Bodhisattvas would lead all beings to the highest bliss.

Evidence for the penetration of Iranian influence is quite clear from the period of the Śaka and Kuṣāṇa domination of the area. It is also clear, however, that even in the time of the Buddha himself the northwestern parts of India, now Pakistan, were dominated by Iran, for there is no question that Gandhāra and an undefined area of the Indus Valley were under the suzerainty of the Achaemenids. Archaeological evidence of Achaemenid domination is scanty, but some years ago Dani discovered fire-altars at Balambat in Swat,[66] and these prove that some form of Zoroastrianism was practised there. About seventy years ago D.B. Spooner put forward arguments in favour of massive Iranian influence on India at the time of the Mauryan empire.[67] Though few modern specialists would go as far as Spooner, the fact remains that in India monumental stone-carving first appears in a distinctly Persepolitan form. The technique of carving large pieces of stone and imparting to them a fine and durable polish must surely have been learnt from schools of Iranian masons and craftsmen who perhaps emigrated to India after the Macedonian conquest of Iran, when there were no longer patrons in Iran wealthy enough to support them. Even the decision of Aśoka to 'set out for Saṃbodhī,' if our interpretation of this phrase is correct, may owe something to ideas coming from Iran in the form of the Zoroastrian resolve to choose to follow the powers of Light. The view that Aśoka's rock-inscriptions themselves were inspired by Achaemenian precedent is well known, and seems reasonable.[68] The first century A.D., when western contacts with India were closer than ever before, saw the emergence of the developed Mahāyāna Bodhisattva doctrine in that part of India which was most exposed to influences from the West, including Iran. We may suggest that not only later parallels with Iranian religion in various aspects of the Bodhisattva doctrine, but also the very doctrine itself, arose in part through the favourable ground prepared for it by Iranian contacts.

Yet another factor which promoted the development of such a doctrine must have been the general religious, social and political climate of India itself. The Buddhist theism of the Mahāyāna arose *pari passu* with the growth of a new type of theism in Hinduism, reflected especially in the *Śvetāśvatara Upaniṣad* and the *Bhagavad Gītā*. It is generally assumed that these two texts are fairly wide apart in time, but we believe that there is no very good reason for this view. Certainly the *Bhagavad Gītā* is more elaborate than the *Śvetāśvatara*, but, except for the theological doctrine of *avatāra* and the ethical doctrine of selfless action, which are peculiar to the *Gītā*, the message is much the same in both texts, namely devotion to a personal god, whether Śiva or Viṣṇu. The texts are evidence of a growing conviction, probably felt much earlier in less educated circles, but now affecting even the intelligentsia, that the ultimate basis of the cosmos was a personal god who felt love for all created things, and to whom they should feel deep love and devotion in return. He could, it was believed, set aside the evil effects of *karma*, so that past sins did not need to be expunged by suffering in later incarnations, and the repentant sinner, even the *śūdra*, could, through devotion, by the grace of God go straight to him on death and be reborn no more.[69]

It is often suggested that theistic Buddhism, especially the cult of the heavenly Buddha Amitābha and the doctrine of salvation by faith which accompanied it, were the response of Buddhism to the rise of Hindu devotional theism. We know from the inscription on the famous Besnagar column that the Bhāgavata sect,[70] with doctrines probably similar to those of the *Gītā*, was an important factor in the religion of Western India by about 100 B.C., and probably had the support of the Śuṅga kings. The Amitābha cult, and the finished Bodhisattva doctrine of the Mahāyāna, are not attested at this early period, and we may thus suggest Hindu theism as an important factor in their evolution.

We must, however, emphasize again that these innovations in Buddhism need not be attributed wholly to the influence of Hinduism, much less to that of Zoroastrianism. We have shown that the Mahāyāna doctrine of the Bodhisattva may be deduced logically from the Buddhology of Theravāda.[71] Moreover the whole new mythology of the Mahāyāna is implicit in the simple phrase *Buddhaṃ saraṇaṃ gacchāmi*, which, taken at its face value, implies that the Buddha still exists as a distinct entity, and is capable of giving protection to those who trust in him. Yet the atmosphere of the times between the fall of Mauryan Empire and the retreat of the Kuṣāṇas from most of India was conducive to theism, to a religion which encouraged simple faith, and which gave hope of divine intervention to alleviate the hardships and dangers which beset the ordinary man.

When we consider the period from 200 B.C. to A.D. 200, the period when in India the seeds of Mahāyāna Buddhism, together with those of devotional Vaiṣṇavism and Śaivism, germinated and developed, we are inclined to look on it as a period of progress. The remains of Bharhut and Sanchi, the Western Caves, Amaravati and Nágarjunakonda, all speak of the flourishing state of Buddhism. The buildings and sculpture of the Gandhāra and Mathura schools seem to show how the invaders were contained and became sufficiently Indianized to endow splendid *stūpas* and monasteries. All the material evidence speaks of prosperity. It is clear, from the vantage point of two thousand years later, that this was a period of cultural progress.

Yet on many occasions during those decisive centuries, the situation must have seemed very different, especially to the ordinary man in those areas of India which came under the rule of the invaders from Central Asia. From all that we can gather about the Mauryan régime it brought stability and peace to most of the sub-continent through most of the 3rd century B.C. It gave way to smaller, less well organized kingdoms, quasi-feudal in structure, which soon felt the weight of foreign attacks. The Bactrian Greeks occupied the Panjab, the Śakas penetrated as far as Mathura and Gujarat, and the power of the Kuṣāṇas under Kaniṣka was felt at least as far as Varanasi. Each of these conquests meant new battles, new hordes of barbarians marching over the land, commandeering corn and cattle, raping and looting. It may be that none of these attacks was as bloodthirsty as the better documented raids of Tīmūr and Nādir Shāh, but they cannot have failed to cause widespread misery and death.

The well known *Mārkaṇḍeya Parvan,* interpolated into the *Mahābhārata*, gives us an idea of how the times appeared to some at least of the orthodox brahmans. In the form of a prophecy, put in the mouth of the *ṛṣi* Mārkaṇḍeya, we are told of impure barbarians overrunning the holy land of Bhāratavarṣa, slaughtering and looting, bringing in their wake insecurity of life and property, banditry, and the disintegration of the norms of family life. In these circumstances the sacrifices and rituals of orthodoxy are neglected, and the only religions to flourish are those of the heretics, who teach the people to worship mounds (*eḍūka*) containing dead men's bones — a clear reference to the Buddhists.[72]

The brahman author of this passage was quite convinced that the end of the *yuga* was very near, and that soon the world would be destroyed by fire, wind and water. His belief in cyclic time, and the return of the *Kṛta Yuga* after this cataclysm, seems in no way to have mitigated the feeling of virtual despair that this passage conveys. Life was already very terrible and precarious and, from the author's point of view, nothing could prevent the ultimate catastrophe. The passage, describing almost every aspect of human misery, must emanate from a period when the barbarians were actually dominant in northwestern India and were making their presence felt elsewhere also. This account of the four ages gives to the *Kali Yuga* only one thousand years, with two 'twilights' of one hundred each. Since the *Kali Yuga* was believed to have commenced with the conclusion of the *Mahābhārata* war, the end, or the author, must have seemed very near indeed.

The views of this anonymous prophet must reflect the views of the times. Here was a fertile soil for the growth of new religious concepts, based on faith and devotion. Men needed help and guidance which they could not find in the traditional mythologies or in the rather cold metaphysics and psychologies of the older Buddhism, Jainism and Upaniṣadic Hinduism. Men needed saviours. They found them in Hinduism in the Kṛṣṇa *avatāra* of Viṣṇu, whose grace set aside the evil *karma* of those who loved him, and in the beneficent aspects of Śiva, who could do the same. In Buddhism the heavenly Amitābha, Avalokiteśvara and other Bodhisattvas, and the future Buddha Maitreya met the need. A few centuries later, when similar conditions prevailed in China, they began to make a strong impression on that land also.

It is not the primary duty of the historian to evaluate on an ethical or any other basis the subjects of his investigation, and we do not consider it necessary to give such an evaluation. Belief in heavenly Bodhisattvas is a fact of history, whether such divine beings actually exist or not. In this light it is an important subject of study. The Theravādins look on the myth of the heavenly Bodhisattvas as a perversion of the original self-reliant atheistic teaching of the Master. Even intellectual Mahāyānists nowadays are much happier with the subtle mystical philosophy of *Śūnyavāda* than with the beautiful mythology of Mahāyāna. I have met Japanese Buddhists who insist that Bodhisattvas have no reality anyway, that they are *śūnya* like every other finite entity in the cosmos, or that they were deliberately invented by clever monks, motivated by *upāya-kauśalya-pāramitā*, to give comfort and courage to their weaker and less intellectual brethren.

Let us look at the question from another angle. It may be that there is nothing in the universe corresponding to the legendary Avalokiteśvara and his fellow Bodhisattvas. Indeed it may be, and many people nowadays formally believe the proposition, that there are no supernatural powers whatever — that God, and Avalokiteśvara with him, is dead. But the question of the objective reality of heavenly Bodhisattvas is not one which we can fruitfully raise. If they do not exist as objective beings, they have certainly existed, and still exist, as subsistent entities or concepts, on the same level at least, for instance, as Santa Claus or the fierce Aztec war-god Huitzilopochtli. The world would be poorer for the loss of Santa Claus, and so he still exists in the minds of millions of small children throughout the Western world; Huitzilopochtli, being bloodthirsty in the extreme and demanding frequent human sacrifice, has served whatever purpose he had and has perished. Surely the heavenly Bodhisattvas are on the side of Santa Claus. Let us clinch the matter by a few rhetorical questions: Would the world have been a happier place if nobody had ever believed in Bodhisattvas? If the vow of the Bodhisattva, an inspiration to selfless service and helpfulness, had never been devised, would there have been more, or less, love and fellowship among men? Is the doctrine of the transfer of merit calculated to comfort and reassure the believer, or to fill him with guilt and fear? There can be no doubt about the answer to these three questions. In many parts of Asia, at least in past centuries, men have needed Bodhisattvas. Perhaps, despite the advance of human knowledge and power, the world still needs supernatural love, help, and compassion. A new twentieth-century pseudo-scientific myth is developing, thanks to popular television programmes, centering round Supermen and Wonder-Women, who are believed in by children and in whom some of their elders would wistfully like to believe, though they cannot suspend their reasons sufficiently to do so. These are the Bodhisattvas of the Space Age. Clearly, even in modern secular society, the Bodhisattva ideal is not dead.

KEY TO ABBREVIATIONS USED IN NOTES

APP	R. Mitra (ed.), *Aṣṭasāhasrika-Prajñāpāramitā-sūtra* (Calcutta: Asiatic Society, 1888).
Bh G.	R.C. Zaehner (ed.), *The Bhagavad-gītā with a commentary based on the original sources* (Oxford: Clarendon Press, 1969).
Bloch	Jules Bloch, *Les inscriptions d'Asoka* Collection Émile Senart, vol. viii (Paris: Les Belles Lettres, 1950).
CHI	K.A. Nilakanta Sastri (ed.), *A comprehensive history of India*, ii, *The Mauryas and Sātavāhanas* 325 B.C.-A.D. 300 (Calcutta: Orient Longmans, 1957).
CII	S. Konow (ed.), *Corpus Inscriptionum Indicarum* vol. ii, pt. i, *Kharoshthī Inscriptions* (Calcutta: Government of India, 1929).
Conze	Edward Conze, *Buddhism, its essence and development* (Oxford: Cassirer, 1st ed., 1951. Later editions and paperbacks).
Dani	Ahmad Husan Dani, 'Report on the excavation of Balambat settlement site.' *Ancient Pakistan* (Peshawar: University of Peshawar, 1967) vol. iii, pp. 237-288.
Divyāvadāna	E.B. Cowell and R.A. Neil, *The Divyāvadāna* (Cambridge: U.P., 1886).
DN	T.W. Rhys Davids and J. Estlin Carpenter (ed.), *The Dīgha Nikāya* 3 vols. (London: Pāli Text Society, 1890-1911. Reprint London: Luzac & O.U.P., 1947-49.)
Eggermont	P.H.L. Eggermont, *The chronology of the reign of Asoka Moriya* (Leiden: Brill, 1956).
EI	Various editors, *Epigraphia Indica* (Calcutta, Delhi: Archaeological Survey of India, 1888 - in progress).
Frye	Richard N. Frye, *The heritage of Persia* (London: Weidenfeld and Nicolson, 1963. Paperback, New York, Mentor Books, 1966).
Gāthās	Jacques Duchesne-Guillemin (trans.), *The hymns of Zarathustra.* Retranslated from the French by Mrs. M. Henning (London: John Murray, 1952).

Giles — H.A. Giles (tr.), *The travels of Fa-hsien (399-414 A.D.) or record of the Buddhistic Kingdoms* (Cambridge U.P., 1923).

Har Dayal — Dayal Har, *The Bodhisattva doctrine in Buddhist Sanskrit literature* (London: Routledge, 1932. Reprint, Delhi: Motilal, 1970).

Jātaka — V. Fausbøll (ed.), *The Jātaka, together with its commentary* 7 vols. (London: Trubner, 1877-97).

Joshi — Lalmani Joshi, *Studies in the Buddhistic Culture of India* (Delhi: Motilal, 1967).

JRAS — *Journal of the Royal Asiatic Society* (London: Royal Asiatic Society, 1834 - in progress).

Khuddaka Pāṭha — Helmer Smith (ed.), *The Khuddaka-Pāṭha together with its commentary* (London: Pāli Text Society, 1915).

Lamotte — Étienne Lamotte, *Histoire du Bouddhisme indien des origines a l'ère Śaka* Bibliothèque du Muséon, vol. 43 (Louvain: Publications Universitaires, 1958).

Life — Samuel Beal (tr.), *The Life of Hiuen-Tsiang by the Shaman Hwui Li* (London: Kegan Paul, 1911. Reissue 1914).

Mallmann — Marie-Thérèse de Mallmann *Introduction a l'étude d'Avalokiteçvara. Annales du Musée Guimet, Bibliothèque d'études* vol. lvii (Paris: Presses Universitaires, 1967).

Mbh — V.S. Sukthankar and others (ed.), *The Mahābhārata* 19 vols. (Poona: BORI, 1933-59).

MN — V. Trenckner, R. Chalmers and C.A.F. Rhys Davids (eds.), *The Majjhimanikāya* 3 vols. (London: Pāli Text Society, 1888-99. Reprint, London: Luzac, 1960-64).

Monier-Williams — Monier Monier-Williams, *A Sanskrit-English Dictionary*, New Edition (Oxford: Clarendon Press, 1899 reprint, 1951).

Oltramare — Paul Oltramare, *La théosophie bouddhique* (Paris: Geuthner, 1923).

Poussin 1930 — Louis de la Vallée Poussin, *L'Inde aux temps des Mauryas et des Barbares, Grecs, Scythes, Parthes et Yue-chih. Histoire du Monde* vol. vi (Paris: Bomard, 1930).

Poussin 1935 — Louis de la Vallée Poussin, *Dynasties et histoire de' l'Inde depuis Kanishka jusqu'aux invasions musulmanes. Histoire du Monde* vol. vi² (Paris: Boccard, 1935).

Reden K.E. Neumann, *Die Reden Gotamo Buddhas aus der Mittleren Sammlung* 3 vols. 2nd ed. (Munich: Piper, 1922).

Rhys Davids T.W. Rhys Davids, *Buddhist India. Story of the nations* vol. lx (London: Fisher Unwin, 1903).

SBE, xlix E.B. Cowell, Max Müller and J. Takakusu (tr.), *Buddhist Mahāyāna texts. Sacred books of the East* (Oxford: Clarendon Press, 1894. Reprints, Delhi: Motilal, 1965, 1968).

SDP H. Kern and B. Nanjio (eds.), *Saddharma-puṇḍarīka. Bibliotheca Buddhica* vol. x (St. Petersburg: Imperial Academy of Sciences, 1912).

Sircar D.C. Sircar, *Select inscriptions bearing on Indian history and civilization* vol. i, 2nd ed. (University of Calcutta, 1965).

ŚS Cecil Bendall (ed.), *Śikṣāsamuccaya of Śāntideva. Bibliotheca Buddhica* vol. i (St. Petersburg: Imperial Academy of Sciences, 1902. Reprint, The Hague: Mouton, 1957).

SV Max Müller (tr.), the *Larger Sukhāvatī-vyūha* In *SBE* xlix, section ii.

Thapar Romila Thapar, *Asoka and the decline of the Mauryas* (Oxford: University Press, 1961).

Van Buitenen J.A.B. Van Buitenen (tr.), *The Mahābhārata* vol. 2 (Chicago: University Press, 1975).

VP H. Oldenberg (ed.), *The Vinaya pitakam* 5 vols. (London: Pāli Text Society, 1879-83. Reprint, Luzac, 1964).

Warder A.K. Warder, *Indian Buddhism* (Delhi: Motilal, 1970).

Zaehner R.C. Zaehner, *The dawn and twilight of Zoroastrianism* (London: Weidenfeld and Nicolson, 1961).

FOOTNOTES

My main reasons for this are briefly as follows:

(i) The Pāli texts contain what appear to be more reliable historical allusions than those in Buddhist Sanskrit;

(ii) in the Pāli scriptures the supernatural element is less in evidence, and numbers less exaggerated;

(iii) the fact that the non-Theravāda literature is in a bastard Sanskrit can be parallelled by the development of epigraphy during the first two or three centuries A.D., when, in Northwestern India, Prākrit slowly gave way to Sanskrit in inscriptions, with various intermediate stages. If any Buddhist Sanskrit text is older than this period, this fact suggests that it is based on a Prākrit original which has undergone much editing, as well as translation;

(iv) the most impressive feature favouring the comparative authenticity of the Pāli texts is their very character and context. The doctrines there ascribed to the Buddha correspond in their general character with those of contemporary systems such as Jainism and Ājīvikism and the teachings of earlier *Upaniṣads*; they are marked by a tendency to reduce the basis of the whole Universe to a single impersonal principle; they are characterized by an intense drive for psychological security and escape from rebirth; and their main methods of argument are analogical rather than logical. The Mahāyāna texts, on the other hand, introduce into Buddhism a theistic element which is foreign to the Pāli texts and suggests the climate of thought of post-Mauryan India. This is accompanied by the growth of logical reasoning for sectarian purposes, culminating in the work of Nāgārjuna.

2 E.g. *APP* 22, 402-3; *ŚS*, pp. 278-297 forms a remarkable anthology of passages from earlier sūtras (*Akṣayamati-nirdeśa, Vajradhvaja-sūtra, Ratnamegha-sūtra* in particular) giving different versions of the great vow of the Bodhisattva. References might be multiplied indefinitely.

3 The light of the *śrāvaka* reaches a fathom, while that of the Bodhisattva reaches 100000 *koṭis* of *yojanas* (*SV*, xxxiv).

4 Dayal Har, *The Bodhisattva doctrine in Buddhist Sanskrit literature* (London: Routledge, 1932, reprinted Delhi).

5 Marie-Thérèse De Mallmann, *Introduction à l'étude d'Avalokiteçvara* (Paris: Presses Universitaire de France, 1967).

6 The Buddha commences his sermon in *MN* i, 114 with the words *Pubbe va me, bhikkhave, sambodhā, anabhisambuddhassa bodhisattassa sato, etad ahosi*. A similar formula is found in *MN* i, 163. In *MN* iii, 119 the Buddha recalls his pre-natal existence as a Bodhisatta in the Tusita heaven (*Tusitaṃ kāyaṃ upapajji*).

7 *Kathāvatthu* pp. 283-90.

8 Har Dayal, pp. 4-9. The suggestion originated with Neumann (*Reden*, i, 620, n5), but was rejected by Oltramare (p. 250) on the grounds that *sakta* is only applied to selfish or undesirable attachments. I have not had time to investigate the question fully, but I believe examples may be found of derivatives of the root *sañj* being used in Hindu literature in connection with *bhakti*. In any case the matter is not very significant.

9 Har Dayal, p. 9.

10 There seems no need to repeat the arguments in favour of the comparative lateness of the *Jātaka* collection, and few scholars would now follow such pioneers as Rhys Davids, who in his *Buddhist India* cheerfully used material even from the prose *Jātaka* as relevant to the time of the Buddha and the two following centuries. His claim that each of the *Jātakas* has a separate history (Rhys Davids, p. 194) is of course true and many of the stories may have been told by the Buddha himself; but even the verse *Jātaka* shows a much wider geographical horizon than the main body of the Pāli canon and even the less sophisticated stories of folk origin may have been adapted and tampered with over the centuries between their first adoption by the Buddhist clergy and their final redaction in Sri Lanka.

11 Sircar, p. 87, q.v. for further references. On the basis of one *akṣara*, D.C. Sircar dates this inscription in '*circa* 2nd half of the 1st century B.C.,' but the evidence is not absolutely conclusive. In any case, even if we accept this very late date, it does not follow that *Jātaka* reliefs of Bharhut are all as late as this.

12 *VP* iv, 164-66 (*Pācittiya*, 85). The Buddha's order does not specifically forbid the telling of stories, but merely entering a village at improper times in order to take part in gatherings for storytelling. It is sufficient, however, to show the disapproval in which such stories were held. The list of 28 types of secular story occurs in various contexts in other parts of the Pāli canon. In *DN* i, 178-79, Poṭṭhapāda, a *paribbājaka*, is described as sitting in the midst of a large gathering of similar ascetics, telling stories which fall under the same 28 heads.

13 Bloch, p. 158; Sircar, p. 68.

14 8th Rock Edict, line 2; Bloch, p. 112; Sircar, p. 27.

15 Bhabra (Bairat) Edict; line 1; Bloch p. 154; Sircar, p. 14.

16 Rhys Davids (p. 195) gives a list of ten stories contained in the *Nikāyas* and the *Vinaya* which are paraphrased as *Jātakas*. These include the stories of Makhadeva (*MN* ii, 75, c.f. *Jātaka* no. 9) and Mahāsudassana (*DN* ii, 169, c.f. *Jātaka* no. 95), in which even in the earlier version the hero is identified as a previous birth of the Buddha.

17 The story of Sumedha occurs in the *Nidānakathā* to the *Jātakas* (*Jātaka* i, 2ff), and in the *Buddhavaṃsa* (ii, 5ff.) The story is known in Buddhist Sanskrit sources, where its earliest occurrence is probably the *Divyāvadāna* (p. 247). Here the Bodhisattva is called Sumati.

[18] Line 2. Bloch, p. 112; Sircar, p. 27.

[19] The most recent study of this phrase known to me is in Eggermont (pp. 79-81), who strongly supports the now conventional interpretation as a reference to a pilgrimage to the Bodhi Tree on the part of Aśoka. He finds that the sacred tree is referred to in the *Dipavamsa* 6 times as *Saṃbodhi*, as against 22 times as *Mahābodhi* and simply *Bodhi*. One *Jātaka* reference (iv.26), pointed out by Bloch (p. 112, n. 6), is also adduced by Eggermont. These seven references, occurring in two texts of much later date which reached their present form in Sri Lanka, are hardly sufficient to prove that the ordinary educated Indian of the 3rd century B.C., on hearing or reading the edict, would interpret it thus — he would almost certainly assume, whether rightly or wrongly, that the emperor had set out to achieve supernal knowledge or enlightenment, and if Aśoka had wished to tell his subjects that he had made a pilgrimage to the Bodhi Tree he would have worded his edict differently, especially when we remember that at the time probably only a few of them had any very deep knowledge of Buddhism. Moreover those who support the now conventional interpretation overlook the fact that the verb *niṣkram*, which in a Prakrit form must have been used by Aśoka in this context, implies setting out on a journey, not arriving at its destination. Earlier scholars such as Senart and Rhys Davids all interpreted the word in a spiritual sense (for references see Eggermont, *loc.cit.*). De la Vallée Poussin, (1930, pp. 104-08) devotes some attention to the problem and tries to make the best of both worlds by suggesting that Aśoka made a pilgrimage to Gayā and also strove for perfect wisdom. The view that *Saṃbodhi* here means the Bodhi Tree was apparently first put forward by D.R. Bhandarkar (*Açoka*, University of Calcutta, 1925, p. 294, *teste* Eggermont, p. 79).

[20] Bloch, p. 111.

[21] 13th Rock Edict, 1.1 Bloch, p. 125; Sircar, p. 34.

[22] Further it should be noted that, if *Saṃbodhi* means the Bodhi Tree at Gaya, this is virtually the only clear reference to Buddhism in the series of the Major Rock Edicts, assuming, with Romila Thapar and others (Thapar, p. 149), that Aśoka's *Dhamma* was not the *Dhamma* of Buddhism.

[23] Bloch, p. 112, n. 6.

[24] 4th Rock Edict, Bloch, p. 100; Sircar, p. 20.

[25] *DN.* iii, 75 ff.

[26] Mallmann, pp. 119-27.

[27] Sircar, p. 133. *CII*, II, i, p. 77.

[28] Sircar, pp. 136-138; Vogel, J. Ph. *EI* viii, pp. 173 ff.

[29] Saraswati, S.K. in *CHI*, ii, p. 697.

[30] Sircar, pp. 157-58; *EI*, x, p. 113; the reading is not wholly certain.

[31] Mallmann, p. 21.

32 Larger *SV*. xxxi, 13-16; xxxiv; Mallmann, pp. 21-22.

33 Mallmann, p. 28.

34 *SDP*, xxiv; Mallmann, pp. 28-36, especially p. 31.

35 *Life*, pp. 17, 21, 22, 23. In his encounter with the river pirates, moreover, Hsüan Tsang is said by his biographer to have meditated on the Bodhisattva Maitreya, and thereby turned the hearts of his captors (*Life*, pp. 87-89). Fa-hsien, on his return voyage from Sri Lanka, on two occasions invoked Kwan Yin, when threatened with shipwreck (Giles, pp. 77-78).

36 Har Dayal, pp. 188-193.

37 Har Dayal, p. 190.

38 *Khuddaka Paṭha, 8*. For further references see Har Dayal, p. 190.

39 The most important of these, from the historian's point of view, will be found in Sircar, pp. 102-162, where reference to other and earlier editions and translations of the same inscription can also be found.

40 Sircar, p. 137.

41 Bloch, p. 109-110, Sircar, p. 25.

42 Sircar, p. 111.

43 Sircar, p. 115, with f.n.5. After examining the facsimile in *CII* (p. 48) we are more than doubtful about this interpretation, but Professor Sircar's reading of the uncertain Prakrit words as equivalent to Sanskrit *mukti-hitāya* (p. 118) is as good as any other. This reading was first suggested long ago by Bhagwanlal Indraji (*JRAS* NS xxvi, pp. 542-44).

44 Sircar, pp. 124-25.

45 *Sarva-budhana puyae mata-pitaraṃ puyay*[*amto*] *kṣatrapasa saputra-darasa ayu-bala-vardhie bhratara sarva* [*ca*] [*ñatiga*]*-dhivasa - puyayaṃto*. The doubtful passages in square brackets are as restored by Sircar, p. 124.

46 Sircar, p. 126.

47 Sircar, p. 133.

48 Sircar, p. 137.

49 E.g. Sircar, p. 141, p. 149.

50 Sircar, p. 518.

51 Sircar, p. 152.

52 Sircar, p. 230. Our translation of *loka* as 'family' is admittedly unusual, but if we take the phrase as meaning 'both worlds' the phrase *sarva-loka hita-sukhāvaha* seems pleonastic. The previous phrase is ...*apano ubhayakulasa atichitam anāgata-vaṭamānakānaṃ pariṇametum* which may mean: in order to ripen the past, future and present (welfare) of both her families (i.e. her husband's and her own) reading the last two syllables of *vaṭamānakānaṃ* as an error for - *āni*. The meaning of 'a company, a community' for *loka* is attested (Monier-Williams *s.v.*), and is common in several modern Indo-Aryan languages in *tadbhāva* form (*log*). By *ubhaya-loka* Śāntiśrī perhaps refers to the individual members of the two families, as distinct from the families taken collectively in *ubhaya-kula*. This interpretation is, however, admittedly uncertain, and is not in any case really important in the context.

53 The idea that the individual who reaches an advanced spiritual state is relieved of the burden of his past deeds is as old as the fairly early *Kanṣītakī Upaniṣad*, where it is explicitly stated in beautiful figurative language (i.4). The idea is in fact implicit in the term *mokṣa*, though in general the *Upaniṣads* seem to take the view that until the effects of past deeds have been fully experienced this state cannot be achieved (e.g. *Kaṭha Upaniṣad*, v. 7). The view that the contemplation of God sets aside evil *karma* is implicit in the *Śvetāśvatara Upaniṣad* and is summed up in a beautiful verse which seems to be the conclusion of the original text (vi.20). The last three verses are in the nature of a colophon giving the name of the author, and seem to have been added later, at a time when the concept of *bhakti* was widespread, since this word occurs in the *Śvetāśvatāra* only in vi, 23. The attitude of *bhakti*, however, is implicit in several passages of this text, for example vi, 18 (*Taṃ ha devam ātma-buddhi prakāśaṃ mumukṣur vai śaraṇam ahaṃ prapadye*). The use of *śaraṇa* in this passage, incidentally, is logically intelligible; in the case of *Buddhaṃ saraṇaṃ gacchāmi*, on the basis of Theravāda Buddhology, it is not. Clear evidence of the setting aside of *karma* by divine grace is to be found in the *Bhagavad-gītā* (see note 54, below), and elsewhere in the Epic.

54 *Bh.G.* ix, 32.

55 E.g. Warder, pp. 352-55; Joshi, pp. 3-4.

56 *Isaiah* liii, 3-5 (*New English Bible*).

57 E.g., Conze, ch. vi, final paragraph.

58 E.g., Frye, ch. 3. (paperback, pp. 153-54).

59 Frye, *loc. cit.* gives Christian parallels. For possible Iranian influence on the Bodhisattva concept see Har Dayal, pp. 38-39; Mallmann pp. 85-95; Lamotte, p. 551.

60 Frye, ch. 2. sec. 2 (paperback, pp. 48-56); Zaehner, pp. 25, 33.

61 Lamotte, p. 551; Har Dayal, p. 39. A brief bibliography of earlier studies on the subject is to be found in Poussin 1930, p. 243. De la Vallée Poussin gives further notes and references in Poussin 1935, pp. 352-53.

62 The most famous of the *Gāthās* in this connection is *Yasna* 29, wherein Geush Urvan, 'The Ox-soul,' the personification of cattle and directly of the earth itself, complains to Ahura Mazdāh of the evils of the times and is promised help through Zarathushtra, who in turn prays for supernatural power and knowledge in order to protect Geush Urvan (*Gāthās*, pp. 56-61).

63 Zaehner, pp. 44, 94-96.

64 Mallmann, pp. 93-95.

65 E.g. *Yasna*, 46, 10-11 (*Gāthās*, p. 79).

66 Dani, pp. 244-46, and plate xliii.

67 *JRAS* 1915, pp. 63 ff; 1916, pp. 138 ff., 362 ff.

68 Poussin 1930, pp. 20-21, quoting Senart and Hultzsch.

69 See note 54, above.

70 Sircar, pp. 88-89.

71 An earlier study on this theme by the author, which may have some relevance, is 'The rise of Buddhism in its historical development', *Asian Studies* iv, (Manila: 1966) pp. 395-411.

72 *Mbh*, iii, 186-188. The passage contains two separate accounts of the end of the *kali-yuga*. In the first Mārkaṇḍeya expounds to Yudhiṣṭhira the doctrine of the four *yugas*, which he enumerates, giving their lengths as 4800, 3600, 2400 and 1200 years respectively, *Mbh* iii, 186, 18-23, without reference to their being, 'years of the gods' as in *Manu* (i. 69-71). Then he describes the miseries of the end of the *kali-yuga*, largely from the point of view of the conservative orthodox brahman who sees the stable society in which he has been brought up crumbling before his eyes. Important for dating this passage around the beginning of the Christian era is *Mbh*, iii, 186, 29-30:

> Many barbarian (*Mleccha*) kings (there will be) in the world,
> Sinners ruling falsely, devoted to false doctrines (*mṛṣāvāda-parāyaṇāḥ*).
> Āndhra, Śaka, Pulinda, and Greek (*Yavana*) kings,
> Kāmbojas and Aurṇikas, Śūdras, and also Ābhīras.

In the second passage Mārkaṇḍeya tells how he encountered Kṛṣṇa in the form of a child at the end of an earlier *yuga*, and how Kṛṣṇa instructed him on the same theme. This contains the following significant passage (*Mbh*, iii, 188, 63-64):

> Śūdras will proclaim Dharma and brahmans, their servants,
> Will become their disciples, firmly under their authority.
> This world will be reversed, turned upside down.
> They will make them worship *eḍūkas* and avoid the gods.

Van Buitenen's translation (p. 596) does not bring out clearly what seems to be the point of this passage, which seems to refer to Buddhists. He takes the verbs *pūjayiṣyanti* and *varjayiṣyanti* as straightforward actives, and thinks their subject is an unwritten 'people;' but in our view they make better sense as causals, their subject being *śūdrā* in the previous verse. The rare word *eḍūka*, translated by Van Buitenen as 'charnel house,' must refer to *stūpas*. Lexicons confirm its association with bones, and with Buddhism (Monier-Williams, svv. *eḍūka*, *buddhaiḍūka*), but charnel houses, in the sense of buildings in which dead bodies were collected and left to rot, are not attested in ancient India.

THE BODHISATTVA RETURNS TO THIS WORLD

Gadjin M. Nagao

In his celebrated book, *The Bodhisattva Doctrine in Buddhist Sanskrit Literature*, Har Dayal elucidated the fundamental differences between Hīnayāna and Mahāyāna ideas. In his work, which was written almost 50 years ago and which is still being used widely by scholars, Dayal summarized the notion of the Arhat as follows:

> An Arhat who was thus liberated, knew that he would not be reborn. He had accomplished what was to be done. He attained undefiled and final emancipation of mind and heart. He was alone, secluded, jealous, earnest, master of himself.[1]

However, as time went on, Buddhist monks began to neglect the important aspect of Arhatship and became overly self-centered. Har Dayal continues:

> They seemed to have cared only for their own liberation ... were indifferent to the duty of teaching and helping all human beings.[2]

In short, theirs was a saintly and serene but an inactive and indolent monastic order.

In contrast to this, Dayal claimed that the Bodhisattva doctrine was promulgated as a protest against this coldness and aloofness of the Arhat. Accordingly, a Bodhisattva was one who criticised and condemned the spiritual egoism of such an Arhat.

As quoted before, "an Arhat ... knew that he would not be reborn," but a Bodhisattva is reborn and returns to this world. Although the differences between Hīnayāna and Mahāyāna ideas can be pointed out in various ways, I will confine myself here to the idea that a Bodhisattva is one who refuses the liberation of nirvāṇa until all sentient beings are saved. In developing this theme, I shall focus my attention on two terms — *apratiṣṭhita-nirvāṇa* and *saṃcintyabhavopapatti* — because these were scarcely noticed by Har Dayal.

I

Although the Bodhisattva's way is different from that of an Arhat, the nirvāṇa, or the highest goal for an Arhat, is never neglected nor devaluated by the Mahāyānists. This is because the Bodhisattva practice is in itself a way of benefitting others by helping them obtain the ultimate "nirvāṇa."

The last two chapters of Asaṅga's *Mahāyānasaṃgraha* are named *Phala-prahāṇa* and *Phala-jñāna*. As fruits of the Three Learnings (*śikṣā*), the former is no other than nirvāṇa (the suppression of defilements, *phala-prahāṇa*) and the latter refers to the four kinds of Buddha-wisdom (*phala-jñāna*) which are none other than the three kinds of Buddha-body (*kāya*). Vasubandhu's *Triṃśikā* mentions two bodies: *vimuktikāya* and *dharmakāya*. The former is the body acquired when *kleśa-āvaraṇa* (i.e., the Śrāvaka's turbidities) are suppressed, and corresponds to the fruit of having suppressed defilements as explained in *Phala-prahāṇa* chapter of the *Mahāyānasaṃgraha*. The latter is the body acquired when *jñeya-āvaraṇa* (i.e., the Bodhisattva's turbidities) are suppressed and corresponds to the fruit of having obtained wisdom as explained in *Phala-jñāna* chapter of the same text. Thus, along with the Buddha-wisdom or the Buddha-body, nirvāṇa is deemed also to be of the highest importance in the Mahāyāna.

However, in Mahāyāna texts, the word nirvāṇa is considered almost always to be qualified by the word *apratiṣṭhita* which means "not dwelling in," "not abiding in," and so on. When this Mahāyānic nirvāṇa, i.e., *apratiṣṭhita-nirvāṇa*, is considered separately from the two kinds of Hīnayānic nirvāṇa: *sopadhiśeṣa-nirvāṇa* and *nirupadhiśeṣa-nirvāṇa*, it becomes the third nirvāṇa. Or, it becomes the fourth nirvāṇa when the name 'nirvāṇa' (of the *Mahavyutpatti*, 1725) is regarded separately from these three nirvāṇas just mentioned and is considered to be "originally pure" (*prakṛti-viśuddhi*) as stated in the *Chên wei shih lun* (*Vijñaptimātratā-siddhi* by Hsüan-tsang), chüan 10.[3] In any case, this *apratiṣṭhita-nirvāṇa* is the sole nirvāṇa to be acquired either by Bodhisattvas or by Tathāgatas.

The two words *apratiṣṭhita* and *nirvāṇa* do not always form a compound, for we can find instances in which both have case-endings. For example, we find such phrases as

1) *na nirvāṇe pratiṣṭhito bhavati na saṃsāre.* [*Mahāyāna-sūtrālaṃkāra* (hereafter, *MSA*), XVII.32.]
2) *nirvāṇe 'pi mano na pratiṣṭhitaṃ.* [*MSA*, XVII.42.]
3) *apratiṣṭhito nirvāṇe.* [*Mahāvyutpatti*, 406.]
4) *apratiṣṭhitaṃ nirvāṇam.* [*Madhyāntavibhāga* (hereafter, *MV*), IV.12, V.1 (Sthiramati's *Tīkā*).]

In most cases, however, the two words are combined to form a compound:

1) *apratiṣṭhita-nirvāṇa.* [*MV*, II.1, IV.12cd; *MSA*, IX.45, XVIII.69, XIX.62, etc.]

In spite of the fact that we most frequently encounter this expression in compound form, we sometimes find the word "*saṃsāra*" added, as for example in:

2) *apratiṣṭhita-saṃsāra-nirvāṇa.* [*MSA*, XVII.32.]

There are also instances when even the word order is reversed, as for example in:

3) *nirvāṇa-apratiṣṭhita, saṃsāra-nirvāṇa-apratiṣṭhatā, -apratiṣṭhāna, -apratiṣṭhitatva,* etc. [*MV*, V.1, V.29; *MSA*, IX.14.]

É. Lamotte[4] admits that a grammatical explanation of the compound *apratiṣṭhita-nirvāṇa* would be difficult, and simply refers to J. Speyer's paraphrase: "*nirvāṇaṃ yatra na pratiṣṭhīyate*," even though he renders it as "le Nirvāṇa instable." Th. Stcherbatsky[5] and E. Obermiller[6] translate this term into English as "altruistic Nirvāṇa," and sometimes as "non-dialectical Nirvāṇa." The latter two translations, however, are interpretative translations, not literal ones. J. Takasaki[7] translates it as "not to stay fixedly in the Nirvāṇa," or "the Unstable Nirvāṇa."

In my opinion, F. Edgerton[8] gives a more proper explanation in his *Dictionary* when he defines the term *apratiṣṭhita* as "not permanently fixed" and adds, "it (*apratiṣṭhita-nirvāṇa*) is the Mahāyānistic nirvāṇa in which the Tathāgata returns (in the capacity of a Bodhisattva) to worldly life to save creatures ...." From this latter definition, it becomes clear that the word *apratiṣṭhita-nirvāṇa* denotes a

Bodhisattva's resolution: "I shall not enter into final nirvāṇa before all beings have been liberated."

Although *pratiṣṭhā* has the meanings of 'to stay,' 'to dwell,' 'to abide' etc. when used as a verb, and 'ground,' 'basis' etc. when used as a noun, the Chinese and Tibetan translators seem to have understood the term to mean 'being attached to,' 'clinging to,' 'adhering to.' In his *Vajracchedikā*, E. Conze[9] always translates *pratiṣṭhita* as 'support' and *apratiṣṭhitaṃ cittaṃ* as 'unsupported thought.' But he also admits that the meaning of *apratiṣṭhita* is ambiguous and proposes 21 'possible translations' for this term. Among those, the meanings "not attached to," and "not clinging to" are enumerated. In the Chinese commentaries on the *Vajracchedikā*, *apratiṣṭhita* is usually interpreted as "not abiding" as well as "not clinging." *Mi gnas pa* (*apratiṣṭhita*), in the Tibetan translation *mi gnas pa'i mya ngan las 'das pa* (*apratiṣṭhita-nirvāṇa*), is apparently considered as an adjective describing nirvāṇa. This suggests a notion of "a nirvāṇa not clung to" derived from the Skt. *apratiṣṭhita-nirvāṇa*. The use of *apratiṣṭhita* as an adjective is reinforced when *apratiṣṭhita-nirvāṇa* is aligned with *sopadhiśeṣa-nirvāṇa* and *nirupadhiśeṣa-nirvāṇa*, because the first part of the two latter compounds clearly functions as an adjective. Further, in Sthiramati's commentary on the *MSA*, XVII.42,[10] *mi gnas* is replaced by *ma chags* (not clinging). Thus, *apratiṣṭhita* can be interpreted as "not clinging to." Also, in Vasubandhu's commentary on the *MSA*, IX.70[11] we read: *apratiṣṭhitanirvāṇe niviṣṭaṃ*, and this can be understood to mean "[a Bodhisattva] enters into a nirvāṇa to which he does not cling."

The two meanings of "not dwelling" and "not clinging" can be clearly seen in the *MSA*, XVII.42,[12] which delineates three levels of attachment and detachment that can be traced among the three types of human beings. Vasubandhu's commentary states:

> With regard to the detachedness of [a Bodhisattva's] compassion, there is a verse which reads:
>
> The mind of compassionate beings [Bodhisattvas], filled with tenderness, does not even dwell in [or cling to] the quiescence [of nirvāṇa].

> How much less will his loving mind dwell
> in [or cling to] worldly happiness or
> his own life?
>
> The loving minds of all worldly beings dwell in worldly happiness and their own life. Although the loving minds of Śrāvakas and pratyekabuddhas do not dwell in such things, their minds dwell in (or cling to) nirvāṇa which is the quiescence of all pains. On the contrary, due to compassion, the minds of Bodhisattvas do not dwell even in nirvāṇa. How much less will their loving minds be attached to the two [saṃsāra and nirvāṇa]?

Here, three kinds of attitudes about love are presented. Ordinary beings covet worldly joys as well as their own life, both of which are saṃsāric. The two *yānikas*, the Śravākas and Pratyekabuddhas, though freed from samsāric things, are still attached to nirvāṇa. The Bodhisattvas dwell neither in saṃsāra nor in nirvāṇa and neither love nor become attached to them. By combining the meanings of "not dwelling" and "not clinging," Vasubandhu makes it clear that the ways of the Bodhisattva, the Hīnayānic saints, and the ordinary beings are different. Hence, in the case of the Bodhisattva, we find the qualification: *apratiṣṭhita-saṃsāra-nirvāṇa*.

This term, *apratiṣṭhita-saṃsāra-nirvāṇatva*, is expounded in the *MSA*, XVII.32,[13] in a very comprehensible and clear manner. The verse runs as follows:

> After realizing all samsāric entities as painful and substanceless, he who possesses compassion and the highest wisdom [i.e., the Bodhisattva], is neither afflicted [by saṃsāra] nor bound by the faults [of saṃsāra].

Commenting upon this verse, Vasubandhu says:

> Since he possesses compassion, a Bodhisattva does not become agitated by saṃsāra, or does not feel weary of saṃsāra; therefore, he does not dwell in nirvāṇa. Again, since he possesses the highest wisdom, he is not bound by the faults of saṃsāra; therefore, he does not dwell in saṃsāra.

From Vasubandhu's commentary, it becomes clear that the term *apratiṣṭhita-nirvāṇa* means to exit from nirvāṇa and to come down into saṃsāra. A Bodhisattva does not dwell in and does not cling to nirvāṇa owing to his compassion. Moreover, a Bodhisattva's activity includes the aspect of *apratiṣṭhita-saṃsāra*, i.e., he neither dwells in nor clings to saṃsāra owing to his great wisdom. These two activities of coming from nirvāṇa and going to nirvāṇa are to be understood to be operating simultaneously in the term *apratiṣṭhita-nirvāṇa.*

The above does not exhaust all possible interpretations of the term *apratiṣṭhita-nirvāṇa*, for there are several others which are either separate interpretations or are derivatives of this term.

(1) In the *MV*, V.29[14] *apratiṣṭhatā* means *avinivartana*, "not turning back." This verse expounds the ten kinds of "attainment [of fruit]" (*samudāgama*) which results from the Bodhisattva's practice, and *apratiṣṭhatā* is mentioned here as the eighth kind of attainment. Vasubandhu says that it means "not dwelling in both saṃsāra and nirvāṇa," and continues to explain it as follows:

> It [*apratiṣṭhatā*] is an "attainment [of fruit]" called the "gaining of the [Buddha's] prediction at the stage of non-turning around," because he [the Bodhisattva] is now not liable to turn back from either saṃsāra or nirvāṇa.

Sthiramati clarifies this further in his commentary:

> Perceiving the sentient beings, a Bodhisattva does not turn back from the way of saṃsāra because of his compassion and also does not turn back from the way toward nirvāṇa because of his wisdom.

These two commentaries make it clear that the term "not turning back," which is another name for *apratiṣṭhatā*, means not only not turning back from the way to nirvāṇa but also not turning back from saṃsāra.

A similar explanation can be found in the *MSA*, XIX. 61-62,[15] where, likewise in terms of ten items, the tenet of Mahāyāna is elucidated. Of these ten items, the seventh and the eighth items are commented upon by Vasubandhu as follows:

> The purification of the [Buddha]-land and not dwelling in nirvāṇa are seen in the three stages of non-turning back.

(2) In *MSA*, IX.14,[16] *apratiṣṭhita* means *advaya*, "non-duality." In this verse Asaṅga explains *āśraya-parāvṛtti*, "evolution of basis," in ten ways. Of these, the sixth is called *dvayā vṛttiḥ*, "evolving of duality," because by means

of this evolution the Buddha Śākyamuni has manifested the two events of Enlightenment (*abhisaṃbodhi*) at Bodhgayā and *Parinirvāṇa* at Kusināra. These two events are also mentioned in Vasubandhu's commentary on the *MSA*, XIX.62,[17] and probably correspond respectively to the *Phala-jñāna* (*abhisaṃbodhi*) and *Phala-prahāṇa* (*parinirvāṇa*) in the *Mahāyānasaṃgraha* quoted above.

This "evolving of duality," however, is in the ultimate sense *advayā vṛttiḥ*, "evolving of non-duality," which the *MSA* explains as the seventh evolution of basis. Because the Bodhisattva dwells neither in saṃsāra nor in nirvāṇa, for him there is no duality between *saṃskṛta*, the compounded, and *asaṃskṛta*, the uncompounded. Owing to his wisdom, a Bodhisattva relinquishes the compounded and does not enter *saṃsāra*; and, owing to his compassion, he denies the uncompounded and does not enter nirvāṇa either.

It is this non-duality that plays a salient role in the notion of the Buddha's *samatā-jñāna*, "Equality Wisdom." The *MSA*, IX.70[18] explains "Equality Wisdom" with the compound: *apratiṣṭhasamāviṣṭa*(*-jnāna*). The Tibetan translation, however, understands this compound as *apratiṣṭha-śamāviṣṭa*(*-jñāna*) (*/ mi-gnas zhi-bar zhugs-pa ni/ mnyam-nyid ye-shes yin-par 'dod/*). *Sama* is another name for nirvāṇa, and, in his commentary, Vasubandhu makes the statement: *apratiṣṭhitanirvāṇe niviṣṭam samatā-jñānam*, "the Equality Wisdom is what had entered the not dwelling (or not clung to) nirvāṇa." We see here a kind of pun on the words *śama* (= nirvāṇa) and *sama* of *samatājñāna*. Sthiramati quotes in his commentary the *Buddhabhūmi-sūtra* and says:

> When the not dwelling nirvāṇa is realized, there is no difference between saṃsāra and nirvāṇa; they are regarded to be of one taste (*ekarāsa*).

Thus, at least, we can say the meaning of *apratiṣṭhita* is related to the meanings of *avinivartana* and *advaya*. With these meanings in mind, it is possible to interpret *apratiṣṭhita-nirvāṇa* as "the nirvāṇa in which the Bodhisattva does not turn back from either saṃsāra or nirvāṇa," and "the nirvāṇa in which the Bodhisattva realizes equanimity and the non-duality of saṃsāra and nirvāṇa."

II

Related to this *apratiṣṭhita-nirvāṇa*, there is a term *saṃcintya-bhavopapatti*. *Saṃcintya*, a gerund used as an adverb, means "intentionally, purposely." *Bhavopapatti* means to be born into the world of existence. Thus the term *samcintya-bhavopapatti* means 'to take birth willingly, volitionally, in the world of existence.' Since not to dwell in nirvāṇa is to get away from nirvāṇa, by implication it means to enter into saṃsāra. Thus, a Bodhisattva voluntarily comes into the saṃsāric world.

Why does he volunteer? It is solely for the purpose of benefitting others, helping others, and making service to others that a Bodhisattva enters saṃsāric life, even though nirvāṇa is the highest bliss to which all aim and even though he is one capable of attaining it or one who does not stay in it depending upon one's perspective. This he does from his unlimited compassion.

Such a birth, therefore, is a miraculous one. It does not take place in an ordinary way, but takes place in the midst of *śūnyatā*; it is paradoxical. For example, in the *Vimalakīrti-nirdeśa-sūtra*, one reads:

> Although there is in reality neither arising nor extinction, they [Bodhisattvas] voluntarily take on births.[19]

There is neither arising nor extinction in ultimate reality; yet a Bodhisattva intends his birth owing to his deep compassion for sentient beings and his sublime wisdom of *śūnyatā*. His is a paradoxical birth because it is non-existent and yet existent.

To express the idea that a Bodhisattva takes birth in the saṃsāric world, the sūtras and śāstras use a variety of different words and phrases. For example, *saṃcintya-bhavapratikāṅkṣī* and *saṃcintya-upapatti-parigraha* are phrases that appear in the *Prajñāpāramita-sūtras*.[20] While one finds the phrase *saṃcintya ca bhavādānam* in the *Abhisamayālaṃkāra*, I.67,[21] the śāstras such as *MSA* (II.9, IV.25) and *Ratnagotra-vibhāga* (I.68, in its commentary)[22] repeatedly employ the expression *saṃcintya-upapatti*. But it is the *MSA* that deals with the idea of the Bodhisattva's birth most frequently and comprehensively. In the *MSA*, then, it seems that *saṃcintya-bhavopapatti* was used as the standard form of expression. In any case, the term *saṃcintya*, "at will," which is common to all these expressions, is the key-word representing the central meaning of the idea.

Generally, the causes of birth for ordinary beings are past deeds (*karman*) and defilements (*kleśa*). But the Bodhisattva's birth is different in that it is caused purely by his will and purpose.

A typical birth of a Bodhisattva is explained in the *Bodhisattvabhūmi*, as follows:

> Wishing to benefit those lowly beings from a *caṇḍāla* up to a dog, wishing to calm their calamity, or wishing to guide them, a Bodhisattva takes any form from that of a *caṇḍāla* up to that of a dog at will.[23]

Here we see how severe and radical the Bodhisattva's rebirth is; it is almost impossible to accomplish. As his 'will' to be reborn gushes forth due to his limitless compassion, his place of rebirth ranges throughout all of the six *gatis*, even including the hells. However, as stated in the *MSA*, IV.24-25,[24] even though his rebirth has been difficult and severe, he goes about it as if going through a joyful garden (*udyāna-yātrā*). Or, again, he looks upon it like a magical creation (*nirmāṇa*) (*MSA*, XI.30),[25] in concordance with the Buddha's teaching: "every being is like *māyā*, like *nirmāṇa*, and so on."

The *MSA*, XX-XXI.8[26] divides the cause for Bodhisattva's birth into four kinds: 1) *karman*, 2) *praṇidhāna*, 3) *samādhi*, and 4) *vibhutva*. Of these, no. 1) *karman* is the cause for birth of a Bodhisattva who is in the stage of *adhimukticaryābhūmi*, i.e., a Bodhisattva who has not yet entered the Bodhisattva's 1st *bhūmi*. This means that he is in a state similar to that of an ordinary being, and, accordingly, *karman* is mentioned as the cause for his birth in accordance with the general rule of birth (although *kleśa* is not mentioned here). But because it is by the force of *karman* that his birth has been determined according to his will (*abhipreta*), his birth by *karman* may be understood in the sense of *saṃcintya-bhavopapatti*. Categories nos. 2) to 4) may be seen as *saṃcintya-bhavopapatti* that is genuine. Of these, no. 2), i.e., birth by the force of his vow, *praṇidhāna*, is related to the Bodhisattva who is already in the first and second *bhūmis*. No. 3), i.e., birth by the force of *samādhi*, refers to the one in the third to seventh *bhūmis*. No. 4), i.e., birth by the force of superhuman power, *vibhutva*, or transformation, *nirmāṇa*, refers to the one in the other *bhūmis*, the eighth and so on.

A Bodhisattva enters such a painful life of saṃsāra, and yet does not embrace the thought of fear or disgust; nor is he contaminated by the defilements of the saṃsāric world even if he has not abandoned them. Thus, for him, saṃsāra is like a joyful garden, or, it is not a place where he becomes agitated nor is bound by its faults.

The *MSA*, XVIII,19-21[27] explains *saṃcintya-bhavopapatti* further as the *dhṛti*, "firmness" of Bodhisattva. Firmness is first seen here in view of various ways of learnings. Then, it is related to *duṣkaracaryā* (austerity) in which the Bodhisattva is engaged; next it is related to *saṃcintya-bhavopapatti* by which a Bodhisattva is reborn at will into saṃsāra and does not abandon it (*saṃsārātyāga*); and finally it is related to *asaṃkleśa*, i.e., he does not suffer from its contamination. All these activities are called the Bodhisattva's firmness.

Or again, according to the *MSA*, XVIII.44,[28] *saṃcintya-bhavopapatti* of a Bodhisattva may mean to be reborn as a *cakravarti-rāja* and other dignitary beings such as Indra and Brahmā. Such a rebirth naturally possesses the prosperity (*saṃpatti*) of supreme body and supreme enjoyment. And yet one so reborn is not contaminated by defilements of desire and so on.

In the *MSA*, XX-XXI.12,[29] the characteristic of each of the eleven *bhūmis* is explained. It is with regard to the sixth *bhūmi* that *saṃcintya-bhavopapatti* becomes an issue. In this discussion, there is a phrase, *saṃkleśasyānurakṣaṇā*, 'guarding or protection of defilements.' The sixth *bhūmi* is characterized by the fact that when a Bodhisattva is reborn at will from having stayed with the view of *pratītyasamutpāda* (dependent co-origination) for a long time, there is the 'guarding of defilements.' In his commentary Sthiramati says:

> A Bodhisattva is reborn, fully mindful and conscious of whatever place where he chooses to be reborn. Because he is not contaminated by the defilements owing to the fact that he has stayed with the view of *pratītyasamutpāda* for a long time, there is the "guarding of defilements."[30]

In spite of these commentaries, the last phrase, "guarding of defilements," is not clear to me. It may mean 'guarding oneself against the contamination by defilements,' or, perhaps more accurately, 'keeping the defilement' as a course for a Bodhisattva's compassionate activity. The *Chên wei shih lun* (*Vijñaptimātratāsiddhi*), *chüan* 9,[31] reads:

> 留煩惱障 助願受生
>
> [A Bodhisattva] retains the obstacle of defilement (*kleśāvaraṇa*) to sustain his vow to be reborn [into saṃsāra].

In view of summarizing the discussion thus far, we have found that the term *apratiṣṭhita-nirvāṇa* included the two meanings of 'not dwelling in saṃsāra' and 'not dwelling in nirvāṇa.' 'Not dwelling in saṃsāra' meant not to indulge in saṃsāra, and not to be stained by saṃsāric defilements. We also saw that this was accomplished through wisdom (*prajñā*). On the other hand, we saw that 'not dwelling in nirvāṇa' meant that saṃsāra was accepted as a 'joyful garden' and that this was owing to the Bodhisattva's deep compassion. This latter characteristic was represented by the term *saṃcintya-bhavopapatti*.

III

In both Mahāyāna and Hīnayāna, nirvāṇa has always been the ultimate aim gained by "wisdom." However, the Mahāyānic idea differs from that of the Hīnayānic, in that a Bodhisattva refuses even nirvāṇa so long as all sentient beings have not yet been saved. This is to say that Bodhisattvas, refusing the bliss of nirvāṇa, come down to this world because of their "compassion." For a Bodhisattva, the ascent of wisdom terminates at the point of nirvāṇa from whence the descent of compassion begins. The Bodhisattva is, therefore, characterized by two activities: 'going up' or 'ascending' and the other 'coming down' or 'descending.'

All Buddhist learnings and practices, including *śīla*, *dhyāna*, and so on, belong to the "ascending" direction; they are all cultivated for the purpose of traversing the way leading to final liberation. The doctrines of the six *pāramitās* and the ten *bhūmis* belonging to the *Bodhisattva-mārga* are also the same.

In contrast to these, the notions of *apratiṣṭhita-nirvāṇa* and *saṃcintya-bhavopapatti* represents the "descending" direction. The Sino-Japanese Pure Land traditions have expressed the same idea, though they used two other terms: 'going-thither' (往相) and 'coming-hither' (還相). These terms were originally innovated by T'an-luan (曇鸞) in the 6th century China and were made popular by Shinran (親鸞) in the 13th century Japan. According to the Pure Land Buddhist tradition, the term 'going-thither' means to be reborn into Sukhāvatī, i.e., to go from this world. The term 'coming-hither' means to return to this world, i.e., those who have been born in Sukhāvatī return immediately to this world. To go from this saṃsāric world corresponds to the 'ascending' direction, and to return to this world corresponds to the 'descending' direction.

Therefore, 'to ascend' means that one negates saṃsāric reality and aspires for the nirvāṇic ideal. Hence, the motivating power of the ascent is always based upon a negation, i.e., on *śūnyatā*. The descent, however, begins from *śūnyatā* and takes place in the midst of it. It affirms saṃsāra in its true character as *śūnyatā*. This is to say, in Mahāyāna, more emphasis is put on the real world of saṃsāra rather than on the ideal world of nirvāṇa.

However, it is not that these two activities of ascent and descent are opposing each other; they, in the final analysis, are one and the same.

For instance, in the *Saddharmapuṇḍarīka-sūtra*, Buddha Śākyamuni himself, who achieved enlightenment after a long period of practice (ascending activity), declares that he had already achieved it in countless aeons past, and as a skillful means (*upāya*) appeared here on this earth (descending activity) for the purpose of benefitting others in the guise of a human being. Thus, the two directions are regarded here as identical. From the Mahāyānic point of view, even the Bodhisattvas presented in the Jātaka tales can be interpreted in this way.

We see in the *MV*, I.13[32] a theoretical basis for the identification of these two directions. According to this text, *śūnyatā* is defined by two terms: 'non-existence' (*abhāva*) and 'existence of [this] non-existence' (*abhāvasya bhāvaḥ*). 'Non-existence' refers to the upward movement (negation of this world). 'Existence of [this] non-existence' refers to the downward movement (affirmation of this world). Thus, the one and the same śūnyatā has these two aspects.

In a like manner, the term Bodhisattva itself is to be understood in two ways: the one is a Bodhisattva as a Buddha-to-be (ascending, from *sattva* to *Bodhi*) and the other is a Bodhisattva as a celestial being, or Bodhi-being, such as Avalokiteśvara, Mañjuśrī, and so on. The activities of such celestial beings who come down from the state of Buddhahood which is inactive and immovable, are seen in this world as the activities of a Bodhisattva.

Generally speaking, in every religious or philosophical thought, the ascending aspect is considered to be of central importance, while the descending direction is often obscured or neglected. In many cases, the term Bodhisattva is understood simply as the 'Future Buddha' or the 'Buddha-to-be.' However, in the Mahāyānic ideal, this is not the case; the descending direction being clearly seen in terms of *apratiṣṭhita-nirvāṇa* and *saṃcintya-bhavopapatti*. In other words, these two activities complement each other, and the Mahāyāna, or the way of a Bodhisattva, will not become a complete and total system without incorporating these two activities.

Similarly, the establishment of the Mahāyāna can be understood as the outcome of the Mādhyamika thought complemented by the Yogācāra thought. Although it is true that the idea of *śūnyatā*, which is a negation of this world, was established through the great achievement of Nāgārjuna and Mādhyamikas, the whole concept of *śūnyatā* was made explicit by Asaṅga and other Yogācāras when they interpreted it to include the 'existence of non-existence' (*MV*, I.13, above).

It is in the Yogācāra interpretation that we find the possibility of establishing the descending direction. The Mādhyamika thought represents, as it were, the ascending of wisdom, and the Yogācāra idea represents the descending of compassion.

In concluding, I would like to re-emphasize the fact that the two activities of ascending and descending are central to the Bodhisattva ideal. Furthermore, it seems to me that a religious system worthy of its name should include these two key philosophical concepts. It seems that they should appear also in other world religions. Could not the terms *fanā'* and *baqā'* found in Sufism be examples of the ascent and descent as understood in the Bodhisattva path?[33]

FOOTNOTES

1 Har Dayal, *The Bodhisattva Doctrine in Buddhist Sanskrit Literature* (Delhi: Motilal Banarsidass, 1970 Reprint) p. 2.

2 *Ibid.*, p. 3.

3 *Chên wei shi lun.* Shindō Edition (Nara: Shōsōgaku Seiten Kankōkai, 1930) *chüan* 10, p. 9.

4 Étienne Lamotte, *La somme du grand véhicule d'Asaṅga (Mahāyāna-saṃgraha)* Tome II (Louvain: Bureaux du Museon, 1938) p. 47*.

5 Th. Stcherbatsky, *The Conception of Buddhist Nirvāṇa* (Leningrad: The Academy of Sciences of the USSR, 1927) pp. 185, 204.

6 E. Obermiller, "The Sublime Science of the Great Vehicle to Salvation," *Acta Orientalia*, 9 (1931) pp. 162, 174.

7 J. Takasaki, *A Study on the Ratnagotravibhāga (Uttaratantra)* Serie Orientale Roma, XXXIII (Roma: Instituto Italiano per il Medio ed Estremo Oriente, 1966) pp. 84, 204.

8 F. Edgerton, *Buddhist Hybrid Sanskrit Grammar and Dictionary* (New Haven: Yale University Press, 1953) vol. II, p. 48.

9 Edward Conze, *Vajracchedikā Prajñāpāramitā* Serie Orientale Roma, XIII (Roma: Instituto Italiano per il Medio ed Estremo Oriente, 2nd ed., 1974) p. 95.

10 See n. 12 below.

11 See n. 18 below.

12 Sylvain Lévi, *Asaṅga, Mahāyāna-sūtrālaṃkāra, exposé de la doctrine du grand véhicle, selon le système yogācāra* (Paris: 1907) Hereafter *MSA*. Tome I, XVII.42:

karuṇāniḥsaṅgatāyāṃ ślokaḥ |

> *āviṣṭānāṃ kṛpayā na tiṣṭhati manaḥ śame kṛpālūnāṃ* |
> *kuta eva lokasaukhye svajīvite vā bhavet snehaḥ* || 42 ||

sarvasya hi lokasya laukike saukhye svajīvite ca snehaḥ | *tatrāpi ca niḥsnehānāṃ śrāvakapratyekabuddhānāṃ sarvaduḥkhopaśame nirvāṇe pratiṣṭhitaṃ manaḥ* | *bodhisattvānāṃ tu karuṇāviṣṭatvān nirvāṇe 'pi mano na pratiṣṭhitaṃ* | *kuta eva tayoḥ sneho bhaviṣyati* |

See also D.T. Suzuki (ed.), *Tibetan Tripitaka, Peking Edition* (Tokyo-Kyoto: Tripitaka Research Institute, 1957) vol. 109, p. 34.5.6 - 35.1.1. Hereafter *TTP*. Sthiramati:

... *'phags pa nyan thos dang rang sangs rgyas rnams 'jig rten gyi bde ba dang srog la chags pa med kyang sdug bsngal thams cad spangs pa'i mya ngan las 'das pa la chags pas mya ngan las 'das pa la gnas pa'o || byang chub sems dpa' rnams ni nyan thos dang rang sangs rgyas rnams kyi zhi ba phyogs gcig pa'i mya ngan las 'das pa 'jig rten gyi bya ba thams cad kyi phul du phyin pa de la yang ma chags mi gnas te |'dis ni mya ngan las 'das pa la mi gnas pa bstan to ||*

13 *MSA*. XVII. 32:

apratiṣṭhitasaṃsāranirvāṇatve ślokaḥ |

> *vijñāya saṃsāragataṃ samagraṃ duhkhātmakaṃ caiva*
> *nirātmakaṃ ca |*
> *nodvegam āyāti na cāpi doṣaiḥ prabadhyate kāruṇiko*
> *'grabuddhiḥ || 32 ||*

sarvaṃ saṃsāraṃ yathābhūtaṃ parijñāya bodhisattvo nodvegam āyāti kāruṇikatvāt | na doṣair bādhyate 'grabuddhitvāt | evaṃ [*na*] *nirvāṇe pratiṣṭhito bhavati na saṃsāre yathākramaṃ |*

14 G.M. Nagao, *Madhyāntavibhāga-Bhāṣya: A Buddhist Philosophical Treatise edited for the first time from a Sanskrit Manuscript* (Tokyo: Suzuki Research Foundation, 1964). Hereafter *MV*. V. 29:

> *avaikalyāpratikṣepo 'vikṣepaś ca prapūraṇā |*
> *samutpādo nirūḍhis ca karmaṇyatvapratiṣṭhitā |*
> *nirāvaraṇatā tasyā 'prasrabdhisamudāgamaḥ || 29 ||*

... saṃsāraṇirvāṇapratiṣṭhata avinivartanīyabhūmivyakaraṇalābha-samudāgamaḥ saṃsāraṇirvāṇābhyām avinivartanāt ||

15 *MSA*. XIX. 61-62:

mahāyānasaṃgrahavibhāge dvau ślokau |

> *gotraṃ dharmādhimuktiś ca cittasyotpādanā tathā |*
> *dānādipratipattiś ca nyāmāvakrāntir eva ca || 61 ||*
> *satvānāṃ paripākaś ca kṣetrasya ca visodhanā |*
> *apratiṣṭhitanirvānam bodhiḥ śreṣṭhā ca darśanāt|| 62 ||*

... tatra satvānāṃ paripācanaṃ bhūmipraviṣṭasya yāvat saptamyāṃ bhūmau veditavyaṃ kṣetrapariśodhanam apratiṣṭhitanirvāṇaṃ cā-vinivartanīyāyāṃ bhūmau trividhāyāṃ | śreṣṭhā bodhir buddhabhūmau | tatraiva cābhisaṃbodhimahāparinirvāṇasaṃdarśanā veditavyā | ...

16 *MSA*. IX. 14:

> *pravṛttir udvṛttir avṛttir āśrayo nivṛttir āvṛttir atho*
> *dvayādvayā |*

samā visiṣṭā api sarvagātmikā tathāgatānāṃ
parivṛttir iṣyate || 14 ||

... *abhisaṃbodhiparinirvāṇadarśanavṛttyā dvayā vṛttiḥ* | *saṃsāra-nirvāṇapratiṣṭhitatvāt saṃskṛtāsaṃskṛtatvenādvayā vṛttiḥ* | ...

17 See n. 15 above.

18 *MSA*, IX. 70:

sattveṣu samatājñānaṃ bhāvanāśuddhito mataṃ |
apratiṣṭhaśamāviṣṭaṃ samatājñānam iṣyat || 70 ||

yad bodhisatvenābhisamayakāle sattveṣu samatājñānaṃ pratilabdhaṃ tad bhāvanāśuddhito bodhiprāptasyāpratiṣṭhitanirvāṇe niviṣṭaṃ samatājñānam iṣyate |

See also Sthiramati, *TTP* vol. 108, p. 263.2.1-2:

... *sangs rgyas kyi sar mi gnas pa'i mya ngan las 'das par zhugs nas* | *'khor ba dang mya ngan las 'das pa gnyis ka la tha dad pa med cing ro gcig par dmigs pa ni mnyam pa nyid kyi ye shes yin par 'dod do zhes bya ba'i don to* || *de bas na sangs rgyas kyi sa'i mdo las kyang* | ...

19 É. Lamotte, *The Teaching of Vimalakīrti (Vimalakīrtinirdeśa)* translated by Sara Boin (London: Routledge & Kegan Paul, 1976) p. 182, v. 13.

20 See E. Conze, *Materials for a Dictionary of the Prajñāpāramitā Literature* (Tokyo: Suzuki Research Foundation, 1967) p. 395.

21 Unrai Wogihara (ed.), *Abhisamayālamkār'ālokā Prajñāpāramitāvyākhyā* (Tokyo: Toyo Bunko, 1932-35) p. 103.

22 E.H. Johnston (ed.), *The Ratnagotravibhāga Mahāyānottaratantra-śāstra* (Patna: Bihar Research Society, 1950) p. 47.

23 U. Wogihara (ed.), *Bodhisattvabhūmi* (Tokyo: 1930-36; Reprinted Tokyo: Sankibo Buddhist Book Store, 1971) p. 226:

saṃcintya caṇḍāla 'ntānām ā śunām arthaṃ kartukāma upadravaṃ saṃśamitukāmo vinayitukāma, ā caṇḍālānām ā śunāṃ sabhāgatāyām upapadyate |

24 *MSA*, IV. 24-25:

cittāvyāvṛttau ślokau |

māyopamānvīkṣya sa sarvadharmān udyānayātrām iva copapattiḥ |
kleśāc ca duḥkhāc ca bibheti nāsau sampattikāle 'tha
vipattikāle || 24 ||

svakā guṇāḥ satvahitāc ca modaḥ saṃcintyajanma
ṛddhivikurvitaṃ ca |
vibhūṣaṇaṃ bhojanam agrabhūmiḥ krīḍāratir
nityakṛpātmakānāṃ || 25 ||

... *saṃcintyopapattir udyānabhūmiḥ* | ...

[25] *MSA*, XI. 30, commentary:

... *nirmāṇopamāḥ saṃcintyabhavopapattiparigrahe 'saṃkliṣṭasarvakriyāprayogatvāt* |

[26] *MSA*, XX-XXI. 8:

upapattivibhāge ślokaḥ |

karmaṇaś cādhipatyena praṇidhānasya cāparā |
samādheś ca vibhutvasya cotpattir dhīmatāṃ matā || 8 ||

caturvidhā bodhisatvānām upapattiḥ, karmādhipatvena yādhimukticaryābhūmisthitānāṃ karmavaśenābhipretasthānopapattiḥ | *praṇidhānavaśena yā bhūmipraviṣṭānāṃ sarvasatvaparipācanārthaṃ tiryagādihīnasthānopapattiḥ* | *samādhyādhipatyena yā dhyānāni vyāvartya kamadhātāv upapattiḥ* | *vibhutvādhipatyena yā nirmāṇais tuṣitabhavanādyupapattisaṃdarśanāt* |

[27] *MSA*, XVIII. 19-21:

dhṛtivibhāge sapta ślokāḥ ... |

vineyadurvinayatve kāyācintye jinasya ca |
duṣkareṣu vicitreṣu saṃsārātyāga eva ca || 20 ||
niḥsaṃkleśe ca tatraiva dhṛtir dhīrasya jāyate |
...

ebhis tribhiḥ ślokair dhṛtiprabhedaṃ darśayati | ... | *punar duṣkaracaryātaḥ* | *saṃcintyabhavopattitaḥ* | *tadasaṃkleśato 'pi prabhedaḥ* |

[28] *MSA*, XVIII. 44, commentary:

katham utpattitaḥ saṃcintyabhavopapattau cakravartyādibhūtasya viśiṣṭakāyavedanādi saṃpattau tadasaṃkleśataḥ | ...

[29] *MSA*, XX-XXI. 12:

upapattau ca saṃcintya saṃkleśasyānurakṣaṇā |
... || 12 ||

... *ṣaṣṭhyāṃ [bhūmau] pratītyasamutpādabahulavihāritayā saṃcintyabhavopapattau tatra saṃkleśasyānurakṣanā* | ...

30 *MSA*, XXI. *TTP*. vol. 109, p. 114.3.8-4.2:

dran pa dang shes bzhin ma nyams par gang nas gang du skye ba de dang der | *'di dang 'dir skye bar bya'o zhes shes bzhin du skye bas na* | *bsams bzhin du skye ba na yang rten cing 'brel te 'byung ba bsgom pa na mang du gnas pas nyon mongs pas mi gos pa'i phyir kun nas nyong mongs pa rjes su srung ba zhes bya'o* ||

31 *Chên wei shih lun*, Shindō Edition, *chüan* 9, p. 31, line 10.

32 *MV*, I. 13:

dvayābhāvo hy abhāvasya bhāvaḥ śūnyasya lakṣaṇaṃ || 13 a,b ||

dvayagrāhyagrāhakasyābhāvaḥ | *tasya cābhāvasya bhāvaḥ śūnyatāyā lakṣanam ity abhāvasvabhāvalakṣaṇatvaṃ śūnyatāyāḥ paridīpitaṃ bhavati* |

33 See Toshihiko Izutsu (tr.), *Rūmī Goroku*, Islam Classics, No. 2 (Tokyo: Iwanami Shoten, 1978). This is a Japanese translation of the *Kitāb Fī-hi Mā Fī-hi* of Jalal al-Dīn Rūmī. In his Introduction, the translator, Izutsu, discusses (pp. 427-35) such Sūfī ideas as *fanā'*(passing away) and *baqā'* (continuously remaining) and *su'ūd* (ascending) and *nuzūl* (descending). He compares and equates them with such Buddhist concepts as 'going-thither and coming hither,' 'returning to the origin and arising from it,' and 'ascending and descending.'

INFLUENCE OF THE BODHISATTVA DOCTRINE ON TIBETAN POLITICAL HISTORY

Turrell V. Wylie

The ancient caravan routes that long linked the literate cultures of Asia avoided the formidable mountains of Tibet and the Tibetan people, although surrounded by Buddhist societies for centuries, remained illiterate followers of an awesome animistic religion. In time military expansion of the ancient monarchy brought the Tibetans in contact with the advanced civilizations of China and India and, finally in the eighth century A.D., a dichotomous spread of Buddhism penetrated the isolated 'Land-of Snows.' From China came Ch'an, the 'mind-only' school of meditational Buddhism referred to in Tibetan tradition as the 'instant method' of enlightenment. This school maintained that enlightenment could be obtained at any 'instant' in meditation and that meritorious deeds and canonical study were not only useless for gaining enlightenment, but actually impediments to it. About the same time, the symbiosis of Mādhyamika and Yogācāra teachings, referred to as the 'gradual method' was introduced from India. This school taught that one advances gradually on the path to enlightenment by means of meritorious deeds and canonical study during the course of many lifetimes. Of particular relevance to the theme of this paper is the emphasis placed by the Indian school on the soteriologic role of the bodhisattva as a faith object who leads the way on the gradual path.[1]

According to late Tibetan sources, conflict between these two schools led to a protracted debate at Bsam-yas monastery with the Indian guru, Kamalaśīla, defending the 'gradual method' and defeating the Chinese monk, Mahāyāna, who argued for the 'instant method.' This traditional account has been shown to be an apocryphal creation of later Tibetan historians.[2] The doctrinal dispute was purportedly resolved in due time when the king, Khri-srong lde-brtsan, issued an edict which proscribed the Chinese system and sanctioned the Indian school alone.[3]

Victory for the Indian school may well have been more the result of political pragmatism than philosophical preference. Assuming that the king wanted to foster a foreign religious system for the advancement of the Tibetan monarchy, then the Indian school of Buddhism would appear to have been the logical choice. While stressing faith in a bodhisattva as an infallible shepherd for the masses in this and later lives, it overtly taught the importance of meritorious deed and canonical study, and covertly, it justified the societal *status quo* as one dictated by the law of karma. The promulgation of such doctrines would enhance a viable and pliable monarchy in Tibet.

In comparison, the 'mind-only' teachings of the Ch'an school of Buddhism could be counterproductive to the advancement of the monarchy. Ch'an masters, particularly those of the T'ang dynasty, were noted for violent anti-traditionalism.[4] The iconoclasm of Ch'an Buddhism could, at best, foster anti-social behavior in the monarchy and, at worst, encourage outright anarchy itself. In view of the political implications inherent in this system, it is not surprising that the Indian school, with its bodhisattva emphasis and karmic reliance, received the royal sanction.

The introduction of Buddhism in the Tibetan court was not without open opposition from the conservative faction representing the non-buddhist, animistic religion of the people. Antagonism between the two factions peaked in the first half of the ninth century during the reign of Khri-gtsug lde-btsan, better known by the epithet Ral-pa-can; i.e., 'Long Hair.' A fanatic patron of Buddhism, this king levied a tax to support the monastic community and he appointed a Buddhist monk as his chief minister at court.[5]

In time the anti-buddhist faction murdered the monk minister and then, in A.D. 838, assassinated the king himself. The king's brother, Glang-dar-ma, also called 'U-dum-btsan; i.e., 'The Hairless Noble,' was elevated to the throne. This king is blamed in Tibetan-tradition for a heinous persecution of Buddhism. Foreign teachers were sent back to their own countries and the translation of canonical texts was put to a stop. Tibetans who had taken

Buddhist vows were forced to renounce them or face death. Finally a Buddhist monk assassinated King Glang-dar-ma in Lhasa in the year 842.[6]

Tibetan histories say the senior queen of Glang-dar-ma was childless so she took another's son and pretended it was her own, while the junior queen was the mother of Glang-dar-ma's son. Dispute in the court over which son was the rightful heir to the throne led to a split in the royal lineage. The faction supporting the son of the junior queen remained in Lhasa, site of the pro-buddhist court. The faction favoring the so-called son of the senior queen returned to the Yar-lung valley and reestablished a court in the traditional center of the pre-buddhist kingdom. Regarding the successor to Glang-dar-ma, the official history of the T'ang dynasty states that he had no sons whatsoever and so a son of the queen's older brother was elevated to the throne.[7] Be that as it may, a dichotomy of the royal lineage fragmented the monolithic loyalty structure upon which the monarchy depended and as a result the great Tibetan empire collapsed, never to rise again.

The ninth-century dichotomy of the monarchy was followed by still further disintegration of the body politic and central Tibet remained fragmented by local hegemons for the next four hundred years. Little is known about the political history of that medieval hiatus due largely to the bias of later 'lama-historians' who compiled *chos-'byung*, a genre of religious historiography concerned all but exclusively with the vicissitudes of Buddhism. These myopic histories ignore central Tibet where Buddhism is said to have died out after the persecution, and they concentrate on events in the Western Kingdom where the renaissance of Buddhism took place.[8]

Pertinent to the theme of this paper is the fact that when Tibet fragmented politically in the ninth century, its society was still dominated by the pre-buddhist, shamanic religion. Buddhism had been introduced into the royal court, but did not control it, nor had its teachings spread widely among the common people.[9] Yet, when central Tibet resurfaced in the main stream of recorded history in the thirteenth century, it is clear that Vajrayāna Buddhism had gained religious supremacy in the land.[10]

The impetus for that cultural metamorphosis may be traced to the soteriologic aspirations embodied in the bodhisattva doctrine. The indigenous animistic religion of the Tibetan people kept the 'life-force' (*srog*) in the hands of the capricious gods and malicious demons while alive, and offered the 'soul' (*bla*) nothing but an eschatological future in the Underworld. Buddhism, on the other hand, offered the common people the hope of a better rebirth through faith in a bodhisattva who served as a model of virtuous behavior while guiding them on the gradual path to ultimate liberation. The profound ontological and epistemological concepts of the symbiotic Mādhyamika-Yogācāra school of Vajrayāna Buddhism appealed to the hieratic intellectuals of Tibet, but it was the bodhisattva doctrine with its hope for a better future life that attracted the common people.

Traditional Tibetan sources compiled not long after the end of the four-hundred-year hiatus in central Tibetan history testify to the pervasive popularization of the bodhisattva doctrine. The general idea that a bodhisattva incarnates in the phenomenal world for didactic purposes had already been adopted by the Tibetans to embellish their own early history. 'Religious historiography' (*chos-'byung*) dating from the early thirteenth century uses the titulary *Chos-rgyal* (Sanskrit: Dharmarāja) in reference to three of the ancient kings; namely, Srong-brtsan sgam-po of the seventh century, Khri-srong lde'u-brtsan of the eighth century, and Khri Ral-pa-can of the ninth century. These three kings are said to have been 'incarnations' (*sprul-pa*) of the bodhisattvas Avalokiteśvara, Mañjuśrī, and Vajrapāṇi, respectively.[11] Acceptance of the doctrine of 'incarnation' became so widespread that it seemed inconceivable to the common people that an ordinary mortal could, in fact, achieve the state of enlightenment. As a case in point, the disciples of Mi-la-ras-pa, attributing his ascetic mysticism to supermundane powers, asked him whose 'incarnation' he was. Replying that he had no knowledge of being the incarnation of anyone, Mi-la-ras-pa then chided his disciples for having doubts about the true efficacy of the Dharma.[12]

By the thirteenth century the cultural milieu in Tibet had become dominated by Buddhism, which had by proselytical necessity adopted many features of the indigenous shamanic religion. Moreover, Tibet still lacked a centralized form of government and its lands were politically fragmented among various local hegemons, both lay and ecclesiastic. It was in this matrix that an embryonic form of hierocratic government was engendered.

The pivotal point in Tibetan history at which the evolution of its body politic was turned in the direction of a theocracy came when the Mongols intervened in Tibetan affairs in the thirteenth century. I have dealt with this intervention at some length elsewhere.[13] Suffice it to say here that it was the policy of Chinggis Khan and his followers to subjugate a foreign land by offering its ruler a choice between submission or annihilation. Continuance of submission and the payment of tribute to the Mongols were assured by taking members of the ruler's family as hostages. In addition, the Mongols preferred to administer subjugated territories through local ecclesiastics wherever possible.[14]

When the Mongols first invaded Tibet circa 1240 they found a politically fragmented land with no identifiable ruler to negotiate a submission. Subsequently, Sa-skya Paṇḍita, the learned hierarch of the 'Khon ruling family of the Sa-skya sect, was summoned to the Kokonor region to submit Tibet (albeit symbolically rather than veridically) to Prince Khöden. Two of his nephews, 'Phags-pa and Phyag-na rdo-rje, were taken along as hostages. Following the death of Sa-skya Paṇḍita in 1251, the two nephews were taken to the camp of Prince Khubilai. In time, Khubilai appointed 'Phags-pa, then heir and successor to the abbatial see of Sa-skya, as his court lama.

The deaths of Güyüg Khan (1248) and Möngke Khan (1259) led to protracted rivalry between princes of the blood over the rights of succession to such an extent that Tibet remained all but ignored by the Mongols. Not until Khubilai became undisputed Khan of the Eastern Mongols was any military attention turned to the veridical subjugation of Tibet. Finally in 1265, 'Phags-pa Lama and his younger brother, Phyag-na rdo-rje, who had been designated as chief of Tibet by Khubilai Khan himself, returned with a Mongol military escort to Sa-skya and began taking steps to establish a centralized government. A census was taken and central Tibet was divided into thirteen myriarchies for taxation and administrative purposes. In keeping with the subjugation policy of the Mongols, most if not all of the thirteen myriarchs appointed were hierarchs themselves or members of hierarchic families.[15] Thus, by the end of the thirteenth century, Tibet once again had a central government, albeit one imposed by a foreign power whose military troops enforced the hierocratic rule of the Sa-skya lama as a 'regent' of the Mongol Khan.

As stability in the Sa-skya regency began to wane early in the fourteenth century due in part to protracted sibling rivalry for ruling power among the numerous offspring of the then late Sa-skya lama, Bdag-nyid chen-po Bzang-po-dpal, the Mongols began to lose interest in the welfare of Sa-skya and, for reasons of their own, turned their military attention elsewhere. Consequently, Sa-skya was overthrown in the middle of that century by the combined Tibetan forces of the Phag-mo-gru myriarch, a lama of the Bka'-brgyud-pa tradition of Tibetan Buddhism.[16]

This lama, commonly known by the title *Ta'i Si-tu* in Tibetan,[17] structurally reorganized the government. He abolished the myriarchal system established by the Mongols and implemented a new administrative unit called a *rdzong*. Basically meaning a 'fortress,' the term *rdzong* was used to define the administrative area around various *rdzong* or 'fortresses,' which were constructed at strategic places throughout the land. Unlike the Mongol system which appointed local leaders to be myriarchs in their own territories, the officials appointed under the Phag-mo-gru system to govern each *rdzong* were those individuals who had proven their loyalty to Tai'i Si-tu himself in the overthrow of the Sa-skya 'regency.' Thus, the independent government established by Ta'i Si-tu was more politically centralized than the administrative system of the Mongol-imposed Sa-skya 'regency.'

The *rdzong* system as implemented by the astute and charismatic lama, Ta'i Si-tu, embodied the same inherent weakness that led to the downfall of the ancient monarchy, that is to say, it depended upon singular loyalty for stability and viability. After the death of Ta'i Si-tu, disloyalty began to appear in the government and finally, in the fifteenth century, open rebellion on the part of officials in charge of the Rin-spungs rdzong marked the beginning of the end of the Phag-mo-gru dynasty.

A radical innovation in Tibetan Buddhism occurred in the fourteenth century that served to channel the evolutionary stream of the body politic irrevocably from a hierocracy towards a theocracy. That pivotal event was the appearance of the unprecedented concept of the 'reincarnation' of a lama. For the purpose of conceptual clarity in this paper, a distinction is made between the terms 'incarnation' and 'reincarnation.'

'Incarnation' is used for Tibetan *sprul-sku* (Sanskrit: *nirmāṇa-kāya*), a term generally and better translated outside of this paper as 'emanation body.' In contrast, 'reincarnation' renders Tibetan *yang-srid*, literally "again exist,"[18] and is used to identify an individual who is considered to be the 'rebirth' of an antecessor. By way of illustration, Tibetan tradition claims that the ancient king, Srong-brtsan sgam-po, was an 'incarnation' (*sprul-sku*) of the Bodhisattva of Mercy, Avalokiteśvara; but it does not regard him as being the 'reincarnation' (*yang-srid*) of any earlier king. By comparison, the fifth Dalai is regarded as having been the 'reincarnation' of the fourth Dalai Lama, who in turn was the 'reincarnation' of the third, and so forth.

The doctrine of 'incarnation,' referring to a discrete phenomenal form emanated by a bodhisattva for didactic reasons, dates from the early days of Mahāyāna Buddhism and is widely accepted by various schools. On the other hand, the concept of 'reincarnation' as defined here is unique to the Tibetan form of Buddhism. Tibetan tradition places the first occurrence of 'reincarnation' in the lineage of the Black-hat Karma-pa hierarchs. Tradition favors the second hierarch, Karma Pakṣi (1206-1283), as the first *yang-srid* in Tibet, but the evidence indicates the idea arose in the time of the third hierarch, Rang-byung rdo-rje, who was born just over four months after the death of Karma Pakṣi.[19] I have dealt in some detail elsewhere with the identification of the first 'reincarnation' and the theoretical reasons why the concept emerged when and where it did.[20] Suffice it to say here that 'reincarnation' was engendered in the Tibetan matrix by the political need to affect a transition from a hierocratic form of government based on 'charisma of person' to an institutionalized one dependent on 'charisma of office.'[21] The establishment of both the Sa-skya regency and the Phag-mo-gru dynasty can be attributed to the charisma of their founding lamas, 'Phags-pa and Ta'i Si-tu, respectively; just as their decline and fall can be blamed on the diminution of charisma in succeeding rulers and their overthrow before charisma of office could become institutionalized. As will be seen later in this paper, the theoretical purpose for the origination of the concept of 'reincarnation' in the fourteenth century became a political reality in the seventeenth century.

Not long after the concept of 'reincarnation' surfaced in Tibetan Buddhism, another religious development began that was to have a long-range impact on Tibetan political history; namely, the great reformation movement led by Tsong-kha-pa (1357-1419). Aiming his reform at the general decline in monastic morality prevalent in his time, Tsong-kha-pa emphasized adherence to the disciplinary vows set forth in the Vinaya and stressed the importance of academic study, while rejecting many of the tantric texts used by the other sectarian traditions as non-buddhist works. These reformed teachings found a receptive audience in a disenchanted society, and within one decade the three major monasteries of the reformed sect in the Lhasa region were founded: Dga'-ldan in 1409, 'Bras-spungs in 1416, and Se-ra in 1419, the year of Tsong-kha-pa's death. This reformed order became known as the Dge-lugs-pa and is popularly referred to as the Yellow-hat sect. In 1447 the monastery of Bkra-shis lhun-po was founded near Shigatse by Dge-'dun grub-pa, a personal disciple of Tsong-kha-pa and the Yellow-hat hierarch revered in Tibetan tradition as the first Dalai Lama.[22]

During the ensuing years, the reformed Yellow-hat sect continued to increase the size of its monastic communities and to receive more patronage from local officials. Meanwhile, conflict between the declining rulers of the Phag-mo-gru dynasty and the rebellious Rin-spungs lords who seized the strategic *rdzong* at Shigatse in Gtsang province in 1435 led to a state of protracted civil war between the two. In time, the Phag-mo-gru patronized the Yellow-hat sect, which waxed in the province of Dbus; and the powerful Lords of Gtsang became patrons of the Red-hat Karma-pa hierarchs. Thus began a general struggle for supremacy between the Red-hats and the Yellow-hats that was to last some two hundred years.

Following the course of sixteenth-century history, Tibet seemed to be headed toward a viable separation of church and state. Unlike the successive hierarchs of the 'Khon family who administered the Sa-skya regency, or those of the Rlangs family who ruled the Phag-mo-gru dynasty, the lay Lords of Gtsang had no familial ties with the lineage of reincarnate hierarchs of the Red-hat Karma-pa sect. Also there was no geographical proximity between the two since Yangs-pa-can, the mother monastery of the Red-hats, was located far from Shigatse, site of the court in Gtsang.[23]

Continuation of this separation of church and state could well have led to a radically different form of government in Tibet, but it came to naught due to a strategem on the part of the Yellow-hat sect. Facing unrelenting military and religious harassment from his Gtsang adversaries, the hierarch of the Yellow-hats, the third Dalai Lama, travelled to Mongolia, where it is said he converted the great Altan Khan.[24] After the third hierarch died in Mongolia, his 'reincarnation' was 'discovered' to be none other than the great-grandson of Altan Khan himself. This, the fourth Dalai Lama, a Mongol and the only one in the entire lineage not ethnically a Tibetan, was brought to Lhasa and installed as the hierarch of the Yellow-hat Dge-lugs-pa sect. Thereafter, the Mongols became devoted followers of the Dalai Lamas and the military might of their cavalry was at their beck and call.

When the fourth Dalai Lama died, his 'reincarnation' was 'discovered' in a powerful family in the Yar-lung region, thus enhancing the geo-political power of the Yellow-hat sect.[25] As the Yellow-hats continued to grow in strength, the then King of Gtsang, Karma Bstan-skyong, entered into an alliance with the King of Be-ri in eastern Khams, with the intention of outflanking the stronghold of the Yellow-hats at Lhasa.

Faced with this dilemma, the fifth Dalai Lama summoned Gushri Khan to lead his Khoshot Mongols from the Kokonor region to attack first the King of Be-ri and then the King of Gtsang. Gushri Khan defeated the enemies of the Yellow-hat sect and then in 1642 he enthroned the fifth Dalai Lama as the spiritual and temporal head of Tibet. The Khoshot Mongols remained in central Tibet to enforce the peace. Thus, once again political unity was imposed on Tibet by the might of the Mongols, and centralization of the body politic under the rule of the Dalai Lamas was to remain intact for over three hundred years.[26]

The single factor perhaps most responsible for the continuous concorporation of church and state in the hands of successive Dalai Lamas was the bodhisattva doctrine. In the beginning, the 'reincarnation' concept in Tibet seemed primarily concerned with the identity of the human antecessor, rather than a superhuman emanator. A further embellishment of the innovative idea of 'reincarnation' emerged when the fifth Dalai Lama became temporal and spiritual head of Tibet. A 'treasure-text' (*gter-ma*) revealed that the Dalai Lama was, in truth, the 'incarnation' (*sprul-sku*) of the patron bodhisattva of Tibet, Avalokiteśvara.[27]

Once the symbiotic nature of his ontological being was revealed by the *gter-ma* text, the Dalai Lama became both 'incarnate' and 'reincarnate;' a phenomenal manifestation of a noumenal reality. Following this 'revelation,' the charisma of the 'office' of the Dalai Lama subordinated his charisma of 'person,' so much so in fact that the 'office' continued to function as an impersonalized governmental institution in spite of the individual actions of a Dalai Lama. As a case in point, the sixth Dalai Lama is said to have preferred 'wine, women, and song' to the ascetic discipline of the Vinaya and finally renounced his monastic vows. Yet, he remained the true 'reincarnation' of the fifth Dalai Lama and the 'incarnation' of the bodhisattva Avalokiteśvara to the Tibetan people even after he died while being taken to China by Manchu imperial troops. The Tibetan people sought out a child as his 'reincarnation,' who was then enthroned in the uninterrupted charismatic 'office' of the Dalai Lama.[28]

Another case in point and one particularly relevant to contemporary Tibetan political affairs focuses on the attempts of the previous Dalai Lama as a 'person' to implement modern social and political reforms in the 1920's. He was forced to abandon his reformation movement by the very monastic structural-power of the Tibetan government which both endowed and sustained the charisma of the Dalai Lama's 'office,' rather than his 'person.'[29]

In conclusion, the bodhisattva doctrine helped transform the religious culture of Tibet from shamanism to Buddhism in the medieval period; it encouraged the development of the unique concept of 'reincarnation' of a lama; and by means of the traditional Mahāyāna acceptance of the 'incarnation' of a bodhisattva, it moulded a symbiotic theocracy in which the 'office' of the Dalai Lama symbolized the inseparable unity of 'church and state.' It also influenced the xenophobic and myopic policies of Tibet's monastic government, reinforcing its political indifference to critical international developments and thereby contributed directly to the decline and fall of the traditional state.

FOOTNOTES

1 For a monographic study of this doctrinal issue, see Paul Demiéville, *La Concile de Lhasa: Une Controverse sur le Quiétisme entre Bouddhistes de l'Inde et de la Chine au VIIIe Siècle de l'Ère Chrétienne* (Paris: Presses Universitaires de France, 1952). For Tibetan data on the 'instant method,' see *inter alia* Dpa'-bo-gtsug-lag, *Lho-brag chos-'byung*, vol. Ja, edited by Lokesh Chandra in the *Śata-piṭaka Series*, vol. 9 (4) under the title *Mkhas-pahi-dgah-ston* (New Delhi: International Academy of Indian Culture, 1962) folio: 114.b-ff; and Fifth Dalai Lama, *The History of Tibet* [in Tibetan] (Varanasi: Burmese Buddhist Vihar, 1967) pp. 87-8. An account of the 'gradual method' is found *inter alia* in Fifth Dalai Lama, *op. cit.*, pp. 73 ff.

2 For a study of this traditional story see Yoshiro Imaeda, "Documents Tibétains de Touen-Houang concernant le Concile du Tibet," *Journal Asiatique*, Tome 263, (Paris: 1975) pp. 125-46.

3 The Tibetan text of this royal edict is found in Dpa'-bo-gtsug-lag, *op. cit.*, folios 118.b-119.a.

4 See Feng Yu-lan, *A History of Chinese Philosophy* (Princeton: Princeton University Press, 1953) vol. II, 386-406.

5 This minister, named Bran-ka Dpal-gyi yon-tan, was instrumental in concluding the peace treaty with China early in the ninth century. For some details, see the translation of the official T'ang history by Paul Pelliot, *Histoire Ancienne du Tibet* (Paris: Librairie d'Amérique et d'Orient, 1961) pp. 130-1. For the bilingual text of the treaty with translations, see Li Fang-kuei, "The Inscription of the Sino-Tibetan Treaty of 821-822," *T'oung Pao*, 44 [Livr. 1-3, 1956] pp. 1-99.

6 This Buddhist monk, named Lha-lung Dpal-gyi rdo-rje, is said to have assassinated Glang-dar-ma out of compassion. See Fifth Dalai Lama, *op. cit.*, pp. 10-12; Tshal-pa Kun-dga' rdo-rje, *Hu-lan deb-ther*, published under the title, *The Red Annals: Part One* (Gangtok: Namgyal Institute of Tibetology, 1961) folio 18.b.

7 Pelliot, *op. cit.*, p. 134.

8 The oldest example of the *chos-'byung* genre extant today is that of Bu-ston Rin-chen-grub, composed in 1322. For a translation in part, see E. Obermiller, *History of Buddhism by Bu-ston*, Parts I & II (Heidelberg, 1931-1932). D. Seyfort Ruegg, "The Life of Bu Ston Rin Po Che," *Serie Orientale Roma* 34 (Rome: 1966) gives an account of this lama's life and times.

9 Even though the chief minister involved in the peace treaty of 821-822 was a buddhist monk, the religious ceremony performed in Lhasa to conclude the treaty was non-buddhist (see Pelliot, *op. cit.*, p. 131).

10 From the number of monasteries mentioned in the course of Atisa's travels in central Tibet in the eleventh century, halfway through the medieval period, it is clear that Buddhism had already made extensive inroads there (Fifth Dalai Lama, *op. cit.*, pp. 111 ff). *Chos-'byung* accounts give the misleading impression that at the time of the Mongol invasion in the thirteenth century most, if not all, of the local hegemons were hierarchs of one sectarian persuasion or another; for example, see Giuseppe Tucci, "Deb t'er dmar po gsar ma," *Serie Orientale Roma* 24 (Rome: 1971) pp. 181 ff.

11 These bodhisattva identifications appear already in the *chos-'byung* of Bu-ston (see footnote 8), as well as in *The Red Annals* (Gangtok edition, folios 17.a, 17.b, and 18.b, respectively), a religious history composed just twenty-four years after that of Bu-ston.

12 | *nga gang gi sprul pa yin nga rang la yang cha med* |, *Mi la ras pa'i rnam thar*, edited by J.W. deJong ('S-Gravenhage: Mouton & Co., 1959) p. 154.

13 Turrell Wylie, "The First Mongol Conquest of Tibet Reinterpreted," *Harvard Journal of Asiatic Studies* 37 (1977) pp. 103-33.

14 Henry H. Howorth, *History of the Mongols from the 9th to the 19th Century*, Parts 1-4 (London: Longmans, Green & Co., 1876-1927) Part 1, p. 109.

15 Wylie, *op. cit.*, p. 126n.

16 For an account of the overthrow of the Sa-skya regency and the establishment of the Phag-mo-gru dynasty, see Tsepon W.D. Shakabpa, *Tibet: A Political History* (New Haven: Yale University Press, 1967) pp. 73 ff.

17 Tibetan *Ta'i Si-tu* is a transliteration of the title *T'ai szu t'u*, one of the three ranks of princes in the Mongol hierarchy. This title was conferred on the Phag-mo-gru lama by the last Mongol emperor of the Yüan dynasty. See Giuseppe Tucci, *Tibetan Painted Scrolls* (Rome: La Libreria dello Stato, 1949) I, p. 22.

18 Melvyn C. Goldstein, *Tibetan-English: Dictionary of Modern Tibetan* (Kathmandu: Ratna Pustak Bhandar, 1975) p. 1035. Another term is *yang-sprul*, 'again incarnated.' See Sarat Chandra Das, *A Tibetan-English Dictionary* (Calcutta: Bengal Secretariat Book Depot, 1902) p. 1127.

19 According to his hagiography (*rnam-thar*), when Rang-byung rdo-rje claimed to be the rebirth of Karma Paksi, a lama said that since Karma Paksi died on the third day of the ninth month of the sheep year (1283) and Rang-byung rdo-rje was born on the eighth day of the first month of the ape year (1284), an interval of less than five months had elapsed; therefore, Rang-byung rdo-rje could not be the rebirth of Karma Paksi. In rebuttal, Rang-byung rdo-rje claimed his consciousness (*rnam-shes*) had entered a four-month-old fetus. See Karma Nes-don bstan-rgyas, *Brief Biographies of the Successive Embodiments of the Black Hat Karmapa Lamas* (New Delhi: Tibetan Bonpo Monastic Centre, 1973) folio 142.

20 Turrell V. Wylie, "Reincarnation: A Political Innovation in Tibetan Buddhism," *Proceedings of the Csoma de Körös Memorial Symposium* (Budapest: Hungarian Academy of Sciences, *in press*).

21 For a detailed analysis of this political process, see Max Weber, *Economy and Society* (New York: Bedminster Press, 1968) III, pp. 1158-1211.

22 For a general account of the Yellow-hat reformation and the rise of the Dalai Lama hierarchy, see David Snellgrove and Hugh Richardson, *A Cultural History of Tibet* (New York: Frederick A. Praeger, 1968) pp. 177 ff.

23 The monastery of Yangs-pa-can was founded in 1490 at a strategic site on the main route from Shigatse to Lhasa, via the Shangs and Stod-lung valleys. See Alfonsa Ferrari, "Mk'yen brtse's Guide to the Holy Places of Central Tibet," *Serie Orientale Roma* 16, (Rome: 1958) pp. 160-61; Luciano Petech, *China and Tibet in the Early 18th Century* (Leiden: E.J. Brill, 1950) p. 85n.

24 The title *dalai lama* actually dates from the meeting in 1578 of the Yellow-hat hierarch and Altan Khan. The Khan gave the Lama a title containing the word *dalai*, which means 'ocean' in Mongolian and connotes the profundity of the Lama's erudition. Since it was Mongolian, this title was not in common use among Tibetans, who referred to the hierarch as *Rgyal-ba Rin-po-che*, 'Great Precious Conqueror' or *Sku-mdun*, 'His Presence.'

25 The fifth Dalai Lama was a scion of the influential 'Phyong-rgyas family of Rnying-ma-pa sectarian tradition. The political importance of this family, whose estates were in the same valley where tombs of some of the ancient kings are located, is shown by the fact the Karma-pa tried to claim the child as a reincarnation of one of their own hierarchs (Snellgrove and Richardson, *op. cit.*, pp. 193-4).

26 From the enthronement of the fifth Dalai Lama as head of Tibet in 1642 until the fall of the Ch'ing dynasty in China in 1911, foreign military forces — at first Khoshot Mongols and later Manchu imperial troops — were garrisoned much of the time near Lhasa to protect the Dalai Lama and his theocratic government. The last of the imperial garrison was deported from Lhasa in January of 1913 (Shakabpa, *op. cit.*, p. 245).

27 *Gter-ma*, or 'treasure-text,' is a genre of literature purportedly concealed as a treasure of prophecy in ancient times and discovered at the appropriate time. For a discussion of the symbolism manifested in the identification of the Dalai Lama with Avalokiteśvara and the building of the Potala, the fortress of the Dalai Lama in Lhasa, see Zahiruddin Ahmad, "Sino-Tibetan Relations in the Seventeenth Century," *Serie Orientale Roma* 40 (Rome: 1970) pp. 139-45.

28 For a detailed study of the fate of the sixth Dalai Lama and the search for the seventh reincarnation, see Luciano Petech, *op. cit.*, pp. 9 ff.

29 The thirteenth Dalai Lama was influenced by what he saw while in exile in British India and many of his reforms grew out of his visit there in 1910-1912. See Charles Bell, *Tibet: Past and Present* (Oxford: Clarendon Press, 1924) pp. 109 ff.

THE VIEW OF BODHICITTA IN TIBETAN BUDDHISM

Lobsang Dargyay

One of the great French Buddhologists Louis de la Vallée Poussin, has said:

> The entire career of a Bodhisattva is to think of *bodhi*.[1]

The structure of this "thought of *bodhi*" is twofold: firstly the wish to attain *bodhi* (*saṃbodhi-kāmanā-sahagatā*), secondly there is the motivation to aspire *bodhi* for the benefit of all sentient beings (*parārthālambanā*) alone. However, I do not wish to discuss the altruistic motivation for aspiring *bodhi* but should rather confine the topic of my paper to *bodhicitta* in the sense of being the mind directed towards *bodhi*.

The phenomenology of *bodhicitta* has been the topic of discussion of many Indian Buddhist scholars. Within philosophical traditions such as the Mādhyamika, different theories are expounded. When the Tibetan scholars, from the seventh century onward, became acquainted with Buddhism, they confronted various diverse theories and had to come to a conclusion for themselves as to how they were to interpret *bodhicitta* and *cittotpāda* that were formulated by the Indian masters.

The approach of a Tibetan scholar differs widely from the approach of a Western scholar who wants to know exactly what a single Indian or Tibetan master has said and what induced him to utter his thoughts and ideas just in the way he did.

In this paper, I wish to demonstrate the Tibetan discussion of *bodhicitta* and how the Tibetans strived to harmonize the divergent views on *bodhicitta*. Long quotations from different Indian Masters are found throughout the Tibetan philosophical texts, and the Tibetan scholars contrast one quotation with another. Based on this elaborate examination of all aspects and of theories related to *bodhicitta*, the Tibetan scholars came to a final opinion, which became — more or less — accepted among all Tibetan philosophers who followed.

For the purpose of this paper I have chosen two prominent Tibetan philosophers who carried on this Tibetan analysis of the Indian views on *bodhicitta*:

1) Tsong-kha-pa (1357-1419), the founder of the youngest Tibetan school, the dGe-lugs-pa, and
2) Mi-pham (1846-1912), a distinguished philosopher of the oldest school, the rNying-ma-pa.

By including the opinions of other Tibetan scholars, who belonged to these respective schools, I will attempt to demonstrate the range of this discussion within Tibetan Buddhism. This topic is very complex and therefore it is my hope that experienced and educated scholars will carry on this investigation.

One of the main problems under discussion by Tibetan scholars was the question of whether *bodhicitta* was to be defined as *citta*, mind, or as *caitta*, a mind-factor or mental event. To understand the details of this discussion it is necessary to delve into the various aspects of *bodhicitta* as they were seen by the Tibetan scholars of the past.

1. <u>Bodhipraṇidhicitta and bodhiprastānacitta</u>

It is a well established assumption that there are two steps with regard to *bodhicitta*:

1) *bodhipraṇidhicitta*, or the wish to attain *bodhi*, and
2) *bodhiprasthānacitta*, which means to have already embarked upon the journey toward *bodhi*.[2]

Throughout Buddhist literature it is usual to compare *praṇidhicitta* with a man's desire and will to undertake a journey; on the other hand, *prasthānacitta* is similar to the attitude of a man who has already set out on his travel. It is clear, then, that in *praṇidhicitta* there is a strong element of desire and will. At this moment the Bodhisattva aspires for enlightenment, but he has not yet taken the essential step toward enlightenment; he is still only wishing to do so. This popular view is expressed by Tsong-kha-pa in his famous commentary on the *Abhisamayālaṃkāra* (*AA*), the *gSer-phreng*:

> Though the very nature of both, the Aspiring Attitude (*praṇidhi*) as well as the Realizing Attitude (*prasthāna*), is to think, 'May I become a Buddha for the benefit of all other Beings,' there does exist an inward difference between these two attitudes; either they had undergone the action for realizing enlightenment or not. This is the same as for instance [a person] who engenders the wish for going to a country and [a person] who has already set forth on the way [to that country].[3] Thus, the aspiration is only the first [step of *bodhi-*] *citta.*[4]

Both stages are characterized by a sincere wish for enlightenment; however, the first stage (*praṇidhicitta/smon-pa'i sems*) is confined to a wishful aspiration by one's mind. Hence, sometimes *bodhicitta* is seen as the wish for enlightenment and is also translated in this sense and this correctly so when the whole context refers to *praṇidhi*. The second stage (*prastānacitta/'jug-pa'i sems*) is characterized by the same mental attitude as *praṇidhicitta*, but it goes a step further than the former in that it starts to realize this aspiration for enlightenment. Thus, the second stage is marked by a more active doing and putting into reality what was hoped for in the first stage. Mi-pham clarifies this in his commentary on the *AA*:

> The difference is that the Aspiring Attitude has not really grasped the practice [of the six *pāramitās*], on the other hand the Realizing Attitude has already grasped it.[5]

The most important task of the Bodhisattva, i.e. the completion of the six *pāramitās*, is linked here with the two stages of *bodhicitta*. There is no development of *bodhicitta* without the development of the six *pāramitās*. This interrelation is suggested by Mi-pham.

When a Bodhisattva is about to take the path towards enlightenment, he has not yet completed the development of the six *pāramitās*; he just begins to strive for their realization. The Bodhisattva cannot generate the Realizing Attitude unless he succeeds in developing the six *pāramitās*. Pondering on this interrelation of *praṇidhicitta* and *prasthānacitta*, along with the development of the six *pāramitās*, the question arises as to how the two stages of *bodhicitta* and the Five Paths (*lam lnga*),[6] i.e. the Mahāyānistic way towards enlightenment, are related and dependent upon each other. The foundation of these Paths and the basis for the Bodhisattva's activity is the primordial element of Buddha-nature, the germ of enlightenment within each being. This germ has to be aroused by 'great compassion' that precedes the beginning of the development of *bodhicitta*. Great compassion is the Bodhisattva's desire to attain Buddhahood not only for his own benefit, but also for the sake of leading others to ultimate enlightenment. With his mental effort directed towards *bodhi*, the Bodhisattva enters the Path of Accumulating Merit (*saṃbhāra-marga/tshogs-lam*). When this ethical attitude is linked with a super-normal, thorough and intrinsic cognition (*vipaśyanā/lhag-mthong*), then the second division of the Path, i.e. the Path of Training (*prayoga-mārga/sbyor lam*) is attained. The third division is the Path of Intuition (*darśana-mārga/mthong-lam*). At this point the Bodhisattva gains his first awareness of *śunyatā* and enters the first stage of the *āryamārga*, the Path of the Noble Ones, the first *bhumi*. The fourth division is the Path of Contemplation (*bhāvanā-mārga/sgom-lam*) and then follows the Ultimate Path (*aśaikṣa-mārga/mi-slob-lam*), where Buddhahood is attained.

A Bodhisattva has, of course, to develop *bodhicitta* before entering the Path of Accumulating Merit. During his gradual progress through the Five Paths he has to develop and deepen his practice of *bodhicitta*. According to the system of Maitreyanātha, *bodhicitta* is to be divided into twenty-two steps[7] and each step is said to be, respectively, like the earth, like gold, like the moon, like fire and so on. The first three steps, compared to the earth, gold, and the moon, are contained within the first of the Five Paths, i.e. the Path of Accumulating Merit (*saṃbhāra-mārga*). The first, earth-like step is related to devotion (*'dun-pa*), and the second one is related to a specific intention (*bsam-ldan*), which will not be altered until enlightenment is attained, and therefore it is called the gold-like one. The third step is related to surpassing intention (*lhag-bsam*) and at this point the Bodhisattva's thinking displays its full depth and therefore is equal to the crescent moon.

The first step, the 'earth-like' one, is related to the most inferior step of the Path of Accumulating Merit, i.e. *tshogs-lam chung-ngu*; the second step, the 'gold-like' one, is related to the medium step of the Path of Accumulating Merit (*tshogs-lam 'bring*); and the third step, the 'crescent-moon-like' one, is related to the utmost step of the Path of Accumulating Merit (*tshogs-lam chen-po*). Regarding this situation, Tsong-kha-pa states in his *gSer-phreng*:

> Furthermore the *bodhicitta* of Aspiration (*smon-sems*) is to be placed on the inferior level of the Path of Accumulating Merit (*tshogs-lam chung-ngu*) and from the medium level upwards there exists the *bodhicitta* of the Realizing Attitude (*'jug-sems*). In the Sūtras it is explained: 'At the occasion of specific intention (*bsam-ldan*) the six *pāramitās* are to be realized.'[8]

From Tsong-kha-pa's words, it becomes clear that the Aspiring Attitude is developed from the very beginning of the Path of Accumulating Merit, but he does not mention how long the Aspiring Attitude will last or when it will become transformed. According to Tsong-kha-pa, the Bodhisattva has already brought forth the second stage of *bodhicitta*, the Realizing Attitude (*prasthānacitta/'jug sems*) in the medium level of the Path of Accumulating. Tsong-kha-pa adds a sentence from a Sūtra which states that at this particular moment the six *pāramitās* are practised. Thus, Tsong-kha-pa agrees with the above mentioned passage from Mi-pham's commentary on the *AA*,[9] where Mi-pham says that the essential difference between *praṇidhicitta* and *prasthānacitta* is the practice of the six *pāramitās*. Besides realizing the six *pāramitās*, the Bodhisattva has to take the *bodhicitta* vow to attain *prasthānacitta*, the Realizing Attitude.

Relying on this commonly accepted definition of *praṇidhi-* and *prasthānacitta*, there still remains a problem related to the process of practising the six *pāramitās*. Though the Bodhisattva is continuously practising the six *pāramitās* during the Path of Training (*prayoga-mārga*) and during the following three divisions of the Path, in actual fact, he still becomes entangled in a view that does not fully realize the open and unsubstantial being of all phenomena. Thus, the Bodhisattva fails to realize the *prajñāpāramitā* and, under this circumstance, he does not develop *prasthānacitta*. Though the Bodhisattva usually has grasped the stage of *prasthānacitta*, and he is on the Path of Training or on the Path of Intuition (*darśana-mārga*), he may still fail to practise it in a specific situation.

To avoid this dilemma the later dGe-lugs-pa philosophers held that both aspects of *bodhicitta* exist simultaneously up to the seventh *bhūmi* or until full enlightenment, a point when the full development of the six *pāramitās* is no longer doubtful.

In later times this view changed to some extent. For instance, the first 'Jam dbyangs-bzhad-pa claims in his commentary on the *AA*[10] that both aspects of *bodhicitta* are to be developed simultaneously on the inferior level of the Path of Accumulating Merit (*tshogs-lam chung-ngu*), and while *praṇidhicitta* has to be sustained only up to the seventh *bhūmi*, the *prasthānacitta* has to be continued until Buddhahood itself is attained. By stating that both aspects originate from the inferior level of the Accumulating Path, 'Jam-dbyangs-bzhad-pa is in disagreement with Tsong-kha-pa.

'Jigs-med-gling-pa, though a rNying-ma-pa like Mi-pham, also developed a different concept. He says that the first three steps of the twenty-two grades of *bodhicitta* are to be connected to the inferior, medium and higher levels of the Accumulating Path, but that they all belong to the Attitude of Aspiration (*praṇidhicitta*). Furthermore, he explains that the Realizing Attitude (*prasthānacitta*) starts from the very beginning of the Path of Training.[11]

'Jam-dbyangs-bzhad-pa states clearly that the *praṇidhicitta* lasts up to the seventh *bhūmi*, but the other philosophers, including Tsong-kha-pa and 'Jigs-med-gling-pa, leave this problem unsolved.

A fervent discussion started among the rNying-ma-pa scholars as to whether *praṇidhicitta* will last only up to the end of the Accumulating Path, as suggested by 'Jigs-med-gling-pa, or continues up to one of the higher *bhūmis*.

The following chart gives a concise overview of the different opinions.

	tshogs-lam chung-ngu	tshogs-lam 'bring chen po	sbyor lam	mthong lam
Tsong-kha-pa	smon-sems	'jug sems		
'Jam-dbyangs-bzhad-pa	smon-sems 'jug-sems			
'Jigs-med-gling-pa	smon-sems		'jug-sems	

Taking into consideration the already cited passage from the *gSer-phreng*, Tsong-kha-kha-pa suggests that *praṇidhicitta* is limited to the inferior level of the Accumulating Path and that *prasthānacitta*, which originates from the medium level of this same Path, will be present up to the attainment of Buddhahood. He states that this interpretation of the problem is the only one acknowledged by the Indian masters:

> This is the way the scholars of the venerable country gave credit to it because this Ācārya [Haribhadra] has explained *praṇidhi* and *prasthāna* by quoting Śāntideva in his *Abhisamayālaṃkāra-ālokā* (*rGyan-snang*).[12]

Thus, the opinion that *praṇidhi* is limited to the inferior level of the Accumulating Path was first propounded by the Indian scholar Śāntideva. In Tibet this school of thought has changed to some extent during the last centuries. Some of the famous scholars, to whom I have already referred and who interpreted the definitions of *bodhicitta* variously, belonged to different schools, and therefore we may not draw the conclusion that there is any connection between the philosophical interpretations of these two steps of *bodhicitta* and the various schools (*chos-lugs*) of Tibetan Buddhism.

2. Bodhicitta in its conventional and ultimate aspects

The *bodhicitta* that is at the very foundation of a Bodhisattva's career is also involved in the ontological reflections of Mahāyāna. Thus, *bodhicitta* is understood to have a conventional aspect and an ultimate aspect. In reference to the former it is also called a '*bodhicitta* that is elicited by signs' (*brda'-las byung-ba*). Such is explained by Tsong-kha-pa in his *gSer-phreng*:

> The kind of *bodhicitta* that is procreated while one is taught and verbally instructed by another person (i.e. a teacher) will be called — after it has arisen — '*bodhicitta* elicited by signs.'[13]

The '*bodhicitta* elicited by signs' is *bodhicitta* as a concept taught and as a teachable concept. The term "signs" refers here to the words of a teacher and to the words of the texts.

Mi-pham makes this more clear by stating that the *bodhicitta* which is connected to the first two grades of the Five Paths (i.e., *tshogs-lam* and *sbyor-lam*) is to be defined as '*bodhicitta* attained by signs,' i.e. by instructions, regardless of whether they are caused by one's own basic virtue or through the instructing words of another person. In either case, the vow of *bodhicitta* has to follow.

In its ultimate aspect, *bodhicitta* is also called '*bodhicitta* that is created by the power of meditation' (*bsgom-stobs-kyis byung-ba*). In this "ultimate" aspect, *bodhicitta* is marked by a mental awareness (*manovijñāna*) of three superior qualities. The first of these qualities is the superiority of having heard many times (*lung dam-pa*); the second one is the superiority of cause, i.e. the two accumulations (*tshogs-gnyis*); the third one is the superiority of a thorough perception of *śūnyatā*.

This means that, in the ultimate *bodhicitta*, compassion as the main feature of *upāya* and wisdom will coincide, owing to and fostered by a thorough knowledge of the traditional teachings. Mi-pham explains this concept in a more detailed manner:

> The *bodhicitta* of ultimate truth is referred to by the seven verses [starting with] 'Venerating all Buddhas.' To venerate all Buddhas by [making] offerings to them, listening to the *dharma*, reflecting and meditating upon it during almost immeasurable aeon [is the superiority of hearing]. And by the very cause of accumulating the total

> *puṇya* and *prajñā* of the six *pāramitās* and because of the wisdom that does not ponder on all phenomena [in the frame of] objective or subjective [references], of stable and unstable, [there is] the superiority of reflection; this *bodhicitta* is called a superior one, or the '*bodhicitta* of ultimate truth.'[14]

3. Bodhicitta — mind itself or an aspiration?

These deliberations about *bodhicitta* lead us to an interpretation of *bodhicitta* as it prevails in the Tantric literature. There *bodhicitta* is the Enlightened Mind, the essence of *saṃsāra*, that is simultaneously the ultimate bliss, *nirvāṇa*. Consequently the mind was seen as a motionless, clear and void element beyond any perception. But I shall not dwell on this point; I will just make mention of it.[15]

Within the framework of Buddhist philosophy, as reflected in the Sūtras and Śāstras, there arose a fervent discussion as to whether *bodhicitta* was originally a *citta*, a mind in its indestructable, uncreated being, or mainly a wish, an aspiration for enlightenment, that will become a mental attitude during the various stages of the Five Paths. In terms of Buddhist philosophy, the question was whether *bodhicitta* was *citta* or *caitta*.

This argument had already started in India and the Tibetans tried later to analyse the different views, to point out their characteristic features, and to harmonize some of these discordant concepts in order to get a common opinion on the matter. How they proceeded to reach this goal will now be shown.

Before becoming involved in this discussion it should be pointed out that most of the philosophers who accept the definition of *bodhicitta* as one leaning towards aspiration, wish and devotion, prefer to use the term *cittotpāda* instead of *bodhicitta*. Though *cittotpāda* is an abbreviated form for *bodhicittotpāda*, it seems to be understood more in the sense of a "development of mind," from which one derives, almost naturally, the idea of wishfulness. However, within this framework, this is not the meaning conveyed by the term, but it is rather an interpretation accepted by a certain group of Indian philosophers. In the Tibetan usage both words are almost synonyms.

Let us turn to the Tibetans, especially to how they have handled this problem.

Those supporting a concept of *bodhicitta* that emphasizes the aspect of wish and aspiration center in the views held by Vasubandhu and Asaṅga. Tsong-kha-pa gives a worthwhile summary of this concept in his *gSer-phreng*. At first Tsong-kha-pa deals with Asaṅga by quoting from his *Bodhisattvabhūmi* and according to him, Asaṅga claimed that the very nature of *cittotpāda* has to be referred to as an aspiration (*praṇidhi/smon lam*). As proof, Tsong-kha-pa quotes the following passage:

> In the *Bodhisattvabhūmi* it is said: 'The Bodhisattva's best aspiration is the *cittotpāda*.' For this reason Asaṅga explained that the nature of *cittotpāda* is a [mere] aspiration.[16]

With reference to Vasubandhu, Tsong-kha-pa concludes that he considered the very essence of *bodhicitta* as lying in the will (*cetanā/sems-pa*). In the *gSer-phreng* he therefore says:

> Vasubandhu explains the essence [of *cittotpāda*] to lie in the will, because in his commentary on the *Mahāyāna-sūtra-alaṃkāra* he states: 'The will that is combined with the perception of two or three good qualities is called *cittotpāda*.' [And these words] comments on the phrase, 'the will of the Bodhisattvas.'[17]

Thus, in the words of Tsong-kha-pa, Vasubandhu might have wanted us to understand the sentence *cetanā bodhisattvānam dvayārthā cittasaṃbhavaḥ* (*MSA* IV,1) in the following way:

> The twofold will of the Bodhisattvas is the orgin of *citta* (here identical with *bodhicitta*).

The interpretation delivered by Tsong-kha-pa is mainly based on Vasubandhu's own commentary on the *MSA* (IV,1):

> *iti triguṇā dvayālambanā ca cetanā cittotpāda ityucyate* A will supported in a twofold manner by three qualities is called *cittotpāda*.

If one defines *cittotpāda* in this way, then *cittotpāda* and even *bodhicitta* itself becomes absorbed in the category of will, i.e. *saṃskāra-skandha*.[18] Mi-pham also follows this scheme of interpretation in his commentary on the *MSA*:

> The essence lies in the will that is one of the five omnipresent[19] [mental factors] arising in the Bodhisattva's mind. If one asks what [kind] of thought or perception is experienced by this *cittotpāda*, then [one may answer] there is the thinking and perception of 'I shall attain the great enlightenment' and also [a further] thought and perception 'I will be active for the benefit of all sentient beings.' If a mental attitude arises where the mental factors are correlated[20] to the mind, and that has a twofold aim, i.e. to experience enlightenment and the benefit of other beings, then it is called the rising of *cittotpāda*. In short, [*bodhicitta*] is to think and aspire devotedly 'I shall strive for the ultimate enlightenment to benefit all sentient beings.'[21]

In this passage the solution of the problem as suggested by the Tibetan scholars is indicated. Mi-pham differentiates the mind (*citta*) from the factors correlated with it, as for instance the will (*cetanā/sems-pa*). But we must not anticipate the final discussion, and for now we shall dwell on the opinions of the Indian philosophers.

In India there was also a second group of Buddhist philosophers, who held a view opposite to the one articulated by Asaṅga and Vasubandhu. The most prominent speakers of this group were Haribhadra, Ārya-Vimuktisena and Bhadanta-Vimuktisena. Because this group of philosophers, their interrelations and their historical surroundings have been analysed and discussed at length by Ruegg,[22] I may by-pass this point.

In the words of Tsong-kha-pa the view of Vimuktisena and Haribhadra was as follows:

> [Referring to] what is called *cittotpāda*, Ārya [Vimuktisena] said: "*citta* ('mind') is consciousness (*vijñāna/rnam-par shes-pa*) and cognition (*vijñapti/rnam-par rig-pa*). And [if one asks] of what kind this consciousness will be, [one may answer] it is a mind-consciousness that is supported by all wholesome phenomena. As far as the concept of *utpāda* ('arising') is concerned, it points to the [hitherto] unproduced as now produced. [Such is stated] because it shows the essence[23] of the first limitation on this phenomenon known by the mind.
>
> Thus he has explained the sense of 'mind' and 'arising.' Hence, a consciousness that is the basis of all wholesome phenomena is explained to be the decisive mark (*mtshan-gzhi*) [for *cittotpāda*];

> the five kinds of sensory consciousness are not referred to, as they are directed outwardly, and the *ālaya-vijñāna* and the 'mind' tainted by *kleśa*'[24] are not to be considered here, as they are indeterminate (*avyākṛta/ lung ma bstan*).[25]

From this passage it becomes clear that Ārya-Vimuktisena suggests that the term *cittotpāda* be qualified as mind-consciousness (*vijñāna*).

One might argue against this opinion by referring to several texts where *cittotpāda* is stated to be an aspiration, a wish. There must be some bases for calling *cittotpāda* a wish, and this reasoning must have been refuted by Haribhadra and the two Vimuktisenas. It is impossible to quote the refutation in total here. Simply stated, Bhadanta-Vimuktisena expresses the same opinion in his commentary *AA-vārtika* (*Nyi-khri rnam-'grel*) as Ārya-Vimuktisena has already uttered. Also Haribhadra holds in his *AA-ālokā* (*rGyan-snang*) and in his *Sphuṭārthā* (*'Grel-ba-don-gsal*) the same view that was discussed in Vimuktisena's *Pañcaviṃśati-sahāsrikālokā* (*Nyi-khri-snang-ba*), namely that *citta* becomes modified by the altruistic and ethical impact of the Bodhisattva, and that afterwards this *citta* is called *cittotpāda* or 'Rising Mind,' i.e., rising for the attainment of enlightenment. This moment of ethical willing and altruistic aspiring is the basis for calling *cittotpāda* or *bodhicitta* a wish, will or aspiration, though its real nature does not consist of any wishful attitude.

Haribhadra explains in his *Sphurṭārthā*:

> If the very wish for full enlightenment is a mental factor (*caitta/sems-las byung-ba*) striving for wholesome phenomena, then isn't it right to say that *cittotpāda* arises as a mind endowed with a very noble object? And what is the way the *cittotpāda* arises? That's true, but if one strives for the sign of wholesome phenomena, then the *bodhicitta* arises, bringing about the fruit from the cause. This is because one must acknowledge that all propitious phenomena of the Bodhisattva will be enlarged by this striving.[26]

The Tibetan scholars gathered together these disparate views and opinions and concluded that mind is lucid, motionless, a mere perceiving. When the wish for enlightenment arises in the Bodhisattva, this motionless *citta* becomes elevated, moved. The cause for this 'Rising Mind' (*cittotpāda*) is the wish for enlightenment (*praṇidhi*). This wish is a mental factor (*caitta*), not mind as such. And along with this wish there originate several other factors, all directed towards enlightenment. Thus, the mental factors bring about the change in the Bodhisattva's personality, though the very basis for this striving towards enlightenment, namely the lucid, motionless mind, remains as such. In the Tibetan commentarial literature the mind is compared to a king and the mental factors to his entourage. And for the activity of this entourage, the king, i.e. the mind, has been labelled the will, a wish or an aspiration. Thus, in Tibet the valid view on this problem was based on the thoughts of Haribhadra and his disciples.

FOOTNOTES

1 Louis de la Vallée Poussin, *Vijñaptimātratāsiddhi, La Siddhi de Hiuang-tsang* in Jean Przyluski (ed.), *Buddhica*, première série: Mémoires (Paris: Library Orientaliste Paul Geuthner, 1929) Tome II, p. 727.

2 E. Obermiller, "Analysis of the Abhisamayālaṃkāra," in *Calcutta Oriental Series* (London: Luzac & Co., 1933) No. 27, p. 19.

3 The full title of Tsong-kha-pa's text is: *Shes rab kyi pha rol tu phyin pa'i man ngag gi bstan bcos mngon par rtogs pa'i rgyan 'grel ba dang bcas pa'i rgya cher bshad pa gser gyi phreng ba zhes bya ba.* See D.T. Suzuki (ed.), *Tibetan Tripitaka, Peking Edition* (Tokyo: Tripitaka Research Institute, 1961; hereafter *TTP*) vol. 155, p. 4.1.8 - 4.2.2. For further information on this text, see E. Obermiller, "The Doctrine of Prajñāpāramitā as Exposed in the Abhisamayālaṃkāra of Maitreya," in *Acta Orientalia* (London: 1932) vol. XI, p. 2 and his "Additional Indices," in *Acta Orientalia* (London: 1933) vol. XI, p. 352.

4 The same idea is stated in Vidhushekhara Bhattacharya (ed.), "Bodhicaryāvatāra of Śāntideva," in *Bibliotheca Indica* (Calcutta: 1960) No. 280.

5 'Jam-mgon Mi-pham-rgya-mtsho, *Sher phyin mngon rtogs rgyan gyi mchan 'grel puṇḍa-ri-ka'i do shal* in Sonam Topgay Kazi, *Collected Writings of 'Jam-mgon 'ju Mi-pham-rgya-mtsho* (Gangtok: 1976) vol. 3, p. 27.5.

6 See E. Obermiller, "The Doctrine of Prajñāpāramitā...," *op. cit.*, p. 33 *ff*.

7 Maitreyanātha, *Mahāyānasūtrālaṃkāra* (hereafter *MSA*) in *TTP* vol. 108, p. 4.3.3 *ff* and E. Obermiller, "Analysis...," *op. cit.*, p. 22 *ff*.

8 Tsong-kha-pa, *op. cit.*, p. 4.3.2.

9 See note 5 above.

10 'Jam-dbyangs-bzhad-pa'i rdo-rje, *bstan bcos mngon par rtogs pa'i rgyan gyi mtha' dpyod shes rab kyi pha rol tu phyin pa'i don kun gsal ba'i rin chen sgron me*, N. Gelek Demo (ed.), reproduced from the bkra-shis-'kyil blocks in *Gedan Sungrab Minyam Gyumphel Series* (New Delhi: 1973) vol. 46, p. 287.2 and 289.4.

11 *Collected Works of Kun-mkhyen 'Jigs-med-gling-pa* in *Ngagyur Nyingmay Sungrab Series* reproduced by Sonam T. Kazi (Gangtok: 1970) vol. 29, p. 483.

12 Tsong-kha-pa, *op. cit.*, p. 4.3.5.

13 *Ibid.*, p. 4.3.7. The same idea is expressed in *Mahāyānasūtrālaṃkāra*, S. Bagchi (ed.) in *Buddhist Sanskrit Texts* (Darbhaṅga: 1970) Hereafter *MSA*.

14 The full title of the text is: *Theg pa chen po mdo sde'i rgyan gyi dgongs don rnam par bshad pa theg mchog bdud rtsi'i dga' ston*, in Sonam Topgay Kazi, *op. cit.*, vol. 2, p. 62.

15 D.L. Snellgrove, *The Hevajra-Tantra — A Critical Study* (London: 1959), pt. I, p. 25.

16 Tsong-kha-pa, *op. cit.*, p. 3.1.6. This sentence quoted by Tsong-kha-pa from the *Bodhisattvabhūmi* is rendered in the *TTP* vol. 110, p. 135.5.5 in a slightly different way: *'jig rten las 'das pa'i don dag la yang dag pa'i smon lam dge ba de dag thams cad kyi nang na yang dag pa'i smon lam gyi mcho bla na med pa yin no* || One has to note that Tsong-kha-pa's quote that is repeated by dPal-sprul O-rgyan 'jigs-med-chos-kyi-dbang-po (b. 1808) in later times is seemingly based on the Sanskrit sentence *samyak praṇidhānam* ... that cannot be detected in the *TTP* edition. For the Sanskrit text, see Nalinaksha Dutt (ed.), *Asaṅga, Bodhisattvabhūmi* in the *Tibetan Sanskrit Works Series* (Patna: 1966) vol. VII, p. 8.11.

17 Tsong-kha-pa, *op. cit.*, p. 3.1.7. For the quotation from *MSA*, see S. Bagchi (ed.), *op. cit.*, p. 15 (Chapter IV.1 with commentary).

18 For this discussion, see E. Obermiller, "Analysis...," *op. cit.*, p. 18 *ff*.

19 tib. *kun 'gro lngs*: See H.V. Guenther/L.S. Kawamura, *Mind in Buddhist Psychology* (Emeryville: Dharma Publishing, 1975) p. 19 *ff*.

20 tib. *mtshung ldan lnga*: *Ibid.*, p. 11.

21 Mi-pham, *op. cit.*, p. 57.6 - 58.2.

22 D.S. Ruegg, "Ārya and Bhadant Vimuktisena on the Gotra-Theory of the Prajñāpāramitā," in Festschrift für E. Frauwallner. *Wiener Zeischrift für die Kunde Südasiens*, vol. XII/XIII (1968/69) p. 303.

23 Tsong-kha-pa's *gser-phreng* reads *dngos po* (lit. 'a thing'), but in the Tibetan translation of Vimuktisena's *AA-vṛtti*, *TTP*. vol. 88 p. 14.4.3 *ff*, we read *dbang po* (lit. 'a power'). As the Sanskrit text of Arya Vimuktisena's *AA-vṛtti*, Corrado Pensa (ed.), *SOR* XXXVII (Roma: 1967) reads *bhāva*, I might suggest here that the Tibetan blockprints show an error. Hence, I substitute the tib. *ngo bo* for *dngos po* and translate 'essence.'

24 For this term, see É. Lamotte, "L'Ālayavijñāna (Le Receptacle) dans le Mahāyānasaṃgraha (chap. II) — Asaṅga et ses commentateurs," in *Mélanges Chinois et Buddhiques* (Brussels: 1935) vol. 3, p. 186 *ff*; E. Frauwallner, *Die Philosphie des Buddhismus* (Berlin: 1969) p. 333.

25 Tsong-kha-pa, *op. cit.*, p. 3.2.2.

26 *TTP* vol. 90, p. 276.2.4 *ff*.

BODHISATTVA — THE ETHICAL PHASE IN EVOLUTION

H.V. Guenther

It is not generally known, although it is an incontestable fact, that the advancement of science was greatly hampered by the influential German philosopher Immanuel Kant (1724-1804) who had declared that there could be no other geometry than Euclidean geometry. Its content, he said, came *a posteriori* from sense perception, while its form was determined by *a priori* categories of the mind. This fixed idea was to continue for a very long time as a very powerful *idée fixe*. Similarly, the advancement of Tibetan and, by implication, Buddhist studies has been hampered by the fixed idea that the Tibetans received everything from India *a posteriori* and that in their more or less 'mechanical' translations they understood, if ever they did so, the Indian terms in the manner in which the Westerners assumed these terms had to be understood by imposing on them their *a priori* demands stemming from either rationalism or empiricism. The former had its origin in René Descartes' (1596-1630) philosophy. As a matter of fact, he was better as a mathematician than as a philosopher, for rationalism soon turned more dogmatic than any other form of dogmatism; and the latter derived from Francis Bacon (1561-1626), Thomas Hobbes (1588-1679) and John Locke (1632-1714), and reached its climax in David Hume's (1711-1776) sense-impression theory. We have only to remind ourselves of what is rendered as 'enlightenment' in order to realize the fateful consequence of a fixed idea, for this translation does not do justice to either Sanskrit *bodhi* or Tibetan *byang-chub*. It merely reflects the user's prejudice which is itself a carry-over of a 17th and 18th century ideology — the so-called Enlightenment — reinforced by the user's blissful ignorance of the roots of his prejudice which is made to look respectable in the guise of philosophical positivism and its derivative — philology.[1] It also stresses his unwillingness to enter into a dialogue by first listening to what somebody or some text has to say to somebody about something. By contrast, the Tibetans were most eager to listen, and listening, as Don Ihde has shown, 'is more than an intense and concentrated attention to sound,'[2] rather it is a 'working its way into what is as yet unheard.'[3]

So, what was it that the Tibetans 'heard' and subsequently expressed when they rendered the Indian term *bodhisattva* as *byang-chub sems-dpa'*? What was it they understood by *byang-chub* and what was its relationship with *sems* and *sems-dpa'*? One of the earliest renderings is found in the *bDe-ba chen-po byang-chub-kyi rmad-du byung-ba'i le'u*, as preserved in the version of Vairocana (8th century):

> Here, *byang-ba* means that all that is and has come from me has been for ever free from the impurity of the emotions; *chub* means that the past, the future, and the present, as well as all the countless realms of the trichilocosm are identical, and since there is not so much as an atom apart from the (triad of) *sku, gsung, thugs,*[4] to understand all that is as being indivisible, is (to have realized) *byang-chub*.[5]

In a later chapter the same text states:

> *byang-ba* means to have been pure (refined) of any obscurations and the tendencies toward them from the very beginning; just as a crystal put into the palm of one's hand; the mind and the realm are certainly pure and lustrous since the pristine cognitiveness which in one moment knows all three world spheres, the three aspects of time, and the three life-worlds, never ceases (to know). *chub-pa* means that just as oil pervades the sesame seed, everything that is is (this) quintessence. Since (this) all-pervasive energy (which is the very meaning of Being) which just is, is the birthplace of the (experience of) 'gestalt' (i.e., structured stability as the founding stratum) and pristine cognitiveness (as the founded), (one speaks of *chub-pa*). *sems* means that since it has turned into understanding pristine cognitiveness as the ground of everything it has not been adulterated in its continuum or mystery (of Being).[6]

This interpretation of a key-term of Buddhism is continued by Klong-chen rab-'byams-pa (1308-1364) who, in addition, clarifies the difference between *sems* and *byang-chub-(kyi) sems*. The term *sems* is synonymous with *ma-rig-pa* 'not-quite *rig-pa*',[7] i.e. a low level performance of the cognitive capacity inherent in a living system such as man, and is also a cover-term for what had been itemized as 'a mind' (*sems*) and 'mental events' (*sems-byung*), all of which referred to the thematizations in experience. By contrast *byang-chub-(kyi) sems* is synonymous with *sems-nyid* 'experience-*qua*-experience,' as yet undisturbed by thematizations, and as such the source, though not in an ontic sense, of the thematizations as Samsara and Nirvana. He says:

> The pure fact of 'intelligence' is termed 'limpid clearness' (*byang*) because Samsara has never been experienced to exist entitatively due to the fact that there has never been any pollution. The very energy (of this 'intelligence') is 'consummate perspicacity' (*chub*) because its qualities are spontaneously present (i.e. they just are), (which means) that it allows for everything and anything to come-into-presence. In view of the fact that responsiveness is all-pervasively present, it is because of (its, i.e. Being's) sheer lucency pervading all of Samsara and Nirvana and because of it becoming an individual experience, that it is termed *sems*. However the complex of (what is said to be) 'a mind' and the 'mental events' with their host of thematizations, is not *byang-chub-kyi sems*, because (this complex) is the occurrence of obfuscation (i.e., the opacity of quantification) from out of the creativity within the playfulness (of Being, *byang-chub*). Inasmuch as this (complex) is samsaric, it contradicts the qualitative (of Being). There is a difference between creativity and the playful that derives from creativity.[8]

If now we turn to the specific term *byang-chub-sems-dpa'* we may begin with a quotation from Rong-zom Chos-kyi bzang-po (11th century) who in his commentary on the *Man-ngag lta-ba'i phreng-ba*, a work attributed to Padmasambhava (8th century), states:

> As to the term *byang-chub sems-dpa'*, *byang-chub* renders *bodhi*. This term has been coined in view of the fact that what it connotes is the ultimate abolishment of all impurities and the (resultant) transparent purity as well as a correct understanding and comprehending. *sems-dpa'* renders *sattva*. (This term) means 'desire,' 'courage,' 'a firm and unbending intention,' 'having a mind,' 'intellectual acumen,' and 'summary.' In the context here it is used in the sense of 'desiring

limpid clearness' or 'limpid clearness' (itself) and 'having a mind (for it).' As has been stated:

> *byang-chub* (limpid clearness) has the characteristics of the clear sky;
> All divisive concepts have been dispersed.
> He who desires to understand this
> Is called a *byang-chub-sems-dpa'*.

Also, in the *Shes-rab-kyi pha-rol-tu-phyin-pa* (prajñāpāramitā literature) it has been stated that

> Since someone who has the mind (for limpid clearness) will have realized limpid clearness, he is spoken of as a *byang-chub sems-dpa'*.

In this sense 'to have a mind (for limpid clearness)' is to understand (mind) as this limpid clearness. Furthermore, there also is the compound *byang-chub sems-can*. Here *sems-can* ('having a mind') means an animate being. Therefore any animate being who has a mind for limpid clearness, is termed a *byang-chub sems-dpa'*. This mind of limpid clearness is, in brief, the combination of appreciative discrimination and compassion.[9]

Similarly, in his commentary on the *gSang-ba snying-po*, he interprets the term *byang-chub sems-dpa'* as follows:

> As to the term *bodhicitta*, *bodhi* is (short for) *avabodhi* which is the word for 'comprehending and understanding.' Since *bodhi* is also used in the sense of cleansing moral defects and restoring the initial transparent quality, one speaks (of him who does so as) *byang-chub sems-dpa'*. *sattva* has six connotations: 'courage,' that is the rousing of an inclination, 'valour and firmness;' 'aspiration;' 'intellectual acumen;' 'an animate being;' and 'summary.' Since in this context there is involved a firm and unbending intention (to realize) limpid clearness there is the desire (to realize) limpid clearness; and since there is a reference to (this) limpid clearness and to someone who has the mind for it, one speaks of *byang-chub sems-dpa'*,[10]

and in the same work he relates the term *sems-dpa'* to *rdo-rje* (*vajra*) which has been the symbol for indestructibility and firmness. He says:

> *rdo-rje* implies indestructibility, and although the term *sems-dpa'* has many meanings as has been shown above, here it implies 'firmness,' 'understanding' and 'summing up.' In this sense 'firmness' means that since *byang-chub-kyi sems* is as firm as a *vajra*, one (can speak of it) as

> *rdo-rje sems-dpa'*. In connection with it in its state of being the mental operation within the framework of a particular affinity with Being (as spirituality or 'intelligence,' *rigs-kyi sems*) it has been said:
>
> > What is the mind (*sems*) of all sentient
> > beings (*sems-can*)
> > Is said to be *rdo-rje* (*vajra*).
> > Because of its firmness one speaks of *sems-dpa'*.
>
> And with reference to it in the state of having reached its climax, it is said:
>
> > The pristine cognitiveness which is cognizant
> > of everything thematic
> > Is here termed *rdo-rje sems-dpa'*.
> > Because of its firmness one speaks of *dpa'*.[11]

A glance at the original text with eyes that have not been blinded by the 'Sanskrit-only' glaucoma reveals that the Sanskrit term *sattva* has been rendered differently in different contexts. In one case it is rendered by *sems-can*, in another by *sems-dpa'*. The former term is usually translated as 'sentient being,' but, on the basis of the Tibetan term, could more precisely be rendered as 'having a mind,' and since 'mind' (*sems*), as we have seen, refers to the thematizations that occur in experience, twisting the latter into a belief-system which we call our 'reality,' the term *sems-can* refers to someone who has such a belief-system, who has 'opinions,' as we might say. By contrast, *sems-dpa'* refers to the dynamics of experience-*qua*-experience (*sems-nyid*) which is as 'indestructible' as a *vajra* and involves 'understanding' (*rtogs*) not 'opinionatedness' (*sems*), the latter being a distortion of or an aberration from the former, yet capable of being restored to its 'original' status of experience-*qua*-experience. One is almost tempted to define *sems* in terms of what A.N. Whitehead so aptly termed 'misplaced concreteness.' By contrast, we may speak of its original, not misplaced status in terms of 'intelligence,' provided we do not confuse it with an IQ. There is nothing ontic about 'intelligence,' or — if you like, 'spirituality,' 'resonance,' which is basic to humanity and in its dynamics manifests itself as a 'concern for limpid clearness and consummate perspicacity' (*byang-chub-kyi sems*), as a 'self-existent pristine cognitiveness' (*rang-byung-gi ye-shes*), although more often it may 'go astray' or 'collapse,' as one would say in physics, into a 'mind' (a veritable 'black hole' — a state of infinite density and zero volume).[12] Again we may quote Klong-chen rab-'byams-pa who clearly brings out this difference:

> *sems* is the incidental 'pollution' ranging over the three 'worlds' and made up by the eight thematizing operations (of the 'mind') with its accompanying 'mental events.' *byang-chub-kyi sems* is 'intelligence,' a self-existent pristine cognitiveness, having nothing to do with (such thematizations as) substance and quality, yet being the source of all that goes by (such judgments as) Samsara and Nirvana.'[13]

It is when 'intelligence' takes over, and only then, that we are entitled to speak of *byang-chub sems-dpa'*, because now 'growth' is the over-riding concern, and this is precisely what the Tibetans were aware of when they understood each of its two components, *byang-chub* and *sems-dpa'*, as a process-product term specifying spiritual operations. In the *sNang-srid kha-sbyor bdud-rtsi bcud-thigs 'khor-ba thog-mtha' gcod-pa'i rgyud phyi-ma*, the joint work (or rendering) by Padmasambhava and sKa-ba dPal-brtsegs, we read:

> *byang* is the cleansing of the taking the without and the within as a duality,
> *chub* is consummateness in ultimate indivisibility.
> *byang* is the cleansing of the percepts related to the five senses,
> *chub* is consummateness in unchangingness, non-discursiveness and non-calculating.
> *byang* is the cleansing of one's conceptual thematizations,
> *chub* is consummateness in the openness of the being divested of the linguistic limitations.
> *byang* is the cleansing of both the objective and the subjective,
> *chub* is consummateness in the non-existence of both the objective and subjective.
> *byang* is the cleansing of the thematization into specific characteristics,
> *chub* is consummateness in the non-existence of these characteristics.
> *byang* is the cleansing of the preoccupations and addictions to eternalistic extremes.[14]
> *chub* is consummateness in the ineffable expanse of Being.
> *byang* is the cleansing of the five or three poisons,

chub is consummateness in the five gestalt experiences and the five pristine cognitivenesses (founded on the gestalten)
byang is the cleansing of whatever thematizations there may occur,
chub is consummateness in ultimate non-thematicness[15]

and

sems is concern with ultimate meaning and value,
dpa' is sovereignty over non-dual meaning and value;
sems is concern with the meaning of unorigination,
dpa' is sovereignty over the meaning of non-cessation.
sems is concern with the absence of birth and death,[16]
dpa' is sovereignty over (the fact that there is neither) transmigration nor metamorphosis.
sems is concern with Samsara and Nirvana,
dpa' is sovereignty over ultimate non-duality.
sems is concern with the reach and range of the unchanging,
dpa' has nothing to do with addiction and pre-occupation which cannot be enacted.
sems is concern with the absence of objects and (a) mind (about them)
dpa' has nothing to do with good and evil, negation or affirmation.
sems is concern with the intrinsic meaning of Being as a mother,
dpa' is the inseparability of mother and child.
sems is concern with the expanse (of Being) as unchangingness,
dpa' is (to be immersed) in the expanse of ineffable ultimate bliss.[17]

The above quotations amply demonstrate that *byang-chub sems-dpa'* is, primarily, a descriptive term for a qualitative (or, if you so prefer, a mental-spiritual) process, not a designatory term for a static or quantifiable entity, a 'concrete' person. Even so late an author as Mi-pham rgya-mtsho (1846-1912) is still fully aware of the fact that *byang-chub sems-dpa'* is a qualifying term. He says:

bodhi has the meaning of understanding from deep within and
sattva has the meaning of having a willingness (a 'mind' for it), which together means 'to deeply understand whatever one may set one's mind upon.[18]

However the fact that this process may be pictured in anthropomorphic images because, after all, this process concerns and involves man himself, merely helps to make it more easily understandable. The danger then is that the images may be concretized and quantified into 'entities,' the proverbial multitude of Bodhisattvas in popular imagination. Nevertheless, the fact remains that the qualitative grasp of form and structural order is more immediate and, in this sense, precedes the quantitative grasp of number and magnitude. Therefore, visualizations and images have always played an important role in dealing with 'mysteries' — man's life being no exception. Let us not overlook the fact that Newton's work in physics was largely geometric in spirit: that James Clerk Maxwell who did so much for the study of electromagnetism, 'pictured' and demonstrated its forces in terms of a field spreading throughout space; that the greatest physicists not only 'picture' the universe in terms of geometrical diagrams such as the Kruskal-Szekeres diagram of the Einstein-Rosen 'wormhole' diagram, but even wax poetic in their descriptive imagery:

> No doubt further caverns are waiting to be discovered by the fell-walker in his hunt for quarks, or, at the other end of the distance scale, in his quest for black holes, and in his investigation of quasars, whose prodigal rate of energy production is scarcely understandable in terms of physics as we know it. But caving and fell-walking are not the only activities. There is the vast task of prospecting fields whose general geography is understood, fields whose mysteries stem rather from the complexity of macroscopic matter than from fundamental structure. Think of the rich veins of ore to be mined from the solid-state field; the curious seams of the low-temperature world; the startling versatile outcrops of the semiconductor and insulator fields; the polymer intrusion. Think of the liquid crystals, the volcanic plasmas; the slanting, deceptively ethereal, laser beams; some territories with jewels lying on the surface waiting to be picked up, some with jewels deeply hidden, none without jewels; the rich fields of chemistry and the vast subcontinent of biology. In them all the basic structure is established, the caves and pot-holes are scarcely visible in the far-off foothills and mountains, and there is overwhelmingly the busy, bewildering complexity of inanimate and animate matter to explore.[19]

This idea of *byang-chub sems-dpa'* being a process and, as such, reflecting the dynamics of reality which, in a narrower sense, becomes human and social life, runs through the whole of the rNying-ma-pa tradition of Tibetan Buddhism

— the 'older' school which presents Buddhism as a live force in contrast with the 'newer' schools which turned ever more 'academic' if not utterly stale. A dynamic view realizes that a process is directional, and this idea which is inherent in Buddhist thought has found its expression in the notion of a 'way' that is being travelled and in the wider conception of *theg-pa* (Sanskrit *yāna*) which is more than what the traditional and 'static' translation of this term by 'vehicle' conveys. It suggests a pursuit in which one allows oneself to be carried on by the stream of evolution whose orientation is not fixed on any place on earth, but has as its *telos* the realization of spiritual organization, the transparency and lucency of Buddhahood, which even as a 'goal' remains dynamic. Thus Klong-chen rab-'byams-pa says of the *byang-chub sems-dpa'i theg-pa*:

> Its essence is its having become the reliable impetus for or expertise in riding the huge wave of social responsibility by means of great compassion through having understood that all that is is (as open, not ontic) as the sky. Its definition is 'a great vehicle' because it leads to the reliable stronghold of ultimate freedom by any expertise one develops.
>
> Its purpose is to make those of superior intelligence reach Buddhahood.
>
> Its goal is the realization of the eleventh level of 'light-everywhere.'[20]

Similarly, Lo-chen Dharmaśrī (1654-1717), echoing the words of Klong-chen rab-'byams-pa, defines this term in these words:

> (Its essence) is to have become the reliable expertise in riding the huge wave of social responsibility by means of great compassion through having understood that all that is has nothing ontic about it.
>
> (Its definition) derives from the word *bodhisattva*, which is *byang-chub sems-dpa'*, because owing to the great mental power (involved) there is absolutely no budging from the realization of unsurpassable limpid clearness and consummate perspicacity.[21]

The evolutionary process passing through various stages as one of which we can explicate the term *byang-chub sems-dpa'* — takes place in a human individual who in his growth (observable, on the physical side in the progression from childhood to adulthood, while not always noticeable, on the mental side) sets up specific norms which reflect the level the process has reached. This does not mean that a higher level supersedes the lower one which then can simply be discarded. On the contrary, each higher level embraces the lower one in a truly hierarchical (stratified) relationship, thus setting up an ever more richly orchestrated reality in which man participates by becoming increasingly this reality.

The *byang-chub sems-dpa'* level is between the *so-sor thar-pa* level which it presupposes, and the *rig-'dzin* level to which the evolutionary process tends as the next higher one.[22] The *so-sor thar-pa* level is characterized by *behavioural patterns*, exemplified by the eight types that make up this level. These types are the monk, the nun, the novice (male and female) as well as a special type of female novice who seems to have been of a studious kind, and the lay person (male and female), as well as the individual who observes fasting and other rites and rules. With the exception of the latter the remaining seven are fit to participate in the evolutionary process. This, at least, is the conception of the followers of the Cittamātra philosophy, while the Mādhyamikas seem to have been broader in outlook by allowing other life forms to participate, even though, in the last analysis, the decisive step could only be taken by the human individual.[23]

On the *byang-chub sems-dpa'* level the behaviour patterns are given new meanings by infusing them with *ethical* considerations which bring out the value of whatever is and which are geared to the preservation and, even more so, to the furtherance of values, but never to a reduction of human beings to a mere response mechanism. This new level establishes a feedback link between the 'I' — as a human being I owe it to myself to act in a human manner — and a 'Thou' (or 'other,' i.e. other-than-myself) — the 'other' being included in and co-constituting a reality or world which is an intricate network of qualities. In addressing the other I establish communication with him or her, — I succeed in getting and remain on speaking terms with him or her, — and thus the other is not a thing to be manipulated but a person to be appreciated, to be understood, to be 'cared for.' This is the deeper meaning of the 'for-oneself' (*rang-don*) and 'for-others' (*gzhan-don*). Social responsibility rests on the emergence of ethical awareness, not on prescriptive sadomasochism.

On the *rig-'dzin* level all duality has been resolved and emphasis is on the union with and unity of the evolutionary force which is active throughout the universe. Here individual ethics gives way to ethics of whole systems which aims at making man to tune-in and to contribute to evolution generating its own norms in its continuous upward sweep. This ethics, too, addresses itself to the individual but it does not close the individual off from the universe. This ethics is grounded in and leads to 'freedom,' not as some static 'thing' or ontic entity, but as the creativity manifesting itself in the creation of a meaningful world — meaningful because it is not the product of preconceived notions which have their root in opinionatedness (*sems*), but because it is an unfolding in primary cognitiveness (*ye-shes*) which is, as the Tibetans noted, an 'intelligence' (*shes*) that has been there all the time (*ye*) to direct, as we might say, the evolutionary process. Thus, these three levels of organization make, each in its own way, for 'fluctuations' which lead to more complex and higher levels of dynamic regimes which themselves induce and guide (from a higher level) the ensuing 'mutations.'

Erich Jantsch[24] has succinctly stated:

> A belief in evolution implies that man, and all mankind, share in a process of which the evolution of mankind is but a temporary aspect. Such a free attitude, going beyond any particular interests of the individual, system, or even species, becomes possible if man is also understood as sharing in a universal mind, of being immortal as spiritual energy.

One may take exception to the term 'universal mind' because it is too apt to suggest an ontic entity with subjectivistic overtones, and also to the qualification of energy by 'spiritual' because the term 'spiritual' has been abused by having it indiscriminately applied to any eccentricity.

Nevertheless, it is this idea of 'energy' in evolutionary perspective that underlies the concept of *bder-gshegs snying-po* or *de-bzhin gshegs-pa'i snying-po*, making itself felt in all its self-evolving norms, the former term emphasizing the 'felt' quality of this process in its optimal (*bde* 'pleasure,' 'ecstasy,' 'bliss') operation, the latter the direction (*de*) it takes.

It is about time that we realize that, first, there is no such thing as 'Buddhism' and never has been, and that what is termed 'Buddhism' is a rich tapestry in the process of being woven. Secondly, this tapestry will not reveal its richness and beauty by being twisted through antiquated positivistic ideologies whose alleged objectivity is a pathological subjectivism, but only by allowing this tapestry to display itself before our eyes as an invitation to enter into a meaningful, ongoing dialogue with its message.

FOOTNOTES

1 To give an example, if someone were to 'translate' the French *il a le mal de tête* as 'he has the evil of the earthenware pot,' which is the correct philological rendering and then were to claim that this is what the French understood by that phrase, he would be considered insane, but when someone proclaims such absurdities as 'embryo of Tathāgata,' 'substantial Body,' 'emanated incarnation Body,' and so on, which are not even philologically correct but merely reveal utter incomprehension of the subject-matter, by a strange volte-face, he is said to be a scholar.

2 Don Ihde, *Listening and Voice. A Phenomenology of Sound* (Ohio: University Press, 1976) p. 49.

3 *loc. cit.*

4 I have left these terms untranslated intentionally. They are qualitative terms, hence the quantitative rendering of them in mechanical dictionary 'translations' by 'body, speech and mind' is certainly false.

5 In *rNying ma'i rgyud 'bum*, vol. 2, pp. 12*f*.

6 *Ibid.* p. 63*f*.

7 There is no negation involved. *rig pa* is still there, though not at its best. The case is different with *'tshe-med* which is the negation of violence. The corresponding Sanskrit words, *avidyā* and *ahiṃsā* respectively, look alike with their negative prefix *a-*, yet quite different functions are involved.

8 *Chos dbyings rin po che'i mdzod*

9 Roṅ-zom Chos-kyi bzaṅ-po, (*gsuṅ thor bu*) Collected Writings (Leh: 1974) pp. 42*f*.

10 *Ibid. fol.* 10 b.

11 *Ibid. fol.* 14 b.

12 This would be the simplest conceivable type of black hole (the so-called Schwarzschild black hole). However, if the 'mind' had been formed from something rotating or something having an electric charge or magnetic field, one would have to speak of a Kerr black hole or a Reissner-Nordstrom black hole with interesting consequences as illustrated by the Penrose diagram. See William J. Kaufmann III, *The Cosmic Frontiers of General Relativity* (Boston: Little, Brown, 1977) sv.

13 *Gnas lugs rin po che'i mdzod, fol.* 10 b.

14 *rNying ma'i rgyud bum.* This edition of early rNying-ma works is full of misspellings, omissions and other defects that mar calligraphic works. The correct version seems to have been *rtag chad zhen chags byaṅ*.

16 The line is one syllable short; it seems *shi* has been left out by the calligrapher.

17 *Ibid.*, pp. 27*f*.

18 Mi-pham rgya-mtsho, *Collected Works* vol. 2, p. 699.

19 B.K. Ridley, *Time, Space and Things* (N.Y.: Penguin Books, 1976) pp. 155*f*.

20 *Theg pa'i mchog rin po che'i mdzod*, vol. 1, pp. 116*f*.

21 Collected Works, vol. 7, p. 46.

22 These three levels are summed up under the term *sdom-gsum*. On the literature about this topic, see my *Kindly Bent to Ease Us* (Emeryville: Dharma Publishing, 197) vol. 2, Bibliography.

23 See for instance *Grub mtha' rin po che'i mdzod*, pp. 190*f*.

24 Erich Jantsch, *Design for Evolution* (N.Y.: George Braziller, 1975) p. 138.

THE BODHISATTVA IDEA IN CHINESE LITERATURE: TYPOLOGY AND SIGNIFICANCE

Yün-hua Jan

Right from the early days when Buddhism was introduced to China, the Bodhisattva idea was one of the most important and popular themes in Chinese Buddhist literature. Chinese attention has constantly and persistently been attracted to this subject, and as a consequence, a large number of works accumulated. However, when one looks to references in an attempt to define what these works are, one will be surprised to find that a definition of Bodhisattva literature in Chinese is rather ambiguous. Taking an early Chinese writer's words as an example, Hsieh Fu (謝敷) of the 4th century A.D. has written, "that a Bodhisattva is the one who has reached deep to the root of existence, and clearly knew the nonexistence of cause and conditions." He further explained that 'reached to root means existence is empty of the Self.' 'Clearly knew the nonexistence' means cause and conditions are ever restful in themselves. It is because of this twofold knowledge, that a Bodhisattva will not "renounce existence in order to enter into nonexistence," nor "put an end to cause-conditions in order to return to emptiness."[1] This statement gives a philosophical definition of Bodhisattva idea, and hence might lead the reader to think that the idea is purely philosophical. Henceforth, the literature itself must be philosophical.

An eighth century Buddhist catalogue *K'ai-yüan lu* (開元錄) has given Bodhisattva literature a manifold definition: As a doctrine, the Bodhisattva literature deals with Dharmakāya which exists permanently: as a philosophy it deals with the principle (*li*-理) which is extensive and real; and, as a precept for spiritual cultivation, the collection of the literature begins with the aspiration of the Mind of Wisdom, and concludes with the Tenth stage.[2]

If one follows the philosophical definition of the Bodhisattva idea, the doctrine of Emptiness (*śūnyatā*) becomes the central problem and that means the idea has no specific meaning of its own, but is a synonym of Mahāyāna philosophy. If, however, one follows the definition given in the catalogue, the scope of the Bodhisattva becomes broader: it deals with religious philosophy, experiences and precepts. In spite of these dimensions, the idea still remains a purely Mahāyāna viewpoint with a strong monastic flavour. The difficulty is that the Bodhisattva idea in China played a much larger and more important role which goes far beyond the aforementioned dimensions.

Keeping this in mind, one would find that there is a variety of literature, both monastic, such as the doctrine of Dharmakāya and the Emptiness, as well as the precept for cultivations. Apart from that, there are collections of literature that praise the compassion and power of individual Bodhisattvas, describe the holy places and tell stories of miraculous manifestations of the Bodhisattvas. Most of this literature is not only concerned with monastic doctrine, but is also meaningful to laymen, especially illiterate masses. Under these circumstances, it is clearly impossible to deal with all this material in this paper, though it is possible to point out typology and its soteriological significance of this massive literature. From the viewpoint of Chinese Buddhism and Chinese civilization as a whole, a discussion on the typology and its significances are, probably, even more meaningful than some other aspects of the subject.

Typologically speaking, the Chinese Bodhisattva literature can be divided into three categories:

1) the translation and composition of the Birth-stories (*jātakas*) which deal with the past lives of the Buddha;
2) the works of the precept of spiritual cultivation leading to the attainment of Bodhisattvahood. Here the Bodhisattva becomes a spiritual goal and is attainable by every serious religious man if he follows and acts upon the precept.

3) the literature on the worship of the Bodhisattvas as celestial beings, who are very compassionate and powerful, responsive to personal call and helpful to everyone.

Typology One

The earliest Chinese translation of the Birth-stories of the Buddha is the work done by Kang Seng-hui, (康僧會) *Liu-tu chi-ching* (六度集經) or "Scripture on the accumulation of the six Perfections." The work contains 91 stories on the past lives of the Buddha. Another translation done in the same period was Chih-ch'ien's (支謙) *Pu-sa pen-yüan ching* (菩薩本緣經 'The Original Causes of the Bodhisattva'), a short work comprising eight stories. The last stage of Chinese translation in this category is represented by the works done in the 11th century A.D.[3] Like all the *Jātaka* stories the main thrust of these works is to portray Gautama Buddha as a perfect being, who has accumulated great virtues through various lives before his last birth and the attainment of Buddhahood. This means his virtues are accumulative and it is impossible to attain it completely in one life span. It further indicates that the Buddha is compassionate and willing to help sentient beings, and is capable of doing so because of the power and perfections he has accumulated in the past.

The portrait of Buddha as presented to the Chinese people through the Birth-stories has many facets: He was a great being with great compassion, he knew the universe and the past, he possessed supernatural powers, had all moral virtues and universal support. Story after story, the Buddhist translators had repeatedly introduced to the Chinese such an image with these qualities of their religious founder. In order to have a more concrete idea of this subject, we may recount a few stories from this massive collection to analyse their meaning and impact on Chinese tradition.

In one story narrated long ago, there were 500 merchants led by Akṛtajñā, a trader from Baranasi, who had a successful mission in search of treasures from the sea. On their return journey, their ships were caught by the sea *rakṣasa* in a whirlpool and thus were unable to proceed. The merchants were frightened and prayed to gods and goddesses for help. At that moment, there was a king turtle who had compassion on the merchants, and saved them by ferrying them to the shore. The turtle was exhausted and fell into a sleep after the ferrying. Akṛtajñā then killed and ate the turtle and as a consequence of that ungrateful action, all the merchants were trampled to death by elephants. Typically in the Birth-stories, the Buddha tells his followers at the conclusion of the story that "the king turtle was me, the Akṛtajñā was Devadatta, and the 500 merchants were the brahmins who are now converted to Buddhism."[4]

In other works of this group, the Bodhisattva also acted as a king called Śivi who had given his own flesh in order to save a pigeon.[5] Various stories of a similar nature can also be found in a number of translated scriptures, especially the *Miao-se wang yin-yüan ching* (妙色王因緣經) ('The story of the king of beautiful body'). It claims that on the demand of the *Yakśa*, King Surūpa first gave his son and his queen to the hungry demon to stop the hunger, and then offered himself for the same purpose. When the demon saw that the king's body and mind remained undisturbed by the bloody demand of human flesh, he knew the bodhisattva king 'would certainly attain the Supreme Wisdom.'[6] The story of the White rabbit king who offered his own body as well as the bodies of his sons to save a religious man's life, is another expression of the great compassion. At the conclusion of the story, the Buddha made the following remarks: "Throughout eons the Bodhisattva has sought the law diligently and laboriously even at the expense of his body and life. After he was reborn as an animal, he was able to give up his body for the cause of the religion and jumped into fire as an offering to the hungry religious man...."[7]

The Bodhisattva is not only compassionate but also knows how to act. This is, of course, required knowledge. The Birth-stories contain some instances of this aspect of the Bodhisattva idea: *Tsa Pao-tsang ching* (雜寶藏經) has two stories to this effect. The first one is called "The Buddha extinguished the three kinds of fire by the Wisdom water." It says that when the Lord was on his way to South India, he stayed over-night in a village. The villagers had a party at which many people became disorderly and drunk. Fire had broken out and people were in a panic. They went to the Buddha and begged: "Oh the world honoured lord, please help us." The Buddha told them that "all the sentient beings have three fires of attachment, anger and delusion, and I can extinguish them by the wisdom water. If this statement is true, the fire should be extinguished immediately." The fire went out at once when the words were spoken.[8]

Apart from the power of wisdom as regards present affairs, the Bodhisattva knows past lives and deeds very well. As a matter of fact, many stories are the testimonies of the Buddha's knowledge of the past. However, the story of the Ugly Princess is worthy of attention as it is dramatic. According to the story, King Prasenajit had a princess called Lai-t'i (賴提) who was extremely ugly. With some difficulty and a generous dowry, the king married the princess to a youth from a poor family. He warned the son-in-law that he should never expose the princess to other people nor take her to any party. Because of this restriction, the husband was often punished by his friends at their parties as he failed to bring his wife with him. The princess was distressed by this, so she prayed to the Buddha day and night continuously. She also asked why, when the Lord appeared in the world, and all beings benefited from the event, that she alone was left unattended. The Buddha was moved by the sincere prayers and so he emerged from the earth. At the moment when the princess saw the handsome hairs of the Buddha, her own hair became beautiful. As the Buddha continued to emerge, her body was beautified accordingly. Meantime, the husband's friends became curious and suspicious. They thought the nonappearance of the princess meant either that she was extraordinarily beautiful or ugly. They made the husband of the princess drunk so that he slept and then broke into the house and found that the princess was extremely beautiful. When the husband awoke from his drunken sleep he went back to his home, opened the door and discovered the beautiful princess. The princess told the story to the husband and the latter reported this to the king.

On an enquiry from the king, the Buddha told His Majesty that in a previous life of the princess, she had made some remarks about a Pratyeka-Buddha while making an offering to the latter. She said that this holyman was very ugly and his skin was like that of a fish, and his hair like that of a horse-tail. Because of the slanderous remarks, she was reborn as the ugly princess; because of her self-repentence she saw me; and because of her admiration of Buddha's handsome body, her own body was transformed beautifully.[9]

The aforementioned story not only pointed out the Buddha's knowledge of past lives, but even suggests that he had supernatural powers that were capable of transforming the form and events of the physical world. This power was also displayed in another story about the mother of deity Hārītī, who lost her son. It states that Hārītī had ten thousand sons and the youngest of them was called Pin-chia-lo (嬪伽羅 Pingala?). All of them were strong and rough, and they hunted and caught babies for their meals. People were frightened and reported this to the World Honoured One. The Buddha caught Pin-chia-lo, confined him and hid him in his bowl. When the mother deity found that her son was missing and was unable to determine where he might be, she visited the Buddha for help. The Buddha said "you have only lost one son out of the ten thousand, why should you worry about one? Are you aware of the pains of those mothers who have only one or two sons whom you have killed?" The mother diety promised to the Buddha that if she could find her lost son she would never kill other people's babies again. With this understanding, the deity saw her son in the bowl, but failed to release the boy with her supernatural strength. So she went back to the Buddha again. The Buddha told her that "if you are willing to take refuge in the Three Jewels, to accept the Five Commandments and never kill again till your death, I will return your son to you."[10] The deity followed and acted on the advice.

The Buddha then told the mother deity that at the period of Kāśyapa-Buddha, she was the seventh and youngest princess of a king called Kai-ni, (羯膩王) who had great merit but had disregarded the commandments. For that reason, the deity was reborn with a ghostly body.

Apart from supernatural power and wisdom the Bodhisattva possessed all human virtues. Taking filial piety as an example, various stories on this subject have repeatedly informed the reader that the Bodhisattva was absolutely perfect in this virtue. It is mentioned that there was a prince whose father and five elder brothers were killed by a disloyal minister. When the prince was warned that his life was in danger, he took his wife and young son and fled. On their way to another country, food ran out. The prince intended to kill his wife in order to save the lives of the son and himself. The son pleaded with his father to give his own flesh instead of his mother's. The story proceeded painfully as the boy cut three pieces of flesh from his body daily to sustain his parents and himself. With the last three pieces of flesh that remained, the boy gave one each to his parents and abandoned himself on the road. At that moment the god Sakro (i.e. Indra) appeared in the form of a hungry jackal and demanded the last mouthful of flesh that the boy had kept as the last ration for himself. The boy gave it to the jackal without any hesitation. Then as usual, Sakro was moved by the filial action and selfless generosity, so he resumed his real identity and helped the prince to regain the kingdom. The readers were told that the boy was the Buddha in a past life and the prince and his wife were the Buddha's parents in past lives. The story of Śyāmaka (Shen-mo-chia 睒摩迦) is another well-known story in this category. As his filial piety is so moving and so popular in China, even Confucian scholars took it over and included it in their book on filial piety.[11] It should be further noted that this story not only credited the virtue to the Bodhisattva, but also had a secondary claim as well; the Bodhisattva's respect and piety towards elderly people. This claim is stated at the beginning of some versions, i.e., that when Bodhisattva was living in the Tuṣita heaven, he constantly watched and reflected on good and evil ways in the ten directions of the three world systems with the power of meditation. "He clearly saw the merits resulting from the deed of filial piety, the worship of the three jewels, the reverence to the elderly, and the retribution [of these deeds in] the five ways of existence." It was in meditation that he discovered an old blind couple who were religious but needed help. Having been inspired by what he saw, the Bodhisattva vowed that, 'If my life ends, I would like to become their son, to support them unto their death.'[12] So it was by his own will, the Bodhisattva was reborn as Śyāmaka.

Some of the *Jātaka* stories also informed the reader that holy men should not be slandered. Anyone going against this would receive punishment in this life or retribution in a future rebirth.[13] On the other hand, if one supported the religion and made efforts to satisfy the needs of holymen, he would be rewarded according to his contribution. The reward not only meant minor things, but even the kingship of a large or small kingdom.[14]

Taking these representations as a whole, the Bodhisattva idea as presented in various collections of the Birth-stories may be regarded as one typology of the literature. Here the Bodhisattva is portrayed as the most compassionate, wise, powerful and virtuous being who could not and should not be denied or slandered. This was a most powerful and dramatic phenomenon in Chinese tradition which certainly has surpassed the ancient Chinese idea of a religious leader.

Typology Two

The Birth-stories not only indicate the great virtues, the great wisdom and the great compassion of the Buddha as the founder and the leader of the religion, but they also implied positively that such virtues, wisdom and compassion are attainable by all the sentient beings through the means of spiritual cultivation. From a soteriological viewpoint, this spirit of attainability is more meaningful to a religious man who strives to get free from suffering. This spirit of attainability through cultivation is fully manifested in a number of translations which has consequently led to a series of commentarial literature. Of them, the "Scripture on the Ten Positions (*Daśabhūmikā/shih-ti ching* 十地經) has been recognized as the most systematic document on the subject. As various studies on this system have been published and continuously investigated,[15] it is unnecessary to repeat the Ten Positions of the Bodhisattva cultivation here. However, what has to be noticed is that when the idea of cultivation for the Bodhisattvahood had attracted more attention, the scope of the idea gradually developed and enlarged. Such an evolution not only explains how the Chinese understood the idea and had cultivated themselves for it, but the evolution may also indicate the Indian development of the idea.

The earliest Chinese translation of this literature was done by Chih-lu-chia-ch'en (支婁迦讖 Lokakṣema?) in the second century A.D. The work is *Tou-sa ching* (兜沙經).[16] As early Chinese translations of Buddhist scriptures were done at the time when the techniques of translation were still underdeveloped, scholars are often reluctant to indicate what its original Indian title might be. Inspite of this difficulty, the topic of the scripture was, however, quite clear:

> The Buddha loves us [and knows] the thought of Bodhisattvas, so he kindly showed us...the Buddha lands in the ten directions, ...the countless teachings...the ten dharmas where the Bodhisattvas were dwelling. Showed us the ten dharmas which the Bodhisattvas were practicing. Showed us the ten methods by which the Bodhisattvas confess. Showed us the ten places of Tao. Showed us the ten towns of Bodhisattvas. Showed us the ten places of Bodhisattvas' vows. Showed us the ten clevernesses of Bodhisattvas. Showed us the Ten Concentrations of the Bodhisattvas. Showed us the ten flying methods of Bodhisattvas. Showed us the ten seals of Bodhisattvas....[17]

As all these items are numbered ten, I suspect that the term *tou-sa* (兜沙) was probably a transliteration of the Sanskrit word *daśa*.

In comparison with the above mentioned, the second existent translation of the group became more concrete in its programme. This word was done by Chih-ch'ien in the early decades of the third century A.D.[18] The work is the *P'u-sa pen-yeh ching* (菩薩本業經) or 'The Original Actions of Bodhisattvas.' Apart from a preface which sets the discourse in its context, the scripture concentrates on two subjects, namely 'Vows and Actions' (*yüan-hsing* 願行) and the 'Ten Positions.' In connection with Bodhisattvas' vows and actions, the fundamental question is "what is the cultivation that accomplishes the sagacious way of the Buddha?"[19] In the chapter on the 'Ten Positions,' the answer is this: "those who searched for Buddhahood, have ten places to dwell. The past, the present and the future are all accomplished by this."[20] This is the earliest list of the Ten Positions in Chinese texts.

By the end of the third century, Chu Fa-hu (竺法護 Dharmarakṣa) had systematically translated a number of new works. Of them, two titles are directly connected with the cultivation of Bodhisattvas: the first is *P'u-sa shih-chu hsing-tao p'in* (菩薩十住行道品), which is in many points similar to and connected with the Ten Positions of Bodhisattvas. The second title is the *Chien-pei i-ch'ieh chih-te ching* (漸備一切智德經) 'the Scripture on the Gradual Completion of all the Virtues of Wisdom,' which has been identified with the Scripture on 'Ten Positions.'[21] These two works, translated by the same person, are very significant as they indicate that the two texts, though related, are not the same. From this point onward, the texts on the practices of Bodhisattvas have been introduced to the Chinese based either on the system of 'the Ten Positions' or on 'the Ten Dwellings.'

The accumulation of Bodhisattvas' practices increased as time went on. This is evident when Buddhabhadra translated the *Hua-yen Ching* (華嚴經 *Avataṁsaka* or 'Flower Ornament'), the sets of the 'ten actions,' the 'ten goals or directions (*shih huo-hsiang* 十迴向)', 'the ten knowledges (or illuminations *shih-ming* 十明)' and 'the ten endurances' were established besides the 'ten dwellings' and the 'ten positions.'[22] Another set of the 'ten concentrations (*shih-ting* 十定)' was added on in the seventh century translation of the same scripture.[23] These sets of cultivation may not have been as significant as the texts claimed, yet the picture is clear that the qualifications and virtues of a Bodhisattva are much more serious and complicated than the well-known Mahāyāna doctrines of 'ten positions' (*daśabhūmi*) or the 'six perfections' (*ṣad-pāramitā*) indicate.

This does not mean that the 'ten positions' and the 'six perfections' were not important in the Bodhisattva doctrine, but only that during a later period the doctrine became richer and more complex. Consequently, more attention should be given to this later development. Such attention would point out that the Bodhisattva idea did not become static even after the formation and maturity of Mahāyāna Buddhism.

The different versions in Chinese translation of the 'Ten Positions' not only provided scholars with evidence of various recensions of the scripture, but also brought forth some problems. However, whatever the problems might be, the intention and the core of the scripture is clear and non-controversial. In order to show this, a passage from different translations of the scripture is put forward as an illustration. The passage quoted from the different versions of the text is arranged in chronological order.

The passage is from the third (or second) paragraph of the *Shih-ti Ching* (十地經). The earliest version in existence is that by Dharmarakṣa which reads as follows:

> At that time, [Vajragarbha Bodhisattva] awoke from the Concentration after a short while. He paid homage to Bodhisattvas and explained:
>
> Oh son of the Most-victorious, I have clearly understood the vows of Bodhisattvas [that] destroy the net of doubts, and cannot be destroyed by anything. Nothing is born (by itself) in the World, neither is there evil nor rift (*hsin* 釁). The realm of *dharmas* is great and extensive, it is neither far nor near. Where they (i.e. Bodhisattvas) travel and dwell resembles empty space, and thereby they relieve or support all the sentient beings of the ten directions. The Sons of the clan should know that these were possible because the past Bodhisattvas and the ancient Buddhas had ferried over by means of the Wisdom Ground (*hui-ti* 慧地). The future and the present ones would also be like that....[24]

The next version is that of Kumārajīva:

> Vajragarbha Bodhisattva then arose from the Concentration, and told Bodhisattvas:
>
> Oh sons of the Buddhas. These are the works of Bodhisattvas. They should be decided first with skill by yourself, without fault or distinction; pure and clear. They are as great and extensive as the realm of dharmas. They are as ultimate as the empty space. They cover all the sentient beings in Worlds of Buddhas in the ten directions. For the sake of saving and ferrying over all the beings of the world, they are protected by the supernatural power of the Buddhas. Why is this so? [Because] Bodhisattvas, Mahāsattvas entered the Ground of Wisdom of the past Buddhas, and will enter the Ground of Wisdom of the Buddhas of present and future.[25]

A few years later appears the version rendered by Buddhabhadra. The version is more or less identical with the translated version of Kumārajīva.[26]

Śikṣānanda's version of the passage reads comparatively simply:

> Vajragarbha Bodhisattva arose from the Concentration and universally told all the Bodhisattvas:
>
> Oh sons of the Buddha, the vow of goodness is decisive, not mixed with infections and invisible. It is as great and extensive as the realm of Dharma. It is as ultimate as the empty space. It is eternal and exists in all Buddhas' lands. It saves and protects all the sentient beings, and protects all the lands of the Buddhas. It enters the Ground of Wisdoms of the past, the future and the Buddhas.[27]

The last Chinese version of the passage was rendered by Śīladharma during the eighties of the eighth century A.D. It represents the last effort on the subject as far as the translation is concerned. The version reads thus:

> [Vajragarbha Bodhisattva] then arose from the Concentration and universally told all the Bodhisattvas:
>
> Oh sons of the Buddhas, this surely is the vow of Bodhisattvas. It is decisive, not mixed and cannot be reflected completely. It is the great and extensive realm of dharma,

> the exhaustive nature of empty and eternal space. It is capable of saving all the sentient beings; only the sons of Buddhas are dwelling peacefully in this vow. Only from here one is able to enter into the Ground of Wisdom of the past Buddhas, Tathāgatas, able to enter into the Ground of Wisdom of the future Buddhas, Tathāgatas, also able to enter into the Ground of Wisdom of the present Buddhas, Tathāgatas.[28]

The five versions of the passages quoted above have illustrated three points: first, that the basic factors are identical. All of these versions inform their reader that the lecture was delivered by the Bodhisattva after he had arisen from the concentration; second, the differences are concerned with the descriptions of the Bodhisattva's vow: in the final version, the confidence of entering into the Ground of Wisdom of Buddhas of the past, the present and the future. Only Kumārajīva's version has rendered the vow as works (*shih* 事), but the rest have all stuck to the central problem of the vow of Bodhisattvas and its power. Moreover, inspite of the different and identical points, the spirit and the focus of the passage is clear; i.e., that the Ground of Wisdom is attainable through the cultivation of the vow. From the religious viewpoint, this confidence of attainment is the most meaningful element, and it has inspired the Chinese Buddhists in their religious pursuits.

The different rendering of certain terms or passages often put scholars in a dilemma: was it a mistake in translation or was it based on a different version of the original text? Both are possible. This dilemma is not only a problem to the critical scholarship of our time, but a constant question in the minds of Chinese Buddhists throughout the ages. In this connection, it is interesting to have a glimpse of how Chinese scholars tackled the problem and the different renderings of the titles of the scripture is a good example.

The title of the text translated by Dharmarakṣa is called *Chien-pei i-ch'ieh chih-te ching* (漸備一切智德經) which may be translated as the 'Scripture on Gradual Completion of all virtues of Wisdom.' In the version done by

Kumārajīva, the title is rendered as the *Shih-chu ching* (十住經) or the 'Scripture on the ten Dwellings.' In the two versions of *Hua-yen ching* (華嚴經), the chapter is called, *Shih-ti p'in* (十地品) or the 'Ten Positions.' When the Chinese commentators discussed these different titles, they did not look into the problem from a historical-textual angle but rather from a soteriological angle. In the *Commentary of Hua-yen Ching* (*Hua-yen Ching shu* 華嚴經疏), Ch'eng-kuan 澄觀 (738-839) explained the problem as follows:

> According to the *Pen-yeh* (本業), the word *ti* (地 ground, earth) means *ch'ih* (持 to hold, to maintain), to hold innumerable merits. It also means the producing and maturing of all fruit from causes, it is therefore called the 'ground.' The *Original Commentary* has explained the meaning 'to produce, to mature and to maintain the Buddha-Wisdom.'[29]

On the rendering of the 'Ten Dwellings,' the commentator quoted from the *Jen-wang ching* (仁王經):

> The entering into the principle (*li* 理) of *prajñā* is called dwelling. The merit from the dwelling is called the ground.[30]

As regards the other title, the 'Gradual Completion of All Wisdom-merits,' the commentary states it is so as 'the later Virtue (of Wisdom) excelled the previous ones; hence, it is called Gradual Completion. Gradual Completion means Accumulation.'[31]

From the foregoing discussion one may conclude that in spite of the textual differences that exist in different versions of the scriptures on the Ten Positions of the Bodhisattvas, the central message of this typology of literature is clear, that the religious goal is achievable. At the time when the Chinese were giving little attention to the spirit of attainability, here and now, through religious cultivation, the introduction of the Bodhisattva idea on spiritual cultivation is of historical significance.

Typology Three

The introduction and the development of Mahāyāna Buddhism in China brought another type of Bodhisattva literature; namely, the belief and the glorification of certain prominent Bodhisattvas as saviours. Compared with the other two, this type of literature was more popular and had tremendous influence on the Chinese masses. As a result of this influence, festival and rites for worshipping these Bodhisattvas have been instituted in China, and centres for pilgrims were established. Of the Bodhisattvas' holy places, four are very famous, *viz.*, the P'u-t'o Mountain (普陀山) which is the centre for the worship of Kuan-yin (觀音), the Wu-t'ai Mountain (五台山), for Wen-shu (文殊 Mañjuśrī), the O-mei (峨嵋) for P'u-hsien (普賢 Samantabhadrā), and the Chiu-hua (九華) for Ti-tsang (地藏 Kṣitigarbha).[32]

Amongst all the eminent Bodhisattvas, Kuan-yin (觀音) is the most honoured. Though this name has been usually identified with its Indian counterpart, Avalokiteśvara, the tradition had drastic developments in China. To a certain extent, the Chinese development transformed the Bodhisattva in Indian characteristics beyond recognition.[33]

The early introduction of the name Kuan-yin is traceable to the *Ch'eng-chü kuang-ming ting-i ching*[34] (成具光明定意經) translated by Chih-yao (支曜) in 185 A.D. However, the more important work on the Bodhisattva is the well-known *Lotus Sutra*, which was first translated into Chinese by Dharmarakṣa in 286 A.D. This text claimed that even when one heard the name of Kuang-shih-yin (觀世音 aloka-loka-svara) merely by chance, it would produce a power which would free one from various afflictions; allow one to remain unhurt in a blazing fire, not drown in turbulent waters, remain safe in natural as well as in human disasters that might occur in sea trades, remain uninjured through actual execution, be undisturbed by demons and spirits; allow one to escape from jails if one is wrongly and unjustly sentenced by a wicked or evil county magistrate, remain safe during a robbery, be free from attachment, anger and delusion, have beautiful children as one wished for.... The powers ascribed to Kuan-yin are indeed potent and extensive.

Centuries after Dharmarakṣa's systematic introduction of the Kuan-yin doctrine, the socio-political situation in China had deteriorated considerably, wars continued incessantly, and great suffering was brought to the nation. The Buddhist doctrine of suffering and impermanence was no longer an abstract philosophy nor a remote dogma, but a living reality which could befall one at any moment. Under these circumstances, the search for safety and the yearning for security was a natural consequence; and Kuan-yin became the most appropriate object for worship. It is then no surprise to find archaeological evidence to support this fact. According to the study of Tsukamoto Zenryu, Kuan-yin worship was the most predominant feature during the North Wei period as there were 197 images of the Bodhisattva counted in the Lung-men (龍門) caves. This is the largest number of individual Bodhisattvas.[35]

As far as literature is concerned, the translation of Indian works on Kuan-yin grew continuously until the 11th century A.D. Though there is no doubt that these translations enriched and substantiated Chinese conceptions of Kuan-yin worship, the influence of the translation at this stage probably only had limited success within monastic circles. In contrast with the translations, the Chinese compositions have played a more important role in the spread of Kuan-yin worship in China. Of the original Chinese compositions, there are records on Kuan-yin's 'miraculous efficacy,' the 'fabricated or spurious translations,' and the gazetteer of pilgrim centres.

The early Chinese reaction to the power of Kuan-yin is represented by the *Ying-yen chi* (應驗記) or 'Records on Miraculous Efficacy' of Kuan-yin. A number of writings on this subject had taken place during the period of the Six Dynasties (220-582). The earliest composition in the series, by Hsieh Fu (謝敷) of the fourth century was lost, but the subsequent works by Fu Liang (傅亮 374-426), Chang Yen (張演), and Lu Kao (陸杲 459-532) were all discovered in Japan.[36] The full text of the discovery along with annotations from Makita Tairyo has been published by Tsukamoto.[37] Apart from these three records, a few other texts of a similar nature were also found, and some of them have fragments from the original text.[38]

Of the miraculous stories, the collection made by Lu Kao is the most lengthy and significant work. It consists of 70 stories which are classified according to the powers of Kuan-yin as described in the *Lotus Sutra*: 3 people were saved from fire, 1 saved from the ghosts, 8 from executions, 22 freed from jails, 14 from robbery, 1 got a male descendant, 5 found the road while lost in the jungle or on the mountain, 4 returned back to their home country after long and dangerous sojourn, 3 were cured from serious diseases, 2 remained unharmed while threatened by animals....[39]

A number of texts related to the worship of Kuan-yin have been suspected by some modern Chinese and Japanese scholars of being 'fabricated' or 'spurious' scriptures.[40] This though is not the place to discuss these complicated problems. As far as the present topic is concerned, one point is quite clear: *viz.*, whatever the origin of these texts might be, their very existence indicates the popularity of Kuan-yin worship beyond any doubt. The reason for the popularity is explained in the material itself. Taking the *Kao-wang Kuan-shih-yin ching* (高王觀世音經) as an example, the text is now universally recognized as an original Chinese composition, which has pointedly claimed that:

> If one recites this scripture for a thousand times,
> And keeps it continuously in mind thought after thought,
> He will not be harmed by flames,
> And sword will break when it is brandished on him.
> Anger turns into happiness,
> He will survive at death.
> Do not think these are empty words,
> For Buddhas speak no lies.[41]

The quotation here recalls the statement in the *Lotus Sutra*: "if, again, a man who is about to be murdered calls upon the name ... then the knives and staves borne by the other fellow shall be broken in pieces, and the man shall gain deliverance.'[42]

The claim of miraculous efficacy is not merely a restatement alone, but is accompanied by a testimony. The testimony claims that during the sixth century A.D. there was a minor officer in North China who was a devoted believer of Kuan-yin, and who made and worshipped an image of the Bodhisattva. Toward the end of the Yüan Wei (元魏) dynasty, the official was captured and tortured by rebels. The night before he faced execution, he prayed to the saviour for help. Suddenly he felt as if he stood in front of the monk who taught him to recite the scripture. And he recited the text. Next day when the execution was being carried out, he remained alive and unharmed as the executioner broke the knives three times. The knives broke into pieces whenever they were brandished on his neck. He again worshipped the saviour's image after he was released safely. To his surprise, he found three traces of knife-chopping on the neck of Kuan-yin's image. Henceforth, the text is also called 'Knife-broken scripture'[43] (*Che-tao ching* 折刀經). At a time of war and anxiety, any claim of rescuing power is always attractive. And when the power is testified with a story such as the one we have just told, its efficacy surely looks more authentic and alluring.

Another form of testimony of the miraculous power of Kuan-yin is the gazetteer of the places of pilgrimage. Such a gazetteer usually contains scriptural evidence of Bodhisattva's powers and merits, geographical guides of the place, miraculous manifestations, historical events, hymns in praise of the Bodhisattva, and poems on the scenery. From these, one may have a glimpse of this type of literature. It combines elements which are of interest to different kinds of pilgrims with different levels of literacy. To the mind of this author, the most important and new element is that the Bodhisattva's compassionate acts are not only described in scriptures and testified to by past experiences, but even more significant is that he or she still responds to prayers at any moment. A sense of this present possibility of response makes the whole pilgrimage and religious concern more immediate, personal and meaningful, especially to those who are in trouble. This is a new dimension in religious literature. It is also a new dimension in the Bodhisattva worship. As far as Kuan-yin worship is concerned, the most widely-known gazetteer is the *P'u-t'o-lo-chia shan chuan* (補陀洛迦山傳 'A Record on the P'u-t'o lo-chia Mountain.')[44]

At a more popular level, there is a fragment of *pien-wen* (變文) from Tun-huang cave now preserved in the Bibliographique Nationale in Paris[45]; though it has been published under the title of *A Discourse on the Lotus Sutra*,[46] the existent fragment focuses on Kuan-yin worship. The text begins with "Those who worship Kuan-yin will have great luck. This has been praised by the Buddha at Vulture Peak Assembly"; and it ends with "those who hearing and reciting the name of Kuan-shih-yin Bodhisattva's name, would obtain such immeasurable and limitless profits from the merit."[47]

The Kuan-yin worship developed continuously during the later period. This development is testified to by the evidence which appears in the *Pao-chüan* (寶卷 'Precious Scroll') literature. Two pieces of the Precious Scrolls have been pointed out by Chen Cheng-to as significant religious composition in folk literature, namely the 'Precious Scroll on Hsiang-Mountain' (*Hsiang-shan pao-chüan* 香山寶卷) and the 'Precious Scroll of the Kuan-yin Fisher-woman' (*Yü-lan Kuan-yin pao-chüan* 魚籃觀音寶卷).[48] On the subject with which the present paper is concerned, the last title is more meaningful and hence is worthy of discussion. The Scroll states that when Kuan-yin saw the inhabitants of the fishing village Chin-sha-t'an (金沙灘) become so greedy that they caught and killed more fish than necessary, the Bodhisattva descended and appeared at the village as a beautiful young girl. Being charmed by her beauty, the village chief fell in love and proposed to marry the girl. She agreed to the proposal with the condition that he had to become a Buddhist; hence, not to take any life. The chief and his cohorts accepted the condition and converted. Though the girl died on the wedding night, the village became virtuous as a result of her appearance. Studies on this story by M. Sawada illustrate that it was a very popular legend of Kuan-yin, because the fisherwoman has often been referred to in Chinese literature from the T'ang dynasty until very recent times.[49]

A special point of interest presents itself in this legend in that the fisherwoman came to the world not in response to a prayer or call, but because she was inspired by her own compassion for the loss of the lives of fish. This means that Kuan-yin is not only responsive to pleas but even descends to the earth by her own will if the situation demands it.

To sum up the discussion on the Bodhisattva's role as saviour as personified by Kuan-yin, one fact is clear: *viz.*, these Bodhisattvas are all-powerful and compassionate. They are capable of and willing to save all sentient beings. Their efficacy is known and attested. This was the case in the past and probably still is at the present time.

Conclusion and Significance

From the foregoing discussion, it is clear that there are three typologies of Bodhisattva literature in Chinese; each typology represents a different aspect of the Bodhisattva idea. When these aspects of the idea are put into a larger context, their significance and contribution to the Chinese tradition as a whole and religious traditions in particular, become very evident.

The Birth-stories represent the first typology. The idea of a Bodhisattva presented there is that of a perfected Being of wisdom and compassion, whose virtue is cosmological in dimension, and who is powerful, willing and capable of sacrificing his own life for the benefit of others. When this image of a religious founder is compared to the pre-Buddhist Chinese tradition, the new dimension and significance of the Bodhisattva idea becomes overwhelming. In ancient China, the outstanding features of a leader are the qualifications of the sage-kings. Emperor Yao and Shun are regarded as the personification of these qualifications. What are they? The Grand Historian has praised Emperor Yao as:

> His benevolence like that of the Heaven, his knowledge like that of gods. Men turned to him as if following the sun, and admired him as if looking on the rain-cloud during a drought .[50]

As for Emperor Shun, he was idealized as a most virtuous and able administrator, and "well-known by his filial conduct."[51]

Compared with these ancient Chinese features of a religious leader, the virtues of the Bodhisattva as represented in the Birth-stories are much more imaginative, comprehensive and positive. The Buddhists claim that their founder perfected all these qualifications not only in the present life but a long time ago. The Buddhist has outweighed the ancient Chinese leaders by many lives as the Chinese concept of the sage-king is limited by the span of present life only and is ambiguous about what is beyond. Taking the benevolence of the exalted sage-king Emperor Yao as an example, he was credited with the invention of the calendar, the selection of good and able officials, etc.[52] These, though great events in the history of civilization, still lack a personal touch as most of the contributions were made by the officials.

The image of the religious leader built up on the Birth-stories is quite different. For example, in one of the past lives of the Bodhisattva, the leader saw and sympathized with the poverty of his people. He appeared in the world as the king, went and experienced many adventures, brought back treasures and relieved the poverty-stricken people with wealth.[53] The Bodhisattva king not only saved his people by personal effort through dangerous adventures, but gave his own blood and flesh to save other people, animals and even demons and humbled himself by being re-born as an animal or bird. In ancient Chinese tradition, man has distinguished himself from the realm of animals by his moral conscience; and sages have distinguished themselves from ordinary men by their perfection in the moral path.[54] One never heard of a sage-king becoming an animal or a bird by his own preference; it is even impossible for him to become an animal for other people's sake. In contrast to the pre-Buddhist Chinese tradition, the Buddhist image of the leadership is more lively, concrete, cosmological and personal.

The second typology of the Bodhisattva literature demonstrates the Buddhist claim that their religious goal is attainable through cultivation. Many Chinese were converted into Buddhism precisely because the Buddhist tradition had its concrete and detailed spiritual map. A Buddhist thinker has questioned the Classical tradition of China by these words: "If, as they say, myriad creatures were generated spontaneously without cause and conditions ... then immortals would not need to rely on elixirs nor a peaceful country or the help of the capable and wise." In that case who needs a religion? On the other hand, if one follows the Confucian doctrine, believing the world to be governed by the Will of Heaven, "then Heaven gives prosperity to those who conform to the Way." Further, "If calamities, disorders, and rebellions are dependent on the Will of Heaven," then what is the use of the sage and his teaching?[55] The principal difference between the Buddhist and classical Chinese philosophy lies in the Buddhist claim that they have a causal philosophy in understanding the corresponding cultivation in achieving the goal.[56]

This does not mean there is absolutely no Confucian program for personal cultivation; one could easily point out the well-known moral programs as mentioned in the *Great Learning* thus disproving the Buddhist criticism.[57] One should, however, remember that the *Great Learning* itself became prominent only after the Buddhist criticism. The text was obscure as a part of the ceremonial manual, the *Li Chi* (禮記) or the *Book of Rites*. It was under the Buddhist pressure, that the Confucian scholars began to read and rediscover the text. In other words the Confucian program in fact became prominent due to the Buddhist stimulus.[58] With this in mind, it may be said that the introduction of the achievability of the religious goal through cultivation was probably a turning point in the history of Chinese religions. This philosophy of action not only played a great role in Chinese Buddhism but also forced other Chinese philosophies to redirect, rediscover and revitalize their traditions.

The third typology of Bodhisattva literature in China is more related to the Chinese masses. As far as illiterate Chinese were concerned, they remained uncared for in traditional China, and were often caught in a terrible situation. For them, the introduction of the Bodhisattva idea represented the concept of much-needed personal deity. The Bodhisattva is a compassionate being that anyone could adore, anywhere, anytime. In return, the Bodhisattva would save the worshipper at the moment of danger and distress as these compassionate beings are more intimate and effective.

Comparing these personal, warm and efficacious qualities as ascribed to the Bodhisattvas in the popular literature with the pre-Buddhist deities in China, the Bodhisattva concept was something new and needed. As far as available evidence is concerned, the ancient Chinese deities could probably be classified into three categories, namely, natural, moral and ancestral. The worship of natural phenomena represented by sacrifices to Heaven, Earth, mountains and rivers, etc., lacked the warmth of personal relationship. Heaven also has a moral dimension, but that was rather remote to the masses in ancient China. In the first place, the sacrifice to Heaven was solely assigned to the Emperor on the throne. Secondly, moral quality was usually explained in philosophical terms, and thirdly, even if one accepted the moral law, the law operated automatically and solely on a moral basis. In that case, worship became unnecessary if one was perfectly moral or hopeless if one possessed no moral qualities. To put it simply, it had no mercy, and it would be meaningless to pray. Ancestral worship though has been a highly regarded practice in China since antiquity. However, this worship was confined to family circles only. Moreover, the efficacy of ancestral influence in a low and poor family is highly questionable.

With this religious background in mind, the introduction and development of the Bodhisattva concept as a personal, intimate and compassionate deity was indeed a great relief and a source of enrichment to the Chinese masses. To look at this concept from a historical viewpoint, this was probably the first time in Chinese history that a clearcut concept of personal deity had emerged. It is no surprise that Bodhisattva worship became so popular in the country and was even incorporated into other native religions in China. It gave the Chinese masses great hope, the hope for salvation. It showed great compassion, the compassion distressed people needed. It represented a great willingness, the willingness of Bodhisattva to help people. It claimed the possession of great powers, the powers that overcome all impossibilities.

To recapitulate, the Chinese Bodhisattva literature has presented three typologies of the Great Being: it introduced a new image of the religious founder through the past lives of the Buddha; it provided a spiritual map to man, and indicated that the religious goal was attainable through cultivation; it brought to the Chinese masses a warm, compassionate and powerful personal deity. As a result of a combination of these new concepts and the Buddhist religious system as a whole, the effects were as accurate as the lamentation of a leading Neo-Confucianist that "the heretical teaching of Buddhism flourished for the one thousand and five hundred years since it was established in the country."[59]

Judging from the evidence presented in this paper, one may even venture to say that, as far as the Bodhisattva idea is concerned, the influence that Buddhism exerted is much longer than the Neo-Confucian thinker thought. Because even long after the Neo-Confucians succeeded in replacing Buddhism as the main stream of influence on the Chinese intellectual, the worship of Bodhisattvas still grew amongst the Chinese masses. Even in the most recent decades, Kuan-yin still appeared in Chinese opera as a helpful and compassionate being. This image was clearly demonstrated in one of the popular operas, *Chui-yü* (追魚、The Romance of the Fish) which was performed.constantly in China during the fifties of the present century.[60]

FOOTNOTES

1 Quoted and translated from *Ch'u-san-tsang chi-chi* 出三藏記集 J. Takakusu and K. Watanabe (ed.) *Taishō shinshū daizōkyō* 大正新脩大藏經 (Tokyo: Society for the Publication of the Taisho Tripitaka 1922-33. Hereafter *T.*), No. 2145, p. 44a.

2 From the *K'ai-yüan shih-chiao lu* 開元釋教錄 vol. xi, *T.* No. 3154, p. 582a.

3 The Chinese translations of *Jātakas* are collected in *T.*, vols. 3-4. The works of Kang Seng-hui (康僧會) and Chih-ch'ien (支謙) are listed as Nos. 152 and 153. For the lives and works of these early translators, see E. Zürcher *The Buddhist Conquest of China* (Leiden: E.J. Brill, 1959) pp. 47ff. There are a few Sung translations which have been enlisted, Nos. 160, 165, 166, 173, etc.

4 *T.*, No. 203, p. 464b.

5 An elaborate version of the story is in *T.*, No. 208, p. 531. The story is also mentioned in *T.*, No. 160, p. 333b; Nos. 155, 160, 192, 200 etc.

6 *T.*, No. 163, pp. 390c-391c.

7 *T.*, No. 183, p. 453 and *T.* No. 203, p. 454b-c.

8 *T.*, No. 203, p. 455a-b.

9 *Ibid.*, pp. 457b-458a.

10 *T.*, No. 186, p. 504a. See *T.*, No. 203, p. 492a.

11 The story of the prince and his filial son is recorded in *T.*, No. 203, pp. 447c-448b. Accounts of Śyāmaka are found in *T.*, No. 152, No. 43, pp. 24b-25a; *T.*, No. 174-175, pp. 436b-443c; *T.*, No. 203, pp. 448b-449a. The story is then included into the 24 Exemplars in Filial Piety (*erh-shih-ssu-hsiao* 二十四孝) though the surname Shen (a transliteration of Śyā [maka] into Tan).

12 *T.* No. 174, p. 436; No. 175, pp. 438-440b, 442a.

13 *T.* No. 203, p. 457a-b.

14 *Ibid.*, pp. 466c-471a.

15 See J. Rahder *Daśabhūmikasūtra et Bodhisattvabhūmi* (Paris: Paul Geuthner, 1926) and his compilation, *Glossary of the Sanskrit, Tibetan, Mongolian and Chinese Versions of the Daśabhūmika-sūtra* (Paris: 1928). The Sanskrit version has been translated by M. Honda, in D. Sinor (ed.), the *Studies in South, East, and Central Asia* (New Delhi: International Academy of Indian Culture 1968) pp. 115ff. Studies on the relationship between the Ten Stages and the Six Perfections, see N. Dutt, *Aspects of Mahayana Buddhism and Its Relation to Hinayana* (London: Luzac & Co., 1930) pp. 259ff.

On the development of the Ten Positions, see K. Mizuno, "Botsatsu jūji setsu no hatten ni tsuite" (On the Development of the Bodhisattva's Daśabhūmi) in *Journal of Indian and Buddhist Studies* I/2 (Tokyo: Japanese Association of Indian and Buddhist Studies, 1953) pp. 63-68.

16 *T.*, No. 280.

17 Translated from *ibid.*, p. 445a-b.

18 See Zürcher, *loc. cit.* pp. 48-49.

19 *pen-ho hsiu-hsing* (本何修行), *ch'eng-fo sheng-tao* (成佛聖道), *T.* No. 281, p. 447b, line 6.

20 *yü-ch'iu-fo che* (欲求佛者), *yu shih-ti chu* (有十地住). *wang-ku lai chin* (往古來今), *chiai yu tz'u-che'eng* (皆由此入). *Ibid.*, p. 449c, lines 13-14.

21 *T.*, No. 285 has noted its connection with other Chinese versions of *Daśabhūmikas*. See *Hōbōgirin fascicule annexe*. (Tokyo: Maison Fransco-Japonaise, 1931) p. 17.

22 See *Hua-yen ching* 華嚴經, *T.* No. 287, pp. 448, 578, 580; *cf.* pp. 444, 542.

23 *T.* No. 279, p. 211.

24 *T.* No. 285, 458c lines 11-17.

25 *T.* No. 286, 498b lines 20-26.

26 *T.* No. 278, 542c lines 19-24.

27 *T.* No. 279, 179b lines 15-19.

28 *T.* No. 287, 536a line 24-536c line 1.

29 *T.* No. 1735, 735a lines 19-21.

30 *Ibid.*, 735a lines 24-25.

31 *Ibid.*, 735a line 27-735b line 1.

32 See Kao Huo-nien (高鶴年), *Ming-shan yu-fang chi* 名山遊訪記 (Tai-pei: reprint of 1934) pp. 187-200; H. Welch *The Practice of Chinese Buddhism* (Mass.: Cambridge, 1967) p. 307ff.

33 J.H. Chamberlayne, "The Development of Kuan Yin, Chinese Goddess of Mercy," *Numen* IX (1962), 45-42 and T. Goto (後藤大用), *Kanseon Bosatsu no Kenkyu* 觀世音菩薩の研究 (Tokyo: 1970).

34 *T.* No. 630, pp. 451ff and Goto, *loc. cit.* pp. 4-6.

35 *Shina bukkyōshi kenkyu* 支那佛教史研究. (Tokyo: reprint 1969) p. 375.

36 Tsukamoto Zenryu (塚本善隆), *koitsu rokki kanseon okenki no shutsugen*, in the *Silver Jubilee Volume of the Zinbun kagaku kenkyusho* (Kyoto: the University of Kyoto, 1954) pp. 245ff.

37 Tsukamoto Zenryu, "Koitsu rikacho senjutsu Kanseon okenki kaidai," in *Shotoku taishi kenkyu* 聖徳太子研究 No. 3 (1967) pp. 130-147.

38 *Ibid.*, pp. 129, 145-7.

39 *Ibid.*, pp. 134-6, 138-143.

40 Chang Hsin-cheng (張心澂), *Wei-shu t'ung-k'ao* 偽書通考 (Shanghai: 1954 reprint) pp. 1078, 1080, 1117-8; and Mochizuki Shinkō (望月信亨), *Bukkyō kyōten seiritsu shiron* 佛教経典成立史論 (Kyoto: 1946) pp. 317, 329, 331-337.

41 *T.* No. 2898, p. 1425c.

42 From L. Hurvitz (trs.). *Lotus Blossom of the Fine Dharma* (New York: Columbia University Press, 1976) p. 312.

43 The story is found in the *Chen-yüan hsin-ting shih-chiao mu lu* 貞元新定釋教目錄 ch. xxviii, *T.* No. 2157, p. 101b.

44 *T.* No. 1201.

45 Pelliot Collection No. 2133.

46 Wang Chung-min (王重民) *et al* (ed.), *Tun-huang pien-wen chi* 敦煌變文集 (Peking: 1957) vol. 2, pp. 502ff.

47 *Ibid.*, pp. 502 and 515.

48 *Chung-kuo so wen-hsüeh-shih* 中國俗文学史 (Peking: 1959 reprint) vol. 2, pp. 328f. See also Cheng's *Chung-kuo wen-hsüeh yen-chiu* (Peking: 1957 reprint) vol. 3, pp. 1072-75.

49 Sawada, *Bukkyō to Chugoku Bungaku* 佛教と中国文学 (Tokyo: 1957) pp. 143-152. See D.L. Overmeyer, *Folk Buddhist Religion*, (Mass.: Cambridge, 1976) pp. 165-6.

50 Translated from *Shih-chi* 史記 (Peking: 1969 new ed.) p. 15.

51 Translated from *ibid.*, p. 33.

52 *Ibid.*

53 *T.* No. 154, pp. 75b-76a.

54 D.C. Lau, *Mencius*, iv/b/19 (Harmondsworth: Penguin Classics, 1970) p. 131.

55 Quoted from the translation of *The Buddhist Tradition* (New York: Modern Library, 1969) pp. 183-4.

56 Translated from *Yüan-chüeh-ching ta-shu ch'ao* 圓覺經大疏抄 VII-A, Hsü Tsang-ching vol. 14, p. 352 last line.

57 See W.T. Chan, *A Source Book in Chinese Philosophy* (Princeton: University Press, 1963), pp. 89f.

58 See author's paper, "Tsung-mi's Questions regarding the Confucian Absolute," read at the Annual Meeting of the American Academy of Religion, New Orleans, November, 1978.

59 This is a summary of Chang Tsai's (張載 1020-2077) statement. See W.T. Chan's translations, *Reflections on Things at Hand* (New York: 1967) pp. 287-88.

60 *Chui-yü* 追魚 was performed by Wang Wen-chuan and other actresses of the Shanghai Yüeh Company. The opera was one of the popular dramas which was constantly performed until the Cultural Revolution. A cassette tape of the performance was reissued last year after a lapse of decades and is available in Hong Kong.

THE BODHISATTVA CONCEPT: A STUDY OF THE CHINESE BUDDHIST CANON

Lewis R. Lancaster

The Buddhism which was first presented to the Chinese was a tradition that had undergone five centuries and more of development in India and Central Asia. With this long period of expansion and history, Buddhism arrived as a system that had evolved into a number of distinct schools in conflict with one another over doctrine and practice. These splits within Buddhism were invisible to the Chinese who first explored the new religion of the barbarians. One of the important elements of these divergent schools centered on the concept of the Bodhisattva. When the 2nd century translation bureau of An Shih-kao started to disseminate texts among the literate Chinese, the complexities of the Bodhisattva doctrine were made available with no concern about the wide range of ideas represented in texts belonging to a variety of sectarian divisions. For example, the term "bodhisattva" appeared in the translated texts of the 2nd and 3rd centuries as the title of the Buddha Śākyamuni prior to his enlightenment, that is to say that it was used in the *jātaka* tales which recounted his long series of births and deaths.[1] In addition to this use of the word as referring to the former lives of Śākyamuni, it was also a designation for beings living in other worlds or at some long distant time period of the past. For this latter type, we may refer to the Mahāyāna *jātaka* tale of Sadāprarudita and Dharmodgata found at the end of the *Aṣṭasāhasrikāprajñāpāramitāsūtra.*[2] This Mahāyāna *jātaka* was used to illustrate the continued life of enlightened beings who were still in the swirling pattern of births and deaths and whose life accounts include the description of great feats of merit making, the cause of the attainment of higher and higher levels of enlightenment and the possession of great power. For both these types of Bodhisattvas, either the Buddha Śākyamuni of our own historical period or those of countless Bodhisattvas of the Mahāyāṇa tradition, the term "Jātaka Bodhisattvas" can be applied, since they are all beings with recorded stories of former existences.

By the 3rd century the Mahāyāna literature being translated in China represented some of the major doctrinal shifts which were taking place in Indian Buddhism. These new texts flowing from India and Central Asia gave the Chinese a glimpse of another type of Bodhisattva, a type differing in important ways from the "Jātaka Bodhisattva." This new conception can be found in the works of such missionaries as Dharmarakṣa,[3] for it is in those translations that we find the first descriptions of Bodhisattvas who are separated from the human birth and death process. In these Mahāyāna *sūtras*, the Bodhisattvas are either the manifestations of a Buddha or they are beings who possess the power of producing many bodies through great feats of magical transformation. Thus such Bodhisattvas are capable of appearing suddenly and with previous birth and maturation. This type is often called the "Heavenly" or "Celestial" Bodhisattvas and among them we find such figures as Avalokiteśvara, Mañjuśrī and Kṣitigarbha. It is among this group of Bodhisattvas that we find a pattern of existence which can best be compared to the docetic traditions of the religions of Western Asia. For example, Jesus of the Naassene Psalm assumes the body of an *archon* and appears in the world and performs for the worldings.[4] It is really only a phantom figure that is caused to appear or disappear and there is no human who has experienced birth and will face death. That such docetic tendencies existed in Buddhism has been discussed in an article written by Anesaki in the old classic *Encyclopedia of Religion and Ethics*.[5] Anesaki limited his remarks to the life of Śākyamuni, but, if we look carefully at the legends and stories related to Śākyamuni, it is apparent that he was never really elevated in a true docetic fashion, at least not in the same manner that we see in Gnostic Christology or among the "Celestial Bodhisattvas." Śākyamuni is a "Jātaka Bodhisattva," born, maturing, going through many lifetimes of merit making before achieving his final enlightenment. If we seek a proper designation for these Bodhisattvas who miraculously appear and disappear, then they might be called "Phantasma Bodhisattvas," distinguishing them from the "Jātaka Bodhisattvas" of the earlier texts.

In addition to the phantomry of Avalokiteśvara, Mañjusrī and similar Bodhisattvas, the Mahāyāna texts which were written and disseminated in East Asia, include hundreds of names of Bodhisattvas who are listed as members of the audiences gathered to hear the Buddhas preach the Dharma. For centuries the Chinese as well as other Buddhists have carefully preserved these directories of Bodhisattva names, even though their significance is not made clear in either the *sūtras* or the commentaries. Examples of names included in these lists are: Vidyutprabhā (Lightning Flash), Kṣitigarbha (Earth Encompassing) and Ratnaketu (Jewel Brightness). An inventory of the appearance of these words in the texts gives us a hint of the process by which they were made into the names of Bodhisattvas. The words *vidyutprabhā* and the like first appear not as the names of specific Bodhisattvas but as *samādhis*, states of meditative trance. Looking at the translations of a century or so later, these expressions no longer are limited to the *samādhis* but appear as the names of Bodhisattvas.[6] How could such a transformation take place? We can imagine that the terms were first taken to be a compound meaning "The One Who Achieves the Samādhi of Lightning Flash." Having once nominalized the compounds into a reference regarding an individual who had achieved the states described, it was a short step to convert the names into an appellation for a particular Bodhisattva. This process of creating the long lists of names of Bodhisattvas who are present at the time of the teachings of the Buddha would help to explain why so little is known about these Bodhisattvas which we can call "Audience Bodhisattvas." Nevertheless, it should be pointed out that while such Bodhisattvas as Mahāvyūha are insignificant, a few of these Bodhisattvas of the audiences acquire a history and an individuality. The most important of them is probably Kṣitigarbha, a Bodhisattva who became so popular in China that he was second only to Avalokiteśvara. It is Kṣitigarbha who lives out his vow to save beings and give aid in the interregnum between the Buddhas Śākyamuni and Maitreya.

A fourth type of Bodhisattva can be identified among the new items included in the Tantric materials which were translated by a group of missionaries dominated by the fame of Amoghavajra. It is in these texts that the name of one Bodhisattva overshadows all others and that is the Vajrapāṇi.[7] His name first appears in the 7th century text translated by Divākara[8] and unlike the names of so many of the "Audience Bodhisattvas," Vajrapāṇi's has no preceding use as a designation of a meditative state. Neither is he a "Phantasma Bodhisattva" for his appearance and disappearance is not within the everyday life and experience of the believer. Rather, Vajrapāṇi is a distinctly new type of Bodhisattva for he is present in the visualizations of the meditator. While visualization is a very early practice in Buddhist meditation and includes producing the imagery of such Buddhas and Bodhisattvas as Avalokiteśvara and Amitābha, it is in the Tantric texts that the visualized Vajrapāṇi is discussed as being completely within the meditative state and having no antecedents among the "Jātaka" or "Audience" Bodhisattvas. In Vajrapāṇi we have not just a mental reconstruction of a being who has another form of existence, for Vajrapāṇi only appears in the mind of the meditator. We might then call his type "Meditation Bodhisattva" since he comes into being and functions only in the trance practices. Tantra had a limited impact on Chinese Buddhism and some of the later developments which reached Tibet never took hold in East Asia. Thus we do not find such ideas as the "Wrathful" aspect which is so marked in the art and iconography of Tibet. It can be suggested that those "Wrathful" Bodhisattvas belong to this type and represent a more developed form of the visualized "Meditation Bodhisattvas."

From the discussion thus far, it appears that the Chinese were receiving texts which tended to remove the Bodhisattva from the realm of human life and experience into the transcendent spheres. The "Jātaka Bodhisattvas" who had to undergo the usual forms of birth and death fade to the background as the "Phantasma Bodhisattvas" come upon the scene. These latter in turn yielded to the visualized Vajrapāṇi of Tantra. While it is true that the docetic tendencies were strong in the Buddhism of these centuries, it would be misleading to say that the Chinese saw the Bodhisattva figure as completely removed from the human situation of daily experience. The Chinese added on yet another type to the list of Bodhisattva variations. In addition to the mystic experiences associated with the Bodhisattvas, the Chinese included in their hagiographic accounts of Buddhist missionaries and teachers stories of living Bodhisattvas. By the 6th century the biographies of the missionary and Chinese monks referred to these individuals as Bodhisattvas. In the *Chu san tsang chi chi*,[9] the oldest extant catalogue and biographic reference, the translator An Shih-kao and his colleague Lokakṣema are given the titles of Bodhisattvas. This notion was not to be limited to a few great saints of the past; by the T'ang dynasty certain ceremonies were instituted during which both laity and monks or nuns could take the precepts and become officially a Bodhisattva. A classic example of such ceremonies is to be found in the *T'an ching*[10] where a description is given of an investiture of the Formless Precepts. One major form of such an investiture has survived to the present day in the ordination ritual. On the day after the baptism by fire (when flammable substances are placed on the scalp and ignited) the monks take part in the Bodhisattva *vinaya* ceremony and at that time they take all of the vows of the Bodhisattva.[11] In Korea the word Bodhisattva is reserved as a title for devout laywomen who have taken the vows; it is never used for men. There is even report of a service in Jōdoshu in Japan[12] where lay followers accept the career of the Bodhisattva. In other words, the Chinese and other East Asian Buddhists came to recognize living people as Bodhisattvas.

This very cursory analysis suggests a variety of Bodhisattva models with which the Chinese had to concern themselves. There were:

1. "Jātaka Bodhisattvas" who could perform miracles and supernormal activities but who remained within the realm of karma with long histories

of activities which had been the cause of auspicious births, powers and insights.

2. "Phantasma Bodhisattvas" are those removed from the ordinary process of birth and death. They may well display all aspects of life, even death, but it is all a mock show put on for the benefit of others. These Bodhisattvas resemble the gnostic savior, that is a savior who does not have to be saved himself, in contrast to the "Jātaka Bodhisattvas" who must strive through long eons of time to achieve a state of enlightenment.
3. "Meditation Bodhisattvas" were of two types; the first being those whose names had first appeared in the lists of *samādhis* and were later attributed as names of individuals and a second, including Vajrapāṇi, belonging only to the realm of the visualizations of meditators. In both cases the Bodhisattva ideal is connected to the trance states.
4. "Living Bodhisattvas" as a separate group can also be divided into two types, those who are recognized by later generations as having lived a life with all the attributes of the Bodhisattva and those who achieve the title through investiture by taking certain vows.

With such a wide range of ideas about the Bodhisattva it is not surprising to find that controversy arose in China regarding this issue. In the 3rd to 5th centuries missionaries of all persuasions came into China, some bringing texts which taught the doctrines associated with "Jātaka Bodhisattvas" and others came with works which discussed the "Phantasma Bodhisattvas." The great magic worker Fo T'u Cheng taught that only the historical Buddha Śākyamuni should receive attention. It was because of Fo T'u Cheng's emphasis of the life and person of Śākyamuni that the Śākya cult became an important feature of Chinese Buddhism and Buddha's birthday one of the most popular festivals of the 3rd and 4th centuries. Other missionaries also focused on Śākyamuni; Saṃghadeva and Dharmayaśas represented a group that was in opposition to Mahāyāna and other schools which held to docetic notions.[13] Chu Fa-tu was a veritable St. Ignaius of Antioch in his insistence that the physical life of Śākyamuni was of prime importance. Just as St. Ignaius cried out against gnostic christology which represented Christ as a phantom being who did not really suffer death on the cross, so Chu Fa Tu vehemently denied the existence of the Buddhas in the ten directions with their retinues of Bodhisattvas. He told the Chinese to stop reading the Mahāyāna texts and to concentrate on following the Buddha. In this way the non-Mahāyāna schools made a great impact on the emerging Chinese Buddhism, insisting on close observation of the *vinaya* and urging the practice of *dhyāna* in order to achieve personal enlightenment. The Chinese were not unmoved by all this and came to call the teaching the "new" Buddhism. The famous Tao-an based much of his approach on this "new" Buddhism and even attempted to write a *vinaya* code in the absence of a full translation of the *vinaya* from Sanskrit. But as we know from history, the Chinese, caught up by the teaching of the *prajñāpāramitā* that had come from the brushes of the scribes working with Lokakṣema and Dharmarakṣa, did not forsake the Mahāyāna even when studying the texts of the *Abhidharma* and *dhyāna*. By the time of Kumārajīva at the end of the 4th century the process of forming the Buddhist tradition was set and China became a Mahāyāna stronghold.

As I have suggested, the Chinese were presented with the difficult problem of the transcendent appearing and being made flesh. It was a problem that west Asian religions faced at approximately the same time. The conflict that raged over the person of Jesus as Christ resulted in a never to be healed split between those who held to his humanness and the docetic groups such as the Gnostics who saw him only as a manifestation devoid of the pollution of a rotting, hurting fleshly body. It is of importance to the study of religion to note that the Chinese when challenged with the problem of the transcendent and mundane bodies of the Bodhisattvas did not split into a divided world of heresies and orthodoxy. They were able to tolerate a tradition which included both aspects. On the one hand they lit their lanterns on the birthday of Śākyamuni and retold the tales of his varied lives and his experiences as a troubled youth fighting to escape the snares of life, and on the other they had an intense interest in the phantomry of Kṣitigarbha and Avalokiteśvara. The relics of the physical body of the Buddha were revered and at the same time the *Śūraṅgamasamādhisūtra* describes the highest stage of Bodhisattva as one who:

> makes a display of *parinirvāṇa* and yet never perishes, displays a variety of physical forms and yet does not suffer the decay of his physical matter.[14]

Professor U. Bianchi in a lecture in Berlin in 1966 recognized that docetistic attitudes are to be found outside of Gnostic Christology and he makes the point that:

> the modes of relation between the divine and the mundane are of first importance in the description of a religious system.[15]

How complicated the issue seems when we consider that the Chinese held such a wide array of opinions regarding the Bodhisattva. Bodhisattvas can be manifested forms conjured up for the benefit of beings or an appearance within a meditative state serving the function of saving or leading beings toward enlightenment or as a kind and effective teacher who lives in the world as a human being — aging and dying. The missionaries coming into China were in conflict over the docetic issues and tended to create a polemic between the Śākya group and Mahāyāna. The Chinese ignored these appeals and happily accepted Śākyamuni as a Bodhisattva (before achieving Buddhahood) being born a baby and slowly awakening to his destiny and call. This did not turn them away from the notion that Bodhisattvas as transcendent beings could appear in the world at anytime — Kṣitigarbha may be a beggar one day and a merchant the next. In meditative states; in personal commitment of devotee taking a vow; in the close encounter of a teacher and disciple, the Bodhisattva ideal was seen and accepted by the Chinese. It was not in any way limited to a particular person or time. The Bodhisattva ideal did not split the Chinese Buddhists into camps based on docetistic attitudes. This fact must be given consideration by all scholars who pursue the study of docetism and who attempt to use the belief structure about the transcendent and mundane to create typological schemes within religious practice.

This survey of Chinese material supports the idea that in China we have an important reflection of developments taking place in India and in addition it gives some information about the way in which the Chinese handled these ideas. In both instances the Chinese Buddhist texts contain material of singular worth in the comparative studies of religions.

FOOTNOTES

1 An example of these collected tales is in the *Jātakasūtra* translated by Dharmarakṣa in A.D. 285. See J. Takakusu and K. Watanabe (ed.), *Taishō Shinshū Daizōkyō* (Tokyo: Society for the Publication of the Taisho Tripitaka, 1922-33). Hereafter *T.*, 154.

2 *Astasāhasrikāprajñāpāramitāsūtra* translated by Lokakṣema in A.D. 179 in Lo-yang. See *T.* No. 224 pp. 470c-478b.

3 A long list of such Bodhisattva names occurs in the *Pañcaviṃśatisāhasrikāprajñāpāramitāsūtra* translated in A.D. 285. See *T.* 222 p. 147b.

4 Hippolytus, *Refutation of all Heresies*, V, 10, 2.

5 M. Anesaki, "Docetism (Buddhist)" in James Hastings (ed.), *Encyclopedia of Religion and Ethics* (New York: Scribners, 1962) vol. 4, p. 835.

6 *Vidyutprabhā* appears as a *samādhi* in the *Drumakinararājaparipṛcchā* translated by Lokakṣema between A.D. 168-172. See *T.* No. 2149 p. 287b:22. In the *Mahāvaipulyamahāsamnipātasūtra* translated by Dharmarakṣa between 414 and 426, the term is used as the name of a Bodhisattva. See *T.* No. 397 p. 60a. The same term is also applied to the Buddha in the *Bodhisattvabuddhānusmṛtisamādhisūtra* translated by Guṇaśāla in A.D. 462. *Kṣitigarbha* is the same of a *samādhi* in *Paramārthadharmavijayasūtra* translated by Gautama Prajñāruci on September 25, A.D. 542. On the other hand the term appears in the *Suvarṇaprabhāsa* [*uttamarāja*] *sūtra* which was translated by I Ching in A.D. 703. *Ratnaketu* is a *samādhi* in the *Pañcaviṃśatisāhasrikāprajñāpāramitāsūtra* translated by Mokṣala in A.D. 291 and as a Bodhisattva's name in the *Suvikrāntavikramiparipṛcchaprajñāpāramitāsūtra* translated by Upaśūnya A.D. 565. These are examples of a pattern which are shown many times over in the texts of the first occurrence of a term being used in the list of *samādhis* and later appearing as the name of a Bodhisattva.

7 The list of appearances is large; one finds the name in texts such as the *Cundīdevīdhāranīsūtra* translated by Amoghavajra sometime between A.D. 720 and 774.

8 The earliest reference known to the writer is in the *Ghanavyūhasūtra* translated by Divākara between the first year of I Geng and the fourth year of Ch'in Kung in the T'ang dynasty (A.D. 676-688). See *T.* No. 2152 p. 368c.

9 *T.* No. 2154 p. 47c is one example of the attribution of the title Bodhisattva to Lokakṣema.

10 Philip B. Yampolsky (tr.), *The Platform Sutra of the Sixth Patriarch* (New York: Columbia University Press, 1967) pp. 145ff.

11 Prip Moller, *Chinese Buddhist Monasteries* (Hong Kong: University Press, 1967) p. 317.

12 Rev. Eidemann of the Institute of Buddhist Studies in Berkeley has kindly given me this information.

13 Dharmayaśas' biography can be found in *T.* No. 2151 p. 358c:10; *T.* No. 2154 p. 517b:13; *T.* No. 2157 p. 814a. His translations are the *Strīvivartavyākaraṇasūtra* and *Śāriputrābhidharmaśāstra*. Saṅghadeva's biographies are in *T.* No. 2145 p. 99b; *T.* No. 2149 p. 246c, *T.* No. 2154 p. 511b and *T.* No. 2157 p. 808. His translations are: [*Abhidharma*] *jñānaprasthānaśāstra* of Kātyāyana and the *Abhidharmahṛdaya* [*śāstra*] of Dharmottara.

14 *T.* No. 642 p. 630a:22-23.

15 U. Bianchi, "Doceticism: A peculiar theory about the ambivalence of the presence of the Divine," in J. Kitagawa and Charles Long (ed.), *Myth and Symbols* (Chicago: University Press, 1969) pp. 265-273.

THE BODHISATTVA DOCTRINE AS CONCEIVED AND DEVELOPED BY THE FOUNDERS OF THE NEW SECTS IN THE HEIAN AND KAMAKURA PERIODS

Hisao Inagaki

1. Introduction

Japanese Buddhism entered a new epoch in the beginning of the Heian period (9-12th centuries) when Kūkai (774-835) and Saichō (767-822) respectively brought back from T'ang China the Shingon and Tendai tradition. Being ardent followers of the Bodhisattva Path, they developed the Bodhisattva ideal in their own doctrinal setting: Kūkai furthered and completed the esoteric system of Bodhisattva doctrine and practice, while Saichō established on Mt. Hiei the Tendai centre for realizing the Mahāyāna ideal and proclaimed the *Ekayāna* (One Vehicle) teaching based on the *Saddharma-puṇḍarīka sūtra*. Saichō's Bodhisattva idealism culminated in an appeal to the imperial court for permission to establish an ordination platform for Bodhisattvas, a project which was fulfilled after his death.

In spite of the lofty Bodhisattva ideal held by Kūkai and Saichō, Heian Buddhism tended to become secular and degenerate. In the face of the collapse of the Bodhisattva ideal, the Kamakura period (12-14th centuries) ushered in three different Mahāyāna sects.

Firstly, Eisai (1141-1215) and Dōgen (1200-1253) brought back from China the Rinzai and Sōtō Zen sects, respectively. The founders of these two Zen sects sought to revive the genuine Bodhisattva tradition by emphasizing the importance of strict observance of the precepts and devotion to meditation.

Secondly, the Jōdo and other Pure Land sects were founded by Hōnen (1133-1212), Shinran (1173-1262) and others.[1] They abandoned the hope of realizing the Bodhisattva ideal in this world and entrusted themselves to Amitābha, the Buddha of Eternal Light and Life, reciting "*Namu Amida Butsu*" (adoration to Amitābha). In so doing, they hoped to attain birth in his Pure Land, Sukhāvatī, where they could achieve full Enlightenment.

Thirdly, the Nichiren sect was founded by Nichiren (1222-1282). He advocated a new Bodhisattva path based on his own interpretation of the *Saddharmapuṇḍarīka sūtra.* He rejected all other types of Buddhism as being wrong and false, and propounded a radical practice consisting solely of chanting the Chinese title of the *Saddharmapuṇḍarīka sūtra*, "*Namu Myōhōrengekyō*" (Adoration to the *Lotus sūtra*).

The founders of these new sects in the Heian and Kamakura periods produced different forms of the Bodhisattva ideal and proposed different methods of realizing it. There are, however, two common features underlying their views. One is an acute sense that it was a time of crisis for the Dharma and the Bodhisattva Path, which originated from the theory that the *mappō* period, or the last of the three periods of Dharma survival, had begun. The other is the *Ekayāna* ideal which existed from early Japanese Buddhism but which was especially highly esteemed in the Heian and Kamakura periods. Japanese Buddhism, in fact, started from the *mappō* period. At first the Dharma crisis was not strongly felt but soon the *mappō* theory became popular. Faced with the problem of how one could attain Enlightenment in this doomed period, a problem which had not been fully dealt with by Indian and Chinese Buddhists, the founders of the new sects proposed theoretical and practical solutions. While the pessimistic *mappō* idea drove serious seekers of the Dharma to despondency and hopelessness, the Ekayāna ideal advocated in various ways by new Buddhist leaders revived their hopes and gave them assurance of Enlightenment. Side by side with the development of the Ekayāna ideal, the *hongaku* theory, the theory that one is originally enlightened, was widely adopted by the founders of the new sects and it served to strengthen the intellectual basis of their new salvation formulas. In the following, we shall discuss these topics and see how the Bodhisattva doctrine took a unique turn in the Heian and Kamakura periods while vacillating between hope and despondency.

2. The *mappō* idea and the problem of the practicability of the Bodhisattva Path, especially of keeping the precepts

The idea existed in India that the Buddha's Dharma would last in its genuine form for a certain period of time, followed by a period when the Dharma would continue to be in its imitative form (*pratirūpaka*). However, it was in China that the three-period theory together with a 10,000-year post-Imitative Dharma period took its definite form. There are different calculations as to the duration of the first two periods: either 500 or 1,000 years for each of the two.[2] As the year of the Buddha's Parinirvāṇa was traditionally fixed in China at 949 or 609 B.C.,[3] the *mappō* or the period of Decadent Dharma would have started in 552 A.D. at the earliest.

Sure enough, a major persecution of Buddhism in China took place from 574 to 578, which wiped out Buddhism in North China. Previously, in 556, Narendrayaśas came to China and produced a translation of the chapter "Moon-Storage" of the *Mahāsannipāta sūtra* which contained a theory that the periods of the Right Dharma and Imitative Dharma would last for 500 and 1,000 years, respectively.[4] Hui-ssŭ (515-577) was among the first to feel strongly about the advent of the Decadent Dharma period. It is believed that he used the term *mappō* (*mo-fa*) for the first time.[5] Chinese Pure Land masters like Tao-cho (562-645) and Shan-tao (613-681) were quick to accept the *mappō* idea in their efforts to advocate the belief in Amitābha's salvation.[6]

In Japanese Buddhism the *mappō* crisis was not strongly felt in its early stages. According to the ancient chronicle, *Nihonshoki* (Chronicle of Japan), 552 A.D. was the year in which Buddhism was officially transmitted to Japan but it is believed that this had little to do with the *mappō* idea.[7] In fact, Buddhism thrived in the 7-8th centuries and there was nothing which indicated degeneration or decline of the Dharma until the end of the 8th century when laxity and violation of the precepts for monks and nuns became so apparent that the emperor issued an edict in 798 to stop this tendency. On this score, Saichō expressed his opinion in the *Mappō tōmyōki* (*The lamp in the period of Decadent Dharma*)[8] that since the *mappō* period was imminent, it had already become difficult for priests and nuns to observe the precepts. He even asserted that the precepts would cease to exist in the *mappō* period, so that there could be no breaking of them.[9] He thus expressed his strong objection to the strict application of the precepts to priests and nuns of his time.

Later, Saichō went to China and received from Tao-sui the 'Bodhisattva vows for perfect and quick enlightenment' (*endon-bosatsu-kai*).[10] In 818 be began his movement to set up a platform for these Mahāyāna precepts on Mt. Hiei. In so doing, he openly renounced the Hīnayāna precepts he had earlier received at the Tōdaiji Temple in Nara[11] and threw away his begging bowl.[12] The Mahāyāna precepts, or Bodhisattva vows, he sought to establish embodied three ideals called *sanjujōkai* (three groups of pure precepts),[13] namely:

1) Abstaining from evil-doings (*saṃvara-śīla*),
2) Performing virtuous deeds (*kuśaladharma-saṃgrāhaka-śīla*) and
3) Giving benefit to sentient beings (*sattvārtha-krīya-śīla*).

In their actual application, the Mahāyāna precepts specifically consist of the ten major precepts and forty-eight minor ones presented in the *Fan wang ching* (*Brahma's net sūtra*).[14] Saichō also claimed that his Mahāyāna precepts did not form a separate element of the three types of learning (*tisraḥ śikṣāḥ*) but were fused together with meditation (*samādhi*) and wisdom (*prajñā*). Such precepts agreed with his Ekayāna ideal which will be discussed later, and so they were called 'Ekayāna precepts.' When the permission to establish a Mahāyāna ordination platform was granted after his death, monks were able to take ordination in the Tendai Mahāyāna precepts on Mt. Hiei.

Saichō's contemporary and the founder of the Shingon sect, Kūkai, had a different view of how the Bodhisattva doctrine was to be practised in the *mappō* period. While admitting that he was living in a time of degeneration near the end of the period of Imitative Dharma, he believed that people could and should abide by the rules even in periods far removed from the Buddha's time.[15] From his esoteric viewpoint, however, the varieties of precept mentioned in the exoteric teachings are considered to be derived from esoteric precepts which harmonize with one's true nature. Indeed, the Bodhi Mind was viewed as the essence of the precepts.[16]

Apart from Saicho's *mappō* theory, the idea that the *mappō* era started in 1052 became popular in the 11th century,[17] so what became known as Kamakura Buddhism began with an intensified sense of Dharma crisis. As I said before, Pure Land masters of the Kamakura period abandoned their hopes of realizing Enlightenment in this world by observing the precepts and performing the Bodhisattva practices. They took refuge in Amitābha's vow of salvation whereby they sought to attain birth in the Pure Land and become Bodhisattvas and, eventually, Buddhas. This crisis consciousness, originating from the *mappō* idea, was especially strong in Shinran, the founder of the Jōdo Shin sect. He quoted the greater part of the *Mappō tōmyōki* in his masterpiece, the *Kyōgyōshinshō* (*Teaching, practice, faith and enlightenment*),[18] to show that only the Pure Land teaching was practicable in the *mappō* period. His master Hōnen, who established the independence of the Pure Land sect, was formerly a Tendai priest and a strict observer of the Mahāyāna rules but did not expect his followers to abide by them.

Eisai who was first to bring back from China the Rinzai tradition of Zen noted in his *Kōzen gokoku ron* (*Discourse on the protection of the state by propagating Zen*) that 2,147 years had passed since the Buddha's Parinirvāṇa, and wrote "this is the 2nd century in the last of the five 500-year periods".[19] This means that he thought that he lived in a time of strife and argument which made it difficult to pursue the Buddhist Dharma. He was, however, very strict in observing the precepts and urged people to do the same. As he says in the *Kōzen gokoku ron*:

> Precepts and rules of conduct come first in the pursuit of Zen.[20]

He had previously taken the Mahāyāna vows on Mt. Hiei and distinguished himself as a Tendai priest but chose to follow the tradition of Chinese Zen rules of conduct. He says in the *Kōzen gokoku ron*:

> I have sincerely set out the Rinzai Zen tradition and have recited the Four-Part Vinaya and the Bodhisattva Precepts.[21]

Dōgen, from his Zen standpoint, took no notice of the distinction of the three periods of the Dharma.[22] He was of the opinion that whoever practised in the right way could realize Enlightenment. Eisai, Dōgen and their followers were convinced that the precepts were the basis of successful practice of the Bodhisattva Path and that no Enlightenment was possible without abiding by them. In emphasizing the necessity of the precepts, Dōgen said:

> Unless one receives the precepts, one cannot claim to be a disciple of the Buddha.[23]

By the precepts he meant the Bodhisattva precepts, and he followed especially the Three Refuges precepts, the three groups of pure precepts and the ten major precepts.[24]

Nichiren adopted a unique standpoint regarding the *mappō* theory and the Bodhisattva doctrine in general. He claimed that the *Saddharmapuṇḍarīka sūtra* was the only sūtra adaptable to the *mappō* period and that the *Daimoku*, or the recitation of "*Namu Myōhōrengekyō*", was the only method of practice one should follow.[25] He thought that the *mappō* era was the time best suited for the recitation of the *Daimoku*, and that thereby the *mappō* period could effectively take on the character of the Right Dharma era. Nichiren had a specially strong pretension to be a leader in the *mappō* period and claimed that he was an incarnation of the Bodhisattva Jōgyō (Viśiṣṭacāritra) mentioned in the *Saddharmapuṇḍarīka sūtra*.[26]

Despite the arrival of the *mappō* period, when the founders of the new sects stood up with a fresh conviction, they provided arguments for their new salvation formulas which did not contradict the Bodhisattva doctrine. Although their theories differed from each other, they shared a common principle — the Ekayāna ideal, which represents the apex of Mahāyāna and, hence, the culmination of the Bodhisattva doctrine. Let us, next, see how it developed in Japan and took different shapes in the Heian and Kamakura periods.

3. The *Ekayāna* ideal

The form of Buddhism transmitted to Japan from the Asian Continent from the 6th century onward was predominantly Mahāyāna. When we speak of Mahāyāna in the context of Japanese Buddhism, however, it is important to note the difference between Mahāyāna and Ekayāna, because the new Mahāyāna sects established after the Heian period were based on the Ekayāna ideal rather than on the Mahāyāna Bodhisattva ideal in the conventional sense of the term.

The term 'Ekayāna' or 'One Vehicle' is found in various Mahāyāna sūtras, such as the *Saddharmapuṇḍarīka*, *Śrīmālasiṃhanāda*, *Avataṃsaka* and *Laṅkāvatāra*. In these sūtras, the term 'Ekayāna' is used in the sense of 'one path' as opposed to the two paths of the Śrāvakayāna and Pratyekabuddhayāna, and also as opposed to the three paths, i.e. these two and the Bodhisattva Path.[27] Although Ekayāna is often used as a synonym of Mahāyāna, it differs from Mahāyāna in that it does not admit Hīnayāna as being distinct from Mahāyāna. Ekayāna is above Hīnayāna and Mahāyāna and yet it incorporates both. Regarding the difference between Mahāyāna and Ekayāna, Prince Shōtoku (574-622) says in the commentary on the *Śrīmālāsiṃhanāda sūtra*:

> Mahāyāna and Ekayāna have nearly the same meaning, but they are slightly different from each other. Mahāyāna is a term used specifically to distinguish it from the rest of the Three Vehicles, whereas Ekayāna is not opposed to the three or to the two vehicles.[28]

In India the view that Ekayāna is different from Mahāyāna was held by Yogācāra masters. Vasubandhu, as one, says in his commentary on the *Mahāyānasaṃgraha*:

> There are three kinds of Right Dharma established by the Tathāgata: 1) Hīnayāna, 2) Mahāyāna and 3) Ekayāna. Of the three the third is supreme.[29]

In explaining this passage, Saichō says in his *Shō gonjutsu kyō* (*The Mirror reflecting the temporary and true teachings*) that Mahāyāna refers to the teachings, such as the Vijñānavāda, and shares some common ground with Hīnayāna whereas

Ekayāna refers to teachings expounded in such sūtras as *Avataṃsaka*, *Prajñāpāramitā*, *Nirvāṇa* and *Saddharmapuṇḍarīka*.[30] He further comments that there are no different *yānas* in Buddhism: they are all merged into one.[31]

In the fact that Ekayāna does not make a distinction between the three vehicles for the three types of people, its aim is the salvation of all beings. The most popular sūtra which emphasizes the Ekayāna ideal is the *Saddharma-puṇḍarīka sūtra*, on which the Tendai Ekayāna doctrine was based and systematized. About 200 years before the foundation of the Japanese Tendai sect, Prince Shōtoku paid special attention to the Ekayāna teaching of the *Saddharma-puṇḍarīka sūtra*. In his commentary on the sūtra, he shows that the Ekayāna ideal of the sūtra aims at bringing all sentient beings to the same ultimate Enlightenment as that of the Buddha and that various teachings provided in other sūtras for the three different types of Buddhist are provisional and temporary.[32]

The first Japanese sect to uphold the Ekayāna ideal was the Kegon or Avataṃsaka sect founded in the Nara period. It claimed that the *Avataṃsaka sūtra* was the direct exposition of the Buddha's Enlightenment and that its teaching was 'the directly expounded Ekayāna' (*jikken no ichijō*) as distinct from other Ekayāna teachings such as the *Saddharma-puṇḍarīka* and *Prajñāpāramitā* which still recognized the provisional Hīnayāna teachings.

It is to be noted that both Saichō and Kūkai at first devoted themselves to the study of the Kegon in Nara. Later, they established their respective versions of the Ekayāna, namely, *Hokke-ichijō* or Saddharmapuṇḍarīka Ekayāna and *Himitsu-ichijō* or Esoteric Ekayāna. Saichō placed the *Saddharmapuṇḍarīka sūtra* above all other sūtras and compared it to an unobstructed flight passage across the sky. He says in the *Shugo kokkai shō* (*On the protection of the state*):

> The predominantly Hīnayāna method of *śamatha* and *vipaśyanā* is like a roundabout way to be followed on foot. The predominantly Bodhisattva method of *śamatha* and *vipaśyanā* is like a path to be followed on foot for many kalpas. Teachings about these two ways exist

> but nobody practises them. People of today have changed so much. There is no Hīnayāna practitioner here at all. The periods of the Right Dharma and Imitative Dharma having nearly past, that of the Decadent Dharma is drawing very near. This is precisely the time for the practitioners of the Saddharma-puṇḍarīka Ekayāna.[33]

Saichō believed that ordinary Mahāyāna teachings, to say nothing of Hīnayāna, could not save people of the *mappō* period. In practice, the Saddharmapuṇḍarīka Ekayāna ideal is to be realized by the Tendai method of *śamatha* and *vipaśyanā*. He, therefore, prescribed for his pupils the practice of the Four *Samādhis*.[34] In advocating the Ekayāna ideal, he considered it of paramount importance to initiate his pupils in the Mahāyāna precepts, which he called '*ichijō-kai*' (Ekayāna Precepts).[35] As his Ekayāna precepts were based on the Tendai concept of 'perfect fusion' (*en'yū*), they were, as I have already explained, not separate from *samādhi* and *prajñā*. Such precepts were in harmony with the Buddha-nature and, in essence, not separate from the attainment of Buddhahood.[36]

While Saichō upheld the Saddharmapuṇḍarīka Ekayāna ideal, Kūkai promulgated Esoteric Ekayāna. He classified the Buddha's teachings into exoteric and esoteric, and considered the esoteric ones to be deeper and superior. He also classified Buddhism into ten doctrines, placing the Shingon teaching above the other nine. According to him, all other teachings are based on the Buddha's spoken words but the Shingon teaching, as shown in the *Mahāvairocana* and *Vajraśekhara sūtras*, is the direct revelation of the absolute truth by Mahāvairocana, the Dharmakāya Buddha. In the *Hizōhōyaku* (*The precious key to the secret treasury*) he divides the Buddha's teachings into exoteric and esoteric, and further divides the exoteric teachings into the One Vehicle and the Three Vehicles. He then explains:

> The One Vehicle refers to the teaching expounded by Sambhogakāyas manifested to Bodhisattvas on the tenth down to first stages. The Three Vehicles refer to sūtras expounded by Śākyamuni's Nirmāṇakāya to the followers of the Two Vehicles and to Bodhisattvas who had not yet reached the first stage. The esoteric teaching is the Dharma expounded by

> the Svabhāva (Self-nature) Dharmakāya, Mahāvairocana Tathāgata, for the sake of his and his attendant deities' enjoyment of the Dharma; this is what is called *'Shingon-ichijō'* (Mantra Ekayāna).[37]

Elsewhere, Kūkai refers to the Shingon teaching as *'Himitsu-ichijō'* (Esoteric Ekayāna) and also *'Kongō-ichijō'* (Vajra Ekayāna),[38] because he believed it enabled one to reach the Buddha's realm which was as indestructible as *vajra*.

The Kegon Ekayāna ideal of the Nara period (8th century) was thus followed by the emergence of the two highest Ekayāna schools of the Heian period (9th-12th centuries). It was from Saichō's Ekayāna system that a few more Ekayāna ideals of the Kamakura period (12th-14th centuries) derived their inspiration.

Firstly, the Zen promulgated by Eisai and Dōgen may be called *'Busshin-ichijō'* (Buddha-Mind Ekayāna), for it does not make a distinction between various teachings provided for different capacities of people but proposes to lead all beings directly to the realization of the Buddha Mind.

Secondly, Hōnen's exclusive recitation of the Nembutsu is, in my view, an Ekayāna teaching for it claims to enable all beings, without distinction, to attain birth in Amitābha's land and become Buddhas. Hōnen did not use the word 'Ekayāna' for his Nembutsu teaching but the Pure Land Ekayāna ideal was revealed by his disciples, for instance Shinran and Kōsai (1163-1247).[39] Shinran, in particular, gave Hōnen's teaching a solid theoretical basis by availing himself of the Ekayāna ideal presented in the *Śrīmālāsiṃhanāda*, *Nirvāṇa* and *Avataṃsaka sūtras*. Basing his words on the *Śrīmālāsiṃhanāda sūtra*, he says in the *Kyōgyōshinshō*:

> In Mahāyāna there is no difference between the Two Vehicles and the Three Vehicles. The Two Vehicles and the Three Vehicles lead into the One Vehicle. The One Vehicle is the Ultimate *Paramārtha* Vehicle. It is solely the One Buddha Vehicle of the Original Vow (*Seigan-ichibutsujō*).[40]

Shinran considered all the other teachings as provisional, aimed to lead less mature people gradually to the Pure Land teaching. There is, in his view, only one true Buddhist teaching and that is the ultimate Ekayāna teaching, the Path of Amitābha's Original Vow which leads all beings to Enlightenment. The *Kyōgyōshinshō* shows the essential character of his Original Vow Ekayāna ideal:

> When I contemplate the ocean-like Original Vow Ekayāna (*Honganichijō*) teaching, I find that it is an all-complete, unobstructed, absolute and non-dual teaching which brings quick results (for realizing Buddhahood).[41]

A clearer expression of the idea that the Original Vow Ekayāna is 'all-complete' and 'brings quick results' (*endon*, originally a Tendai term) can be found in his *Wasan* (*Hymns*):

> The All-complete Original Vow Ekayāna which
> brings quick results (*Hongan-endon-ichijō*)
> Embraces even the most wicked people and evil-
> doers, so are we taught.
> We shall quickly come to see
> That evil passions are not different in essence
> from Bodhi.[42]

Lastly, Nichiren's teaching is meant for all beings, including Hīnayānists and wicked people, and promises quick attainment of Buddhahood based on the idea of 'the original Buddha-state' (*honmon*) revealed in the second half of the *Saddharmapuṇḍarīka sūtra*.[43]

It may be pointed out that all these Ekayāna ideals not only provided ways of attaining Buddhahood for all humankind, even in the *mappō* period, but also simplified and shortened the process by which they might become Buddhas. Three *asaṃkhya kalpas* are no longer required, and the six *pāramitās* are not all required in order to reach Buddhahood. Especially, in Kamakura Buddhism, traditional, difficult practices were replaced by simple ones, such as the recitation of Amitābha's name, the recitation of the title of the *Saddharmapuṇḍarīka sūtra* and the sole practice of meditation (*shikan-tada*) in Dōgen's Zen. Therefore, the common emphasis of all these founders was the quick attainment of Buddhahood. Indeed, it became the central theme in their proposal of a new Ekayāna ideal.

4. The quick attainment of Buddhahood

First of all, Saichō claimed that his Saddharmapuṇḍarīka Ekayāna was a shortcut to Buddhahood. In the *Hokke shūku* (*Excellent phrases from the Lotus sūtra*)[44] he contends that all sentient beings, even ordinary people, can become Buddhas in their present bodies, and mentions as an example of this the story of a young female dragon who instantly became a Buddha by the merit and power of the *Saddharmapuṇḍarīka sūtra*. He, however, admits that the quick attainment of Enlightenment is limited to men of supreme spiritual capacity, for he says in the *Hokke shūku*:

> Men of first class intelligence can become Buddhas in their lifetime. Those of middle intelligence can become Buddhas in the next life. Those of lower intelligence can become Buddhas in the life after the next.[45]

Kūkai's theory of instantaneous attainment of Buddhahood was more systematic and thorough. In the *Sokushin jōbutsu gi* (*On the attainment of Buddhahood in the present body*) he attempted to show that man and Mahāvairocana Buddha were essentially identical by applying the theory of the interpenetration of the six elements, i.e. earth, water, fire, wind, space and consciousness.[46] In practice, the aspirant can attain unity with the Cosmic Buddha through the Three Mystic Practices (*sanmitsu*), i.e. making a *mudrā*, reciting a *mantra* and entering a *samādhi*.[47]

The quick realization of Enlightenment was also emphasized by Shinran and Nichiren. According to Shinran, when a firm faith in Amitābha is awakened in us, our saṃsāric condition ends at once and we are established in the state of non-retrogression (*avinivartanīya*) which promises attainment of Buddhahood in the next life.[48] Like Saichō and Kūkai, Nichiren asserted that we can realize Enlightenment while having human bodily forms but emphasized that his teaching was deeper than theirs. He believed that, by the power of the *Saddharmapuṇḍarīka sūtra*, Buddhahood could be actualized when we recite the title of the sūtra. Here are three quotations from his works and letters to show his views on the attainment of Buddhahood in the present life:

1. Without any practice whatsoever on our own side, we become a Buddha in this body.[49]
2. In this life, the originally enlightened Tathāgata is quickly revealed in this body; this we call '*sokushin jōbutsu*' ('becoming a Buddha in the present body') ... we become a Buddha endowed with the Three Bodies.... Though there are different capacities, upper, middle and lower, [followers of the teaching] will realize this oneness and non-dualness with Buddhas and Tathāgatas in their present life.[50]
3. Though I have expounded various teachings at various places for the past twenty-seven years from the 5th year of Kenchō to the 3rd year of Kōnin, what I have intended to reveal is this [i.e. *sokushin jōbutsu*].[51]

Nichiren also emphasized the importance of belief and often talked about *anjin* 'settled mind' in this life. From what he said in his works and letters to his disciples, it is evident that he also believed in the Great Bliss in the next life.[52]

Now, we may ask, "What has become of the Bodhisattva Path?" and "What justifications were there when the exponents of various Ekayāna ideals claimed quick attainment of Enlightenment without following the ordinary Bodhisattva career?" These questions lead us to our next topic — the new interpretations of the Bodhisattva Path made in the Heian and Kamakura periods as a result of the exaltation of Ekayāna ideals.

5. New interpretations of the Bodhisattva Path

A Bodhisattva is one who seeks *Bodhi* for himself and, at the same time, seeks to help other sentient beings to attain salvation. From the beginning of the Bodhisattva ideal it was generally believed that a Bodhisattva must perform various *pāramitā* practices for an incredibly long period of time before he achieved his objectives and, thereby, became a Buddha. As Mahāyāna Buddhism developed, this set pattern of a Bodhisattva's career was not necessarily followed. The idea that man possessed Buddha-nature was already extant in Indian Buddhism but it was in China that this idea was expanded into the theory that man is originally a Buddha. The Avataṃsaka, Zen and Esoteric sects were the first to develop this theory. With the popularity of this theory the Bodhisattva concept underwent a drastic change. The Buddha-aspect of the practitioner was now more strongly emphasized than the human-aspect, and Enlightenment was to be attained by the Buddha's power rather than by the practitioner's efforts. In Japanese this theory is called '*hongaku*' (originally enlightened) in contrast to '*shikaku*' (becoming enlightened.)[53] As is easily surmised, the *hongaku* theory is compatible with the Ekayāna ideal, whereas the *shikaku* idea is the basis of the other Mahāyāna teachings, such as the Vijñānavāda. In terms of cause and effect, the *shikaku* theory follows the normal process of rising through the Bodhisattva stages (cause) toward Buddhahood (effect) but the *hongaku* theory starts with the 'effect' or perfect stage of a Buddhahood and looks upon Bodhisattva practices as part of it. From the *hongaku* viewpoint, Buddhahood is not the final objective but the reality to be experienced here and now. Further, it may be noted that the common Mahāyāna principle of non-duality which identifies *saṃsāra* with *nirvāṇa* and *kleśa* with *bodhi* is here more concretely expressed in terms of the man-Buddha identity. In the following we shall see how the *hongaku* theory was employed by the founders of the new sects to justify their new Bodhisattva theories.

As we have already seen, before the Heian period there was a prototype of Ekayāna thought in the doctrine of the Kegon or Avataṃsaka sect. The *Avataṃsaka sūtra* itself contains the germ of the *hongaku* theory, for it says:

> Mind, Buddha and sentient beings —
> these three are not discriminated.[54]

Elsewhere, the sūtra abounds in descriptions of the Buddha's glory in terms of the Bodhisattvas' activities. Moreover, all phenomenal worlds are seen reflected in the Buddha's Enlightenment. From the Kegon standpoint, all the causal practices of the Bodhisattvas are interrelated with and comprised in Buddhahood. At the initial stage of the Bodhisattva's career, therefore, he attains Enlightenment. Hence, the *Avataṃsaka sūtra* says:

> At the time of the first awakening of the Bodhi
> Mind, one realizes Enlightenment.[55]

Also it says:

> A Bodhisattva who has first awakened the Bodhi Mind is a Buddha.[56]

The Kegon teaching is believed to have paved the way for Kūkai's *hongaku* theory. Apart from the *Mahāvairocana* and other esoteric sūtras which already contained some aspects of the *hongaku* idea, he extensively employed the *Shih mo hê yen lun*,[57] a commentary on the *Awakening of faith in Mahāyāna*, as scriptural evidence. In the bibliographical introduction to the *Mahāvairocana sūtra*, Kūkai says:

> Mahāvairocana is the Svabhāva Dharmkāya, namely, the originally enlightened Noumenal Body which has been in existence from the eternal past.[58]

Again, he says in the introduction to the *Vajraśekhara sūtra*:

> The originally enlightened Buddha in one's self and others is naturally self-enlightened and is originally possessed of the Three Bodies and Four Virtues;[59] from the beginningless past it has had perfect merits as numerous as the sand-grains of the River Ganges.[60]

Man is originally possessed of the Three Bodies of the Buddha which he realizes in his human body when he completes the Three Mystic Practices, as Kūkai says in the *Sokushin jōbutsu gi*:

> If the practitioner meditates on this principle well, he will quickly reveal and realize the innate Three Bodies in his present body by virtue of the perfection of the Three Mystic Practices.[61]

However, the Buddha's power (*adhiṣṭhāna*) is indispensable for the realization of this mystic truth. It is the externalized activity of one's innate Buddhahood, which works in correspondence with one's practice-power to realize the original cosmic unity.

Since Kūkai also emphasized the importance of the *Bodhi* Mind and the precepts, he did not abolish the conventional Bodhisattva doctrine. What distinguished his teaching was the esoteric interpretation he made of other Buddhist teachings that he considered exoteric. Kūkai's Bodhisattva doctrine, therefore, can be understood in two dimensions:

1) On the phenomenal plane, the Shingon practitioner is supposed to be a Bodhisattva who must awaken the Bodhi Mind, receive and observe the precepts, engage in meditation, etc., and
2) On the noumenal or esoteric side, he has only to realize what he really is through the prescribed mystic practices; then he will see that all the Bodhisattva practices have already been completed in his innate Buddhahood.

The *hongaku* theory is more popularly known in the Japanese Tendai. The germ of this theory is sometimes sought in Saichō's teaching. From what he says in his works, Saichō did uphold the Saddharmapuṇḍarīka Ekayāna ideal and talked about instant enlightenment, but we cannot find any clear indication that he held the *hongaku* theory.[62] In Tendai, all phenomenal manifestations are considered to be comprised in a momentary thought, and contemplation of the immanent principle underlying phenomena is to be practised by a prescribed method. Following this general line of Tendai philosophy, Saichō accepted the view that the noumenal essence or principle was still distinguishable from phenomenal manifestations. This means that Saichō did not totally identify man with Buddha. We may, therefore, safely conclude that, however lofty his Ekayāna ideal may have been, his Bodhisattva doctrine still had the conventional pattern of proceeding toward Buddhahood through the causal stages of a Bodhisattva's career.

Besides the Tendai, Zen and Ritsu (precept) traditions, Saichō brought back from China a sort of esoteric tradition and showed a great interest in the esoteric teaching. It was, therefore, natural that his successors should have become more inclined to the esoteric, and from within the general tendency toward esotericism, from the end of the Heian period, Tendai masters on Mt. Hiei developed and popularized particular *hongaku* theories. They claimed that men were originally enlightened, that phenomena were identical with noumena, that the present moment was eternity, and so on. The Tendai *hongaku* theories exerted a great influence on Buddhist masters of the Kamakura period, and it may not be too much to say that Zen, Nembutsu and Nichiren's teaching were all cultivated on the soil of the *hongaku* theory.[63]

Firstly, though Hōnen did not take a *hongaku* view, his followers, especially Shinran, adopted certain *hongaku* elements. Hōnen recognized this world as defiled and the people living in it, particularly in the *mappō* period, as utterly incapable of Bodhisattva practices. He abandoned all Bodhisattva practices, even the Bodhi Mind, in choosing the way of salvation through Amitābha's vow.[64] He dedicated himself to the *Nembutsu* or recitation of Amitābha's name based on the belief that this practice was in agreement with the vow which Amitābha made when he was a Bodhisattva. Instead of practising the Bodhisattva Path himself, Hōnen availed himself of Amitābha's vow-power and expected to be born in Amitābha's Pure Land by virtue of it. He hoped to become a Bodhisattva in the Pure Land and, eventually, a Buddha.

Hōnen's disciples shared the basic Pure Land principle with their master but, in the face of criticisms levelled at him by other Buddhists, they found themselves in a position where they had to justify the Pure Land teaching. It is understandable that they in fact adopted Ekayāna ideals and *hongaku* theories in their doctrinal systems. We have already found that Shinran took a specific Ekayāna standpoint, but his *hongaku* theory is not so obvious as that. However, it is possible to trace a *hongaku* way of thinking in his works. Though we are not enlightened, he says, our salvation has already been accomplished by Amitābha. So, if we are awakened to this fact and, thereby, attain firm faith, we are at once made one with Amitābha. Firm faith does not come from within but is Amitābha's Mind transferred to us. Such a faith is the Bodhi Mind and the Buddha-nature; it is the Tathāgata itself, as Shinran says in the *Wasan*:

> One who rejoices in Faith
> Is equal to the Tathāgata, says the Buddha.
> The Great Faith is Buddha-nature;
> Buddha-nature is the Tathāgata.[65]

Also,

> Faith awakened by the inconceivable Vow-Power
> Is the Great Bodhi Mind.[66]

Shinran gave the Nembutsu a deeper meaning. For him, it was no longer a practice based on man's power but it was the Buddha's practice. He clarifies this in the *Kyōgyō-shinshō* as follows:

> The Great Practice is to utter the name of the Tathāgata of Unhindered Light. This practice embodies all good and contains all virtues. It enables sentient beings to attain the supreme and consummate virtues very quickly. It is the treasure-sea of the virtues of True Thusness and the One Reality. Hence, it is called the Great Practice.[67]

Since firm faith is the *Bodhi* Mind and all the Bodhisattva practices required for attaining Buddhahood are transferred to us through Amitābha's name, we can become Buddhas as soon as the residue of our conditioned life has been exhausted at death. In Shinran's view, we become Bodhisattvas after having first attained Buddhahood in the Pure Land; we then engage in endless altruistic activities.

Secondly, when we turn our attention to Dōgen's Zen, we find that the *hongaku* theory is expressed throughout his works. Although he was aware of the danger of the *hongaku* view, which was in fact abused by many, he advanced a peculiar Zen theory along *hongaku* lines. According to him, practice is not different from Enlightenment, as it is said in the *Shōbōgenzō* (*The eye-treasury of the Right Dharma*):

> To think that practice and Enlightenment are not the same is a non-Buddhist view. In the Buddhist teaching, practice and Enlightenment are one and the same. Because practice is carried out on the plane of Enlightenment, a beginner's study of the Path embodies the original Enlightenment in its entirety. For this reason, when [a master] gives an instruction about practice, he teaches that one should not expect Enlightenment apart from practice, for practice is itself the original Enlightenment which is directly indicated [in one's mind].[68]

When Dōgen emphasized 'mere sitting' (*shikan-tada*), he did not mean it to be taken as a causal practice leading to

Enlightenment. Ultimate Enlightenment is the basis on which the real sitting practice is carried out. Buddhahood, in fact, acts upon the practitioner and enables him to perform an endless practice of Zen. Since in Zen all the Bodhisattva practices are comprised in the single practice of meditation, the practice-Enlightenment identity can be interpreted as the Bodhisattva-Buddha identity. Dōgen's standpoint, therefore, is a reversal of the traditional course a Bodhisattva takes in proceeding towards Buddhahood. Although the idea that one is originally a Buddha is common to all Zen masters, Dōgen emphasizes the positive activity of Buddhahood which 'realizes' the Bodhisattva practices. When mere sitting is practised on the plane of ultimate Enlightenment, the sitting practitioner is himself an acting Buddha. He now dwells in the Buddha's Self-Enjoyment *Samādhi* (*jijuyū-zammai*),[69] from which all Bodhisattva practices emanate.

Lastly, we shall see how Nichiren interpreted the Bodhisattva doctrine. When he claimed that he who recited the title of the *Saddharmapuṇḍarīka sūtra* could realize Enlightenment in this life, he did not emphasize the practitioner's capacity to become a Buddha, but believed in the Buddha's power embodied in the title of the sūtra. He says in the *Kanjin honzon shō* (*On the Buddha image to be perceived in meditation*):

> Both the causal practices and the resultant merits of Śākyamuni Buddha are embodied in the five characters, '*Myō-hō-ren-ge-kyō*' (*Saddharma puṇḍarīka sūtra*). If we hold on to these five characters, we are naturally given both his causal and his resultant merits.[70]

Like Dōgen, who saw perfect Enlightenment in the practice of meditation, Nichiren recognized attainment of Buddhahood in the recitation of the title of the sūtra. This interpretation is in line with the *hongaku* theory. He also says in the same work:

> At the time of the Buddha's Enlightenment the *Sahā* world was the Pure Land of Eternity freed from the three calamities and above the changes of the four cosmic periods. The Buddha did not perish in the past, nor will he appear in the future.[71]

Because, he says, "the time when the Buddha was alive is found in the present moment, and the present moment is the time when the Buddha was alive,"[72] this moment is the eternal present and this world is the land of eternity.

The recitation of the title of the sūtra in accord with the Buddha's activity must be based on the practitioner's firm belief. According to Nichiren, belief is a substitute for wisdom, one of the three types of learning (*tisraḥ śikṣāḥ*). He says in the *Shishin gohon shō* (*On the four beliefs and the five merits*):

> Question: Should a beginner in the *mappō* period necessarily follow the three types of learning of the Perfect Teaching?
>
> Answer: ... the Buddha prohibits the observance of the precepts and the practice of meditation and only encourages the cultivation of wisdom. Further, since he is not capable of wisdom, belief is used as its substitute.
>
> If the beginner practises the other five Pāramitās as well, the right practice of belief is hampered.[73]

It is clear that Nichiren admitted the difficulty of practising the Six Pāramitās in the *mappō* period, so he proposed the simple practice of reciting the title of the sūtra based on belief which was a substitute for wisdom.

Nichiren considered himself to be a seeker of the Bodhisattva ideal and, indeed, he felt himself to be specially commissioned with the task of propagating the *Saddharmapuṇḍarīka sūtra* in the *mappō* period with a belief that he was an incarnation of the Bodhisattva Jōgyō (Viśiṣṭacāritra). He also maintained the belief that the state could be protected from calamities and foreign invasion if people believed in his teaching.

Now the summary of this paper. In discussing the subject of the Bodhisattva doctrine as conceived and developed in the Heian and Kamakura periods, I have surveyed both the general tendency and the views of individual masters. In dealing with the former, the *mappō* idea, the Ekayāna ideal and the *hongaku* theory have been discussed. We found that various views about the Bodhisattva Path entertained by the founders of the new sects reflected the influence of these tendencies. Furthermore, in each of the new systems, the Bodhisattva doctrine was very much alive, even though it had undergone drastic transformations.

TABULATED SYNOPSIS

	Name of the sect	Main object of worship	Fundamental sūtra(s) used	Precepts	Bodhi Mind	Form of practice	Specific Ekayāna system proposed
Saichō (767-822)	Tendai	Śākyamuni (Sambhoga-kāya)	Saddharma-puṇḍarīka	Required	Required	Meditation (śamatha & vipaśyanā)	Hokke (Saddharma-puṇḍarīka)
Kūkai (774-835)	Shingon	Mahāvairocana (Dharmakāya)	Mahāvairocana & Vajraśekhara	do.	do.	mudrā, mantra & samādhi	Himitsu (Esoteric) Kongō (Vajra) Shingon (Mantra)
Eisai (1141-1215)	Zen (Rinzai)	(Śākyamuni)		do.	do.	Meditation	
Dōgen (1200-1253)	Zen (Sōtō)	(Śākyamuni)		do.	do.	Meditation	
Hōnen (1133-1212)	Jōdo	Amitābha (Sambhoga-kāya)	Sukhāvatīvyūha & Meditation on Amitāyus	Not Required	Not Required	Nembutsu recitation (Faith)	
Shinran (1173-1262)	Jōdoshin	do.	Sukhāvatīvyūha	do.	(=Faith)	Faith (Nembutsu)	Hongan (Original Vow) Seigan (do.)
Nichiren (1222-1282)	Nichiren	Śākyamuni (Sambhoga-kāya)	Saddharma-puṇḍarīka	do.		Daimoku recitation (belief)	

FOOTNOTES

1 'Others' refers to Ryōnin (1072-1132) and Ippen (1239-1289) who founded the Yūzū-nembutsu and Ji sects, respectively.

2 See E. Inaba, *Mappō tōmyō ki kōgi* (Kyoto: 1960) pp. 70-71.

3 The theory that the Buddha passed into Parinirvāṇa in B.C. 949 appears in the *Kuang hung ming chi.* in *Taishō Shinshū Daizōkyō* (hereafter *T.*). See *T.* vol. 52, p. 100, etc. The second theory appears in the *Li tai san pao chi*, *T.* 49, p. 23, where the author gives six different views current at his time regarding the year of the birth of the Buddha. *Cf.* K. Yabuki, *Sangaigyō no kenkyū* (Tokyo: 1927) p. 224.

4 *Ta fang têng ta chi ching* *T.* 13, p. 279.

5 See Hui-ssŭ's vow, *T.* 13, pp. 786-7, where he says he was born in the 82nd year of the *mappō* era. According to this, since he was born in 515, the *mappō* period started in 434.

6 See, for example, Tao-cho's *An lê-chi*. *T.* 47, p. 13, where he quotes from the *Ta fang têng ta chia ching* and says, "This is the *mappō* era and the evil world marked with five signs of corruption. There is the Pure Land Path which is the only passable way."

7 Modern scholars are of the opinion that 538 is the more probable year of the first official transmission of Buddhism. As for the motives behind the *Nihonshoki's* description, see, for example, S. Ienaga, *Nihon bukkyōshi* (Kyoto: 1967) vol. I, pp. 46-50.

8 Eizan Gakuin (ed.) *Dengyō Daishi zenshū* (Tokyo: 1965) vol. I, pp. 415-426. Saichō's authorship is doubted by some scholars, including E. Tamura. See his article, Tendai gakkai (ed.) *Dengyō Daishi kenkyū* (Tokyo: 1973) pp. 765-8. For E. Inaba's view in favour of Saichō's authorship, see *Mappō tōmyō ki kōgi*, pp. 8-29. As for the exact year when the *mappō* period was thought to have started, there are some conflicting views in the works attributed to Saichō:

1) Two different calculations appear in the *Mappō tōmyō ki*, according to which the *mappō* era started either in 552 or 892. The author was in favour of the latter. See *Dengyō Daishi zenshū*, I, p. 417.

2) The *Shōzōmatsu mon* has the following remark: "This (i.e. 812 A.D.) is the 240th year of the *mappō* era." This means the *mappō* era started in 573. See *Dengyō Daishi zenshū*, I. p. 442.

3) The *Kenkairon* mentions that the author's time was near the end of the period of Imitative Dharma. See *Dengyō Daishi zenshū*, I, p. 82.

4) The *Shugo kokkai shō* has this to say: "... the periods of Right Dharma and Imitative Dharma having nearly passed, the *mappō* period is imminent." *Dengyō Daishi zenshū*, II, p. 349.

Except for the *Shōzōmatsu mon*, the above pieces of evidence indicate that Saichō considered his time was near the end of the period of Imitative Dharma, and, if we accept Saichō's authorship of the *Mappō tōmyō ki*, he believed that the *mappō* period would start in 892.

9 *Dengyō Daishi zenshū*, I, p. 417.

10 For the tradition of the *endon* precepts, especially in its relationship to the precepts used in Zen, see G. Kagamishima's article, "Endonkai to zenkai" in *Dengyō Daishi kenkyū*, pp. 261-276.

11 *Eizan Daishi den*, in *Dengyō Daishi zenshū*, V. Appendix, p. 23.

12 *Enkai hidan*, quoted in G. Fukuda, *Tendaigaku gairon* (Tokyo: 4th ed., 1963) p. 525.

13 For a recent study on the *sanjujōkai*, see H. Hadano's article, "Yugagyōha no bosatsukai o megutte," in *Suzuki gakujutsu zaidan kenkyū nenpō* (Tokyo: 1977) pp. 12-33.

14 *T.* 24, pp. 1004-9. Saichō gives full scriptural references for the Tendai precepts in the *Tendai hokkeshū gakushōshiki mondō*, in *Dengyō Daishi zenshū*, I, pp. 363-8.

15 *Hizō hōyaku*. *T.* 77, p. 366.

16 S. Katsumata (ed.) *Yuikai*, *Kōbō Daishi chosaku zenshū* (Tokyo: 1970) vol. II, p. 164.

17 See *Fusōryakki*, *Teiō hennenki* and *Genpei seisuiki*.

18 *T.* 83, pp. 633-5.

19 *T.* 80, p. 4. The theory classifying the history of Buddhism after the Buddha's death into five 500-year periods appears in the *Ta feng têng ta chia ching*, *T.* 13, p. 363. According to this, the 1st 500-year period would be strongly marked by the attainment of Enlightenment; the 2nd 500-year period, by the serious practice of meditation; the 3rd 500-year period, by much recitation and hearing of the Dharma; the 4th 500-year period, by the construction of many temples; and the last 500-year period, by strife and argument which would obscure the Dharma.

20 *T.* 80, p. 2.

21 *T.* 80, p. 10.

22 *Shōbōgenzō* *T.* 82, p. 20.

23 *Ibid.*, p. 307.

24 *Ibid.*, p. 307.

25 See *Hokke shuyōshō* *T.* 84, p. 279, and *Kanjin honzon shō*, *T.* 84, p. 276.

26 See "Jakunichi-bō gosho," *Nichiren Shōnin ibun zenshū* (Kyoto: 1934) vol. II, p. 1787, and *Jūhachi enmanshō*, *Nichiren Shōnin ibun zenshū*, vol. II, p. 1916.

27 See K. Fujita's article, "One Vehicle or Three," tr. L. Hurvitz, *Journal of Indian Philosophy* (Holland: Dordrecht 1975) pp. 79-166. See also G.M. Nagao's article, "Ichijō sanjō no rongi o megutte," in *Chūgan to Yuishiki* (Tokyo: 1978) pp. 526-541.

28 *Shōmangyō gisho*. *T*. 56, p. 8.

29 *Shê ta shêng lun shih*. *T*. 31, p. 212; quoted by Saichō in the *Shō gonjitsu kyō*, *Dengyō Daishi zenshū*. II, p. 3.

30 *Shō gonjutsu kyō*. *op. cit.*, pp. 3-4.

31 *Ibid.*, p. 4.

32 *Hokke-gisho*, *T*. 56, pp. 64ff.

33 *Dengyō Daishi zenshū*, II, pp. 348-9.

34 The Four Samādhis are:

1) sitting in meditation for a period of 90 days,
2) invoking Amitābha Buddha's name while circumambulating in the hall for a period of 90 days,
3) a combined practice of seated meditation and circumambulation for a period of 7 days and
4) unspecified meditation.

See *Kenkairon*, in *Dengyō Daishi zenshū*, I, pp. 73-4.

35 See *Ichijōkai kenganki*, in *Dengyō Daishi zenshū*, I, p. 429, and *Kenkairon*, *op. cit.*, p. 26.

36 See *Kenkairon*, *op. cit.*, p. 25, and *Ichijōkai kenganki*, *op. cit.*, p. 431.

37 *Hizō-hōyaku*, *T*. 77, p. 367.

38 *'Himitsu-ichijō'* appears in the *Unjigi*, *T*. 77, p. 407. *'Kongō-ichijō'* appears in the *Jūjūshinron*, *T*. 77, p. 361; *Dainichikyō-ryakudai* in *Kōbō Daishi chosaku zenshū*, II, p. 121; and *Hizōki* in *Kōbō Daishi chosaku zenshū*, II, p. 643.

39 Kōsai, one of Hōnen's chief disciples, is believed to have stressed the importance of 'one thought of faith' as opposed to 'many utterances of the Nembutsu.' From what he says in the *Gengibun-shō*, he considered that the Pure Land teaching was the true Ekayāna in compliance with Amitābha Buddha's Original Vow and referred to it as 'the Ekayāna of quick efficacy provided for ordinary men' (*bondon-ichijō*). See K. Yasui, *Hōnen monka no kyōgaku* (Kyoto: reprint, 1968) Appendix, p. 80. For further details, see M. Ishida, *Nihon jōdokyō no kenkyū* (Kyoto: 2nd ed. 1973) pp. 226, 235-6.

40 *T*. 63, p. 598. See *Shêng-man-ching*, *T*. 12, p. 220. Immediately after this, Shinran quotes four passages from the *Nirvāṇa Sūtra* and one from the *Avataṃsaka Sūtra* as scriptural evidence to support his Ekayāna standpoint.

41 *T*. 83, p. 599.

42 *T.* 83, p. 661.

43 The *Lotus sutra* is divided into '*shakumon*', or the section on the temporal Buddha, and '*honmon*', or the section on the original state of the Buddha. Nichiren claimed that his doctrine was superior to that of the Tendai sect because it centred in the *honmon* Buddha, whereas the Tendai teaching was based on the contemplation of the immanent reality-principle presented in the *shakumon*.

44 *Dengyō Daishi zenshū*, vol. III, pp. 260-67.

45 *Ibid.*, p. 266.

46 *T.* 77, p. 382.

47 *Ibid.*, p. 383.

48 See *Kyōgyōshinshō*, *T.* 77, pp. 608, 609, 594, etc.

49 *Kaitai sokushin jōbutsu gi*, *Nichiren Shōnin ibun zenshū*, I, p. 14.

50 *Jūnyoze ji*, *ibid.*, I, pp. 206-7.

51 *Myōichi-nyo gohenji, Ibid.* p. 1891.

52 *Kaimokushō*, *T.* 84, p. 232, etc. Also, Nichiren says, "In future I shall go to the Pure Land on Mount Vulture." See "Shijō Kingo-dono gosho," in *Nichiren Shōnin ibun zenshū*, I, p. 692. For further details of Nichiren's views on the attainment of Buddhahood, see K. Mochizuki *Nichirenkyōgaku no kenkyū* (Kyoto: 3rd ed., 1965) pp. 225-247.

53 For a fuller discussion on this subject, see D. Shimaji *Bukkyō taikō* (Tokyo: 8th ed. 1940) pp. 3-231. Also, see Y. Tamura's article, "Tendai hongaku shisō gaisetsu" *Tendai hongakuron, Nihon shiso taikei* No. 9 (Tokyo: 2nd ed., 1974) pp. 477-548.

54 *T.* 9, p. 465.

55 *Ibid.*, p. 449.

56 *Ibid.*, p. 452.

57 *Shih mo hê yen lun*, *T.* No. 1668.

58 *T.* 58, p. 2.

59 The Four Virtues of the Dharmakāya, i.e., ever-lastingness, bliss, freedom and purity. See *Kongōchōkyō kaidai*. *T.* 61, p. 5.

60 *T.* 61, p. 3.

61 *T.* 77, p. 383.

62 In the *Shugo kokkaishō* Saichō mentions '*hongaku*'. See *T.* 74, p. 152. But he did not incorporate the *hongaku* theory in his doctrinal system. See E. Tamura's article, *op. cit.*, pp. 508-9.

[63] See D. Shimaji. *Bukkyō taikō*. pp. 226-231.

[64] See *Senjaku hongaku nembutsu shū*. *T.* 83, p. 7.

[65] *T.* 83, p. 659.

[66] *Ibid.*, p. 659.

[67] *Ibid.*, p. 590.

[68] *T.* 82, p. 18.

[69] *Ibid.*, p. 15, etc.

[70] *T.* 84, p. 275.

[71] *Ibid.*, p. 275.

[72] *Shuju o furumai sho*, *T.* 84, p. 295.

[73] *Ibid.*, pp. 287-8.

JAPAN'S NEW RELIGIONS (1945-65): SECULARIZATION OR SPIRITUALIZATION?

Minoru Kiyota

1. Target of Investigation, Approach and Suppositions

The term 'new religions' (*shinkō-shūkyō*)[1] is employed in contrast to established religions (*kisei-shūkyō*). But, unless otherwise indicated, in the context of this paper the term refers to and is limited to Buddhist-derived new religions in contemporary Japan, such as Sōka Gakkai. Sōka Gakkai is selected solely because it is one of the most popular among the new religions in terms of the number of its converts. The new religions represent a lay *saṅgha*, not a monastic *saṅgha*, and they are examined from a historical perspective.

First, the rising popularity of the new religions is described as a response to the socio-political upheaval of the postwar period — 1945-65 — a period of Japan's transition from military defeat to her emergence as one of the world's economic powers. Second, the new religions are identified as an integral entity of the Japanese Buddhist tradition. That tradition is identified as the Ekayāna bodhisattva doctrine, a form of experiential philosophy and a developing process of lay Buddhism.

The first part presupposes that the new religions emerge from the lower social strata at a time of socio-political crisis and, as such, they represent a mass movement directed against the establishment. The second part presupposes that the *Sangyō-gisho*[2] — the *Commentary on the Saddharma-puṇḍarīka-sūtra* (hereafter cited as the *Lotus Sūtra*), *Vimalakīrtinirdeśa-sūtra*, and *Śrīmālādevīsiṃhanāda-sūtra* — allegedly composed by Prince Shōtoku[3] in the early 7th century, laid the foundation for the development of a lay *saṅgha* based upon the principle of Ekayāna, and that Buddhism in Japan attempted to implement that principle in each successive historical period.

In all fairness, it must be noted that the first approach was observed by Shigeyoshi Murakami,[4] originally a left-wing writer, who describes Tenri-kyō, Kurozumu-kyō, Konkō-kyō, etc. — the Shinto-derived new religions of late Tokugawa and early Meiji — as the masses' attempts at political expression. It is also observed by Horoo Takagi,[5] an eminent historian of religion, who examines the new religions of postwar Japan as a form of mass movement.

The second approach, though seemingly a sound approach, has not been observed in interpreting the new religions of postwar Japan, at least to my knowledge. This is probably because of a general disinterest in the subject of new religions on the part of Buddhologists and a seeming disinterest in finding a model for religious renewal within the Japanese Buddhist tradition on the part of phenomenologists of Japanese religion.[6] This approach, at least in my view, is valuable and perhaps even necessary to explain the historical roots of the new religions' mass movement. For here we are not dealing with a social phenomenon which can be explained away by simple statistics, but a religious phenomenon with deep roots in the past. This paper intends to prove that the principle underlying the new religions is the bodhisattva doctrine based upon the Japanese Buddhist historical tradition. But the crucial issue we face in a study of this sort is not that the bodhisattva doctrine underlies the new religions, but whether that doctrine has secularized the *saṅgha* or spiritualized the laity. More important is the question of whether spiritualization is a historical possibility. These questions, I feel, have significant bearing on this Conference, for how are we, as scholars of Buddhism and historians of religion, to reconcile the ideal bodhisattva doctrine with actual historical facts? We shall examine these questions by describing the new religions as a socio-religious phenomenon which arose in response to the socio-political upheaval of the postwar period, and by contextualizing the new religions as an entity of the Japanese Buddhist historical tradition.

2. The Socio-Political Upheaval

Japan's military defeat in 1945 produced great confusion

among the Japanese, for the principle that contributed to the emergence of Meiji Japan as a modern state — nationalism based upon the dogma of the divinity of the emperor and ethical concepts based upon the Shinto-Confucian *Imperial Rescript on Education*,[7] promulgated in 1890 — were totally discredited. It also produced great confusion within the Buddhist *saṅgha*, for Japanese Buddhism passed through the period of Japan's emergence as a modern state without eliminating feudalistic elements within it (e.g., the hierarchical institutional organization, the *danka* parish system, adherence to sectarian dogmas — all of which developed during Tokugawa feudalism) or adequately familiarizing itself with the development of modern institutions. It allied itself with the state in suppressing democratic movements in the 1920's and endorsed the principle which contributed to the destruction of the Japanese empire. Because these principles were shattered by external forces, primarily the United States, and not forces within Japan, the Japanese in the period immediately following the surrender were bewildered as to the course that needed to be taken and were totally unprepared to undertake the task of social and political reform. A spiritual vacuum developed and Japan's surrender generated problems of mammoth complexity for her citizens.

The occupation policy was intended to create the conditions stipulated in the Potsdam Declaration and to eliminate elements unfavorable to the development of a modern democratic state. Thus, politically, the Meiji Constitution, which supported an absolute monarchy, was repealed and a new constitution, based upon the principle of a democratic government, was introduced. But the concept of democracy remained completely alien to the minds of many Japanese. It simply meant the rejection of the 'old' and the acceptance of the 'new'. 'Old' meant feudalism, that which bound the citizens to the state. 'New' meant the American way of life, that which guaranteed unlimited personal freedom. The 'old' ethic was based on the premise that the *iye* (household) was the basic piety, virtues which were articulated in the *Imperial Rescript on Education*. The 'new' meant liberation from the 'old' and the freedom of self-expression, matters which permeated the masses through the media. This was the period when the masses, enraptured by the sounds of Tokyo Boogie-woogie, blared incessantly through the public address systems in public places, deliriously danced to the bouyant tune of American jazz. And this is when General Douglas MacArthur, the Supreme Commander of the Allied Powers, arrogantly remarked that the Japanese were of the mentality of a twelve-year-old. Beneath the bewilderment of that period, however, seeds of violent revolution were brewing, for the new period liberated tenant-farmers and industrial laborers from economic oppression, freed the Communists and Socialists from prison, and provided the masses an opportunity to expose themselves to the Marx-Engels classics. Labor unions mushroomed, not as defenders of the rights of laborers, but simply as organizations to indoctrinate the masses for a proletarian revolution.

3. Left-Wing Organizations and Activities

In the early period of occupation, the Japanese Communist Party was led by Tokuda Kyūichi (1894-1953), who was liberated by MacArthur from an 18-year imprisonment. Tokuda was a political activist, not a theoretician. But left-wing organizations took many forms, from the moderate *Shutaisei* group to various shades of radical Marxists.

Shutaisei[8] (literally, 'internalized experience'), a postwar Japanese proletarian theory which attempted to combine Nishida philosophy and Marxism, emphasized the merits of internalized experience based on Zen discipline and Kantian idealism. It became popular among a group of proletarian writers immediately after Japan's surrender, and by 1948 it spread to the ranks of laborers and farmers. The *Shutaisei*-ists claimed that Marxism is not just an economic theory, that dialectic materialism is not just an objective method of investigating society and all its ills, but that they are a way of life. They accused other proletarian writers of having failed to develop a type of Marxism that could be translated into a practical way of life based on the worth and dignity of the individual. The Marxists retorted that the *Shutaisei*-ists were intellectual egoists, each selfishly pursuing his own well-being, and that the meaning of life was to be found only by joining the proletarian revolution. The *Shutaisei*-ists asserted self-independence, the Marxists collective political action. The *Shutaisei* theory offered an alternative to the 'old' ethics based on the *Imperial Rescript on Education* without resorting to the violence of a revolution. Though short-lived, the success of the *Shutaisei*-ists was simply due to the fact that neither the Conservatives nor the Socialists — the two major political parties in postwar Japan — offered anything positive to enhance the material and spiritual needs of the masses. The *Shutaisei*-ists managed to organize a congenial group of comrades, but they failed to formulate a collective disciplinary code of action and received no support from any political party. As a result, their movement faded into obscurity even before the outbreak of the Korean War.

The *Minshushugi kagakusha kyōkai* (Association of Democratic Scientists), the *Nihon minshushugi bunka renmei* (Japan Democratic League), and other Communist organizations also appeared immediately after Japan's surrender. These organizations published their own journals, such as the *Minshu no hata* (People's Banner), *Shakai hyōron* (Social Review), *Jimmin hyōron* (People's Review), etc. The purposes of these organizations were to spread revolutionary ideas among the working class, to destroy capitalistic societies, and to bring about a proletarian government. They failed, however, to realize a popular front and most of them faded into obscurity by the time the Korean War broke out. The ease with which the Red Purge of 1950 was accomplished is eloquent testimony that Japanese proletarianism of this period had not established roots among the laboring class. Nevertheless, in that very year the Japan Socialist Party advocated a radical left policy which resulted in the masses swinging to the conservative Liberal Democratic Party. The failure of the Communists and Socialists was simply due to the fact that the average citizen was indifferent to indoctrination and to a radical form of socio-political revolution. What he demanded was something that offered economic security and a meaningful way of life, without a violent revolution.

After 1950, left-wing movements took different approaches. Union-affiliated choruses and essay-writing groups were organized and both became popular. Although a chorus might be an effective vehicle to introduce and even stimulate an ideology, it can hardly be expected to sustain and develop it. Hence, many members who became dissatisfied with Russian songs when the novelty of them wore off seceded from union-affiliated chorus groups and established their own. They preferred 'old' Japanese folksongs and popular American ones. Essay-writing was more effective.

Essay-writing was a part of the Meiji educational curriculum and was employed as a vehicle to inculcate nationalism and patriotism. Communist leaders took over this tradition to indoctrinate the masses with proletarian ideology. It was particularly effective in elementary school classes where teachers affiliated with the Communist teachers' unions presided. Topics, simple but reflecting distinct traces of left-wing ideology, included "Strength in Unity," "Collective Action," "Labor Improvement," etc., which when translated into children's language came out as "Let's Work Together," "Let's March Together," "Let's Think Clearly," etc. Because government directives on education failed to provide an alternative to the 'old' ethics, the impact of these teachers' thought upon school children was significant. And because of its success in schools, essay-writing was encouraged at adult education classes sponsored by labor unions, youth organizations, women's leagues, etc. The rapidity with which it spread, however, deprived the Communist leaders of controlling it. Essay-writing proved effective as a vehicle of indoctrination only within the confines of elementary and even secondary school classes, where members of the Communist teachers' union presided, instructed, and controlled the thought of children. In adult classes, it simply provided a chance to express one's troubles, anxieties, and dissatisfaction; and afforded dialogue between members who needed companionship and consolation, and even an occasion to dwell in a fantasy of literary romanticism. It provided no intellectual stimulus and it failed to resolve social and political issues. Eventually, the Communists became quite aware that indoctrination, a prerequisite to proletarian revolution, required a guideline. Unions, therefore, established a department of "education and culture." The *Kokumin bunka kaigi* (People's Cultural Conference), consisting of members of labor unions and prominent left-wing writers, was organized to formulate an "educational" guideline in 1956. But even with an officially sanctioned party guideline, the working class proved indifferent to indoctrination.

In sum, the Japanese were forced to abandon a way of life dictated by the *Imperial Rescript on Education*, and the Communists and Socialists, who were freed from prison, employed the opportunity brought about by socio-political changes to seek the support of the masses. But the masses were seeking means to satisfy their personal needs rather than involve themselves in a revolution based on a theory which they failed to fully appreciate. Initially, they willingly took to chorus-singing and essay-writing, but eventually they became indifferent to indoctrination. Thus, whereas some 400,000 copies of the *Akahata* (Red Flag) were sold in 1946, demands for it consistently declined, and by 1958 only 40,000 copies were sold. Socialist publications also dwindled to an insignificant number. The majority of the working class failed to support the Communists and Socialists. The prefectural elections and the election for the Upper House held in 1955 revealed the emergence of a new political power, the Sōka Gakkai, supported by the working class, small and medium-size businesses, shopkeepers, housewives and youth. In the 1959 election of the Upper House, the Communists received a total of 550,000 votes, the Sōka Gakkai 2,500,000. An examination of the new religions, of which Sōka Gakkai is the most prominent, is now in order.

4. The New Religions

The democratization of religion under the Allied Occupation branded state Shinto as the contributing ideology which led to war and defeat, implemented the principle of separation of state and Shinto, and forced the emperor to renounce the dogma of his divinity. How did the Japanese religious consciousness react to these new events? A survey taken by the *Jiji Press* in 1947[9] reveals the following:

Table I

Jiji Press Survey of 1947

Affirm belief in some form of religion	39.3%
No time to think about religion	20.8%
Do not believe in religion	9.9%
Religion misleads people	1.5%
Dissatisfied with current forms of religion	14.9%
Unable to find a religion suited to personal need .	13.4%

A great number of laborers, students and intellectuals were either critical or indifferent to religion, while the rural population and shopkeepers, among whom strong family ties existed, comprised the bulk of the believers. The survey conclusively revealed that, although Shinto had been imposed upon the people by the state with the greatest of zeal since the Meiji Restoration, its impact was hardly felt upon the people after Japan's surrender. Statistically, the fact that there were close to 30% who were "dissatisfied with current forms of religion" and "unable to find a religion suited to personal need" may shed light on the causes of the new religions' rise to popularity. But statistics merely indicate a trend; they neither establish the causes for that trend nor explain the cause-to-effect process leading to that trend.

Historically, Japan's new religions emerged at a time of socio-political crisis, as has already been pointed out by Murakami.[10] But the emergence of the new religions is not a social phenomenon which appears abruptly in a period of socio-political crisis. The new religions of postwar Japan all have their roots in the past. The Reiyū-kai, Risshō kōsei-kai, and Sōka Gakkai, for example, all have their doctrinal roots in the *Lotus Sūtra* and are, in fact, offshoots of the established Nichiren school of Buddhism. Added to this doctrinal affiliation is the fact that, due to a government ordinance which controlled all aspects of religious organization, many new religions, which became prominent and independent in postwar Japan, were identified as units within an established school of religion before the war. The postwar constitution reaffirmed the principle of freedom of religion, which the Meiji Constitution theoretically but not actually guaranteed, and freed religious organizations from government control. It gave rise to what McFarland aptly refers to as the "Rush Hour of the Gods."

The *1959 Yearbook on Religion* (published by the Ministry of Education) records that, whereas 44 religious sects were registered with the Ministry in 1945, the number jumped to 186 in 1950. Even government attempts to consolidate minor sects with major ones proved futile, for a total of 380 religious sects were registered with the Ministry in 1957. The *1965 Yearbook on Religion*[11] gives the following breakdown of the number of believers in major established schools of Buddhism as of 1964. (See Table II)

Table II

Number of Believers in Major Established Schools of Buddhism as of 1964

Schools	Number of Believers
Jōdo and Jōdo Shin	16,899,547
Nichiren	26,779,144
Shingon	12,146,092
Tendai	4,283,755
Zen	9,634,736

The numbers given above include believers in the established schools, in sub-schools within the established schools, and in new religious sects affiliated with sub-schools. Thus, the Nichiren schools claim a phenomenal total of over 26 million, simply because that number includes the Sōka Gakkai believers. The *1965 Asahi Yearbook*[12] gives 11,904,726 as number of Sōka Gakkai believers. This figure, if taken at its face value, essentially means that roughly one out of every ten Japanese is a Sōka Gakkai believer. But the number given both in the *Yearbook on Religion* and in the *Asahi Yearbook* was provided by the headquarters of various religious organizations, and is most likely inflated. Many religious organizations automatically include the members of the entire household as believers in arriving at a final tally. But even so, there is no doubt whatsoever of the overwhelming strength of the Nichiren school over other established schools, simply because many new religious sects are derived from the Nichiren school.

The number of believers in major Nichiren-derived new religious sects selected from the list given in the *1965 Yearbook on Religion*,[13] together with an approximate number of believers in these sects in the late 1950's, are provided below to indicate the phenomenal rise of these sects in popularity within a period of about 10 years. (See Table III)

Table III

Number of Believers in Major Nichiren-derived New Religious Sects

Sects	Approximate Number in the mid-1950's	1964
Nichiren shōshu (Sōka Gakkai)	439,000	15,234,136
Reiyū-kai	3,465,000	4,719,988
Risshō kōsei-kai	1,349,000	2,042,590

Nichiren shōshu is a branch of the Nichiren school and Sōka Gakkai is technically affiliated with Nichiren shōshu. A near 40-fold increase in the number of believers was realized by Nichiren shōshu within a period of about ten years, simply because of Sōka Gakkai's phenomenal rise to popularity during this period. Many new religious sects are derived from the Nichiren school which, notwithstanding its traditional pugnacious stand, has consistently championed the causes of the underdogs and identified itself as an anti-establishment group since it was founded in the 13th century. This is so because of the extremely powerful message that the *Lotus Sūtra*, the canonical basis of Nichiren doctrine and practice, projects. It emphasizes universal enlightenment (making no distinction between monks and laity, men and women), direct involvement in problems related to social injustice and human tragedy (rather than in the pursuit of wisdom as the condition to realize enlightenment), belief in the theory that persecution awaits the Lotus practitioner (the *sūtra* therefore emphasizes the cultivation of discipline in order to bear all forms of persecution), and, above all, faith in the supremacy of the Lotus Dharma.

The Nichiren-derived new religious sects follow the spirit of the Lotus Dharma and have thereby established, firmly, a lay saṅgha. Their doctrines are eclectic and simple and, unlike the ministers of established schools, the founders (or more frequently the founderesses) make claim to unusual spiritual power in divination, sorcery, and faith healing. They are of humble origin, share the day-to-day problems with the masses, offer an intimate sense of belonging to their followers, and are seriously devoted to their faith. Despite their pseudo-intellectualism, they offer the masses solutions to their problems which are satisfactory at their intellectual level. Critics accuse these sects of spreading superstitious ideas and perverted doctrines, but enviously claim that they are exceedingly successful business enterprises, which they undoubtedly are. But in the final analysis, what is important to note is that these sects offer a way, agreeable to the masses, of solving their immediate problems without resorting to a violent revolution. Their doctrines may be non-intellectual, but so is their audience, the masses. Ironically, the development of technology and industry has not wiped them out. On the contrary, it has stimulated the demand for them because stress and anxiety (which modern living associated with modern technology and industrial development brings about) are the conditions under which the masses exist. We are now ready to examine Sōka Gakkai, the most prominent among the Nichiren-derived new religious sects.

5. Sōka Gakkai

Sōka Gakkai was founded by Makiguchi Tsunesaburō (1871-1944), a Tokyo elementary school principal in the 1920's, who initially founded the Sōka Kyōiku Gakkai (Value-Creating Education Association) and through that Association attempted to merge education and Nichiren teachings. He was most active during the period of depression in the early 1930's. Though the Association was nationalistic, it was suppressed by the government because its members refused to submit themselves to state Shinto. Makiguchi, together with twenty-one of his followers, was charged with *lèse majesté* and imprisoned in 1943. He died the following year. Toda Jōsei(1900-58), one of the trusted lieutenants of Makiguchi, began propagating Makiguchi's ideas immediately after the war and proved himself an exceedingly capable man. By 1951, he had gathered around him some 5,000 followers, changed the Association's name to Sōka Gakkai (Value-Creating Association) and became its president. The current president is Ikeda Daisuke. Forceful personality, unflinching determination and single-minded *daimoku* faith (i.e., faith in the *Lotus Sūtra*) characterize Makiguchi, Toda and Ikeda. They are the charismatic personalities of Sōka Gakkai and the center of unity of that organization. (The *daimoku* actually involves the chanting of the formula, "*Nammyō-hō-renge kyō*," that is, "Homage to the Lotus of the Good Law.")

Sōka Gakkai employs a distinct method of conversion. A preliminary investigation of the target-subject, including illness, if any, his financial and professional status, the family composition and its problems, is made through a reconnaissance in preparation for an attack on the most vulnerable element of the subject. The standard solution to any problem with which one might be troubled is "to change one's mental attitude," that is, to change the way of looking at the problem. The Sōka Gakkai doctrine is that mental attitude can be changed by chanting the *daimoku*. The effect of the *daimoku* is "validated" by the personal experience of the converter, who speaks with convincing eloquence and force. The subject is urged to "try it." The missionary assault is repeated at regular intervals, often with the aid of an army of converters, until the subject succumbs. If he does not, the subject is threatened with the prophecy that illness, poverty, and even death would strike him or his family and bring discord to the family. This is *shakubuku* (crushing and bringing into submission), one of the key words in the Nichiren lexicon.

In the meantime, the subject is exposed to loads of propaganda literature, written in a style and on a level convincing to the subject, usually taking the form of a confession of another convert's experience, documented with name, address and a photo. The literature makes the subject aware that his problems are not peculiar to him, that they are shared by others, and that if others are "saved" perhaps he might be too. He is now receptive to the idea of visiting a discussion session at a local center. Because the problems discussed there are very familiar to him, he immediately gains a sense of belonging. Sōka Gakkai caters to the "troubled" mind whether of the worker, shopkeeper, farmer, housewife, or youth. Confession is convincingly presented because it comes out of one's own experience. Once the subject is converted and misfortune strikes, he himself is responsible, the theory being that he has not chanted the *daimoku* faithfully enough.

Sōka Gakkai is structured along military lines. It is hierarchical, from corps leaders to squad leaders, executives and branch-heads. Unlike the ministers of established schools, branch-heads make frequent rounds of their assigned territories to insure order and to promote unity. The annual visit by its members to Taiseki-ji, the Sōka Gakkai mecca at the foot of Mount Fuji, is an occasion for gaiety, unity and demonstration of the vitality of the organization; and the life of the founder and of the successive presidents is dramatized. It is very probable that the president of Sōka Gakkai does not have the freedom to make decisions — and mistakes. Lectures and articles are delivered and written by executives in the name of the president. Sōka Gakkai intends to create a new code of ethics and a way of life which are considered true and infallible by its members because they come from the thought of their charismatic leaders.

6. Komeitō: The Political Arm of Sōka Gakkai

In 1955 and 1956, the *Sōka gakkai seiji remmei* (Sōka Gakkai Political Federation) experienced a fair amount of success in the national elections. In 1959, it acquired six new seats, bringing the total seats occupied in the Upper House of the Diet by Sōka Gakkai members to nine. The *Sōka gakkai seiji remmei* then changed its name to Komeitō (Komei Party). Elections for the Upper House took place in July, 1965 and all nine Komeitō candidates placed on the national constituency were elected. Of the five placed on the prefectural constituency, two were elected. The addition of eleven new members gave a total of twenty Komeitō seats in the Upper House. Among the 37,276,789 votes cast in the national constituency, the Komeitō captured 5,097,677, or 13.7% of the total. (This means that roughly one out of every seven electors voted for a Komeitō candidate.) In the 1967 election of the Lower House, it placed 32 candidates and gained 25 seats. The Komeitō is the political arm of Sōka Gakkai, a recognized third power in the political arena of Japan, and a force not to be ignored. Its platform is:

> To promote the principles of *ōbutsu-myōgō* (unity between secular and ecclesiastic law) and democracy and to build the foundation for world peace; to respect the dignity of man, to bring about the well-being of the individual and the prosperity of the society through "humanistic socialism" and thereby to promote the welfare of the masses; to establish the basis of *buppō minshu-shugi* (Buddhist Democracy), in order to guarantee the basic rights of men, such as the freedom of speech, thought and religion; to eradicate political corruption through fair parliamentary practices and to establish a democratic government.[14]

In spite of what the platform says, the Sōka Gakkai leaders privately claim that their own brand of religion is the only way to bring about the well-being of mankind and the prosperity of the state, and that to realize these goals, the conversion of all citizens is necessary. When questioned as to the possibility of converting all citizens to the Sōka Gakkai faith, its leaders shrewdly remark that only one-third of the citizens need to be converted because among the remaining two-thirds, one-third would be half-way sympathizers and only the remaining one-third would be downright opponents to the Sōka Gakkai faith and to the political aims of the Komeitō.[15] Be that as it may, a multi-party political system, which requires consideration of issues of all citizens, exists in Japan today. But, ironically, the multi-party system works in favor of the Komeitō because neither the Liberal Democrats nor the Socialists maintain an overwhelming majority in the Diet. The deciding vote on many issues is cast by the Komeitō.

In full recognition that Komeitō represents the hopes and aspirations of a large segment of the electorate, it would perhaps be to its advantage to sever relations with Sōka Gakkai. *Ōbutsu-myōgō* smells of immanent theocracy.

Granted the right of a political party to be backed by a religious body, however, the employment of a religious slogan as a political instrument terrifies the intellectuals in whose minds the ghost of Shinto theocracy still hangs on. *Ōbutsu-myōgō* essentially means mass conversion to Sōka Gakkai through political means. Thus, whereas the Komeitō tacitly recognizes the principle of religious freedom as guaranteed in the constitution, the Sōka Gakkai doctrine challenges the very principle to which it pays lip-service. *Shakubuku* means, in the context of the Sōka Gakkai doctrine, the total suppression of all forms of "perversion."

The success of the Komeitō is not due to their past political performance. It does not have a history to document its performance adequately; it has not yet developed a political stature mature enough, relative to that of established political parties, to involve itself in responsible issues, or even to become the target of the "black-mist" corruption which toppled the Lower House in 1967. Its success is due to the electors' desire to see a new hand in government. The Komeitō leaders speak of "clean" politics, a matter which probably attracted many floating votes, but how long they themselves would remain "clean" from the influence of "black-mist" as their political responsibilities increase, as it most certainly will, is uncertain. Komeitō members have heretofore neither legislated any meaningful policy nor have they shouldered any significant political responsibilities, as of the mid-1960's. Nevertheless, the popularity of Komeitō cannot be ignored. Its popularity was simply due to the support it received from Sōka Gakkai. Sōka Gakkai had attracted the masses because it provided an alternative to the violent revolution of a kind advocated by left-wing elements against which the established religion was incapable of responding, positively and creatively. Why was this so?

7. Established Schools of Buddhism

The stronghold of the established schools of Buddhism lies in the rural communities, but only one-third of Japan's total population resides there. Moreover, there was a population decrease of about 300,000 annually in rural communities in the early 1950's. This rate increased rapidly from the mid-1950's through the 1960's, simply because the young preferred to move to cities where employment possibilities had become more abundant with Japan's accelerated industrial development. Thus, the *Sōto Paper*[16] states that in 1955, 70.2% of its believers were the aged rural residents. We can assume that other schools of established Buddhism also showed a high rate of aged rural believers during this period. This assumption is supported by the fact that among the 18 million faithful who assembled at the time of the 750th anniversary of Hōnen and the 700th anniversary of Shinran, both of which were held in Kyoto in the spring of 1961, the majority were the old who, by and large, came from rural communities. The fact that a great majority of the believers in the established schools of Buddhism are aged rural residents means that they represent a very conservative element of the population.

The diminishing attraction to the established schools of Buddhism is in part due to their changed economic status, for when the tenant-farmers were liberated, temples — whose income was largely derived from the land they owned — were deprived of their major source of income. The *Sōto Paper*[17] says that whereas 299,680 *bō* (one *bō* equals 3.9 square rods) of land were in the hands of their local temples in 1936, only 54,983 *bō* of land remained under their ownership in 1958, a total loss of 244,698 *bō*. Added to this was the loss of land by landlords, who were the loyal patrons of village-parish-temples, simply because a village-parish-temple was an effective instrument to maintain the solidarity of a village. Both secular and ecclesiastic landlords favored the *status quo* and traditionally endorsed conservative views. But when the tenant-farmers were liberated in the postwar period, and when that period encouraged freedom of expression, the *raison-d'être* of village-parish-temple became meaningless. Hence, temples were forced into poverty and the parishioners openly criticized the conservative views of their former secular and ecclesiastic landlords.

The *Sōto Paper*[18] says that the monthly income of rural temples ranged from a low of ¥7,765 to a high of ¥21,817, an average of ¥12,365, or about $35.99 (calculated at ¥360 to the dollar) in the late 1950's. With this kind of income, a clergy could not be expected to attend to his parish duties full-time. A similar situation existed in urban areas. The *Laymen's Association Study*[19] reports that 26.9% of the clergy in Tokyo and 19.9% in Osaka maintained side-jobs, mostly teaching and civil service posts in the mid-1950's. Though this study does not give specific income figures, it can be assumed that the cost of maintaining buildings and supporting the family exceeded clerical service fees. Thus, many of the clergy, both in rural and urban areas, were part-time keepers of temples. This served to weaken the relationship between the parish clergy and parish members (a relationship which remained cohesive prior to Japan's surrender) to the extent that the former either had no interest in or was no longer capable of understanding the problems of his parish members. The major function of the clergy was simply to conduct funeral rites and memorial services.

Interestingly, the *Laymen's Association Study*[20] shows that, although buildings within an established temple compound are significantly larger than those of new religious sects, the frequency with which these buildings are employed by the established schools falls far short of that of the new religious sects which, by rule, employ lesser space. It further says that 14.9% of the temples of the established schools in Tokyo and 5.1% of those in Osaka are equipped with non-ritual facilities, the major ones being kindergartens, nurseries, and classrooms for flower-arrangement, tea ceremony, calligraphy, etc. (It can be assumed that the percentage rate indicated in this study will show a marked increase in the 1960's.) Obviously, the services associated with these facilities were rendered by the temples to supplement family income, not as public services.

We can conclude that parish temples were not lively centers of community activities devoted to enhancing community quality or designed to enrich the spiritual qualities of the individual. And because the main function of a parish temple is to conduct funeral rites and memorial services, the religious behavior of the average Japanese is not imbedded in a spiritual experience; it is formalized and ritualized.

8. Japanese Religious Behavior

We have seen that in the face of industrialization and constantly demanding ideological advances, the masses simply select and utilize those things which give them immediate and profitable meaning. Reason rarely has any meaning. But established Buddhism, which maintains no marked function other than to perform funeral rites and memorial services, and the new religion, which is dedicated to curing the sick and to realizing secular benefits in dubious manners, exploit the unspiritual qualities of folk religion. (The term 'spiritual' will be examined in detail subsequently.) The fact that this form of religion does play a significant role in the lives of the present Japanese means that, although Japan has made remarkable industrial progress, she continues to maintain a breeding ground of outdated modes of thought at the lower levels of her social stratum. It is at these levels that organized religion, whether established or new, manages to exercise considerable influence. Thus, a Japanese would continue to pay respect to a Shinto shrine at the birth of a child in order to receive the blessings of a parish deity; and that child, upon reaching maturity would exchange marriage vows at a Christian church to demonstrate his "modernity,"; and, at the end, he would most likely receive the traditional Buddhist funeral rites with hopes to realize a favorable rebirth. Even teenagers armed with portable radios blaring the sounds of 'rock' would continue to visit Shinto shrines and ancient Buddhist temples to receive the blessings of the gods and buddhas; and the "I" novelists would continue to be moved by the bell of Nikolai Cathedral, located in the heart of Tokyo without being aware of its spiritual value, and romanticize the delicacy of human emotion. Japanese religious behavior follows a folk tradition without due criticism, because this tradition, like the traditional public bathhouses and modern *pachinko* parlors, is a form of therapy built into the Japanese social structure, effectively cushioning the shock of intense psychological stress associated with modern urban living, inherent in an industrialized society.

Even the Japanese intellectuals are not immune from this type of socio-religious behavior, because they do not attempt to seriously consider the socio-psychological implication of religious thought. As such, though they would maintain a non-religious attitude individually, they would not publicly criticize, for example, Buddhist services, but would instead participate in them when the occasion calls for their presence. Very few would seriously consider the conflict between their personal outlook on life and that represented by institutionalized religion. Even if they do, they would quietly suffer the agony of their own conscience. This does not mean that the Japanese intellectuals are unaware of contradictions. On the contrary, they take extreme delight in discussing them, but make no serious effort to come to a logical and reasonable solution. To them, contradiction is not necessarily a source of conflict that needs to be resolved, but an object of intellectual curiosity. They drift away from all forms of institutionalized religion and find consolation in the agony of their own intellect. They do not seek the spiritual. But what do we mean by the spiritual, a term which we have been using rather frequently.

9. The Secular and the Spiritual

We now face a crucial question raised in the early part of this paper: is spiritualization a historical possibility? Before we can respond effectively to this question, we need to define what we mean by the terms 'secular' and 'spiritual.' Mahāyāna conceives wisdom and compassion as correspondent: wisdom is insight into emptiness, but that insight has no validity whatsoever if it is not implemented in practice; the implementation of wisdom through skill-in-means is compassion. Thus, the *Mahāvairocana-sūtra*[21] says, "skill-in-means is the ultimate." The term 'ultimate' (*paryavasāna*) means the peak of wisdom. The *Sukhāvatīvyūhôpadeśa*[22] says, "[the purpose of] the primary vow is to transfer merits," the process of which is identified as the "gate of exit [from *nirvāṇa*.]" What is important to note in these two passages is that the Buddhist notion of wisdom is not limited to an intellectual apprehension but is that which is cultivated progressively and experientially. In this context then, wisdom is not the goal; practice is the goal. And, as said before, practice is the implementation — and, it must now be added, the conditioner — of wisdom.

We are now able to define what we mean by the 'spiritual,' at least within the context of Buddhist tradition. Spiritual refers to the domain of wisdom, that is, insight into emptiness. It lies within the domain of supreme truth (*paramārtha-satya*). Secular refers to the practice of compassion, that is, the empirical implementation of that insight. It lies within the domain of conventional truth (*saṃvṛtti-satya*). The former refers to the process of bodhisattva's perfecting wisdom, the latter to bodhisattva practice *per se*, one supplementing the other as organic entities of the total life and experience of man. We now return to the initial question: is spiritualization a historical possibility? Inasmuch as we conceive the terms 'spiritual' and 'secular' as a dichotomy, the answer is no, simply because the intellectual apprehension of emptiness is beyond historical reality. It is an insight, more than anything else. But if we were to conceive these terms as organic entities of total life and experience, spiritualization is a historical possibility because, within that context, the secular (on which level compassion is practiced) derives its insight from the spiritual (on which level wisdom is achieved) and the spiritual derives its *raison-d'être* from the secular. Wisdom is *noesis* and compassion is the experience based upon that *noetic* principle.

Thus, "can the spiritual be realized historically?" is a question which presupposes that the spiritual is transhistorical and that the secular is historical. Actually, total life and experience consist of the feedback between the secular and the spiritual, between the ideal and the real. This feedback process is most succinctly described in terms of the three *svabhāva* theory: *parikalpita-svabhāva* (the discriminated), *paratantra-svabhāva* (the relative), and *pariniṣpanna-svabhāva* (the non-discriminated).

To go from discrimination to non-discrimination is the process of perfecting wisdom; to go from non-discrimination to discrimination is the process of implementing that wisdom. Shinran calls this feedback process "*ōsō-ekō*" and "*gensō-ekō*."[23] The mind is capable of going in these two opposing realms because it in itself is the relative, not the absolute. The mind creates history. But the mind involves the real and the ideal, the spiritual and the secular, the pure and the impure, *nirvāṇa* and *saṃsāra*. The tension between these two extremes is "total life and experience." That is, "the total life and experience" refers to human anxieties arising from dichotomies resulting from this tension, and the will to overcome anxieties that these dichotomies bring about. The term 'spiritualization' then requires redefining: the spiritual is not a realm of human experience divorced from the secular; problems arising from the secular stimulate the spiritualizing process; these problems provide the *raison-d'être* of the spiritualizing process; and the spiritual cannot exist without the secular, just as enlightenment cannot exist without non-enlightenment. In this kind of life and experience, it is now apparent, there is no goal, as there is no goal in history, simply because we are referring to an experiential process.

In the context of the history of the development of Japanese Buddhist thought, this experiential process is described in the *Sangyō-gisho*. The *Sangyō-gisho* articulates Ekayāna, the principle of human equality, and explains that that principle is to be realized experientially. It establishes the doctrinal basis for the development of lay Buddhism. These themes — human equality, the experiential, and lay Buddhism — are emphasized successively in the history of the development of Japanese Buddhist thought.

In the Heian period, Kūkai advocated *sokushin-jōbutsu* (the body, just as it is, is that of the Buddha), making no distinction between one's mental (or spiritual) capacity, between men and women, between monks and the laity; and Saichō established the Mahāyāna platform of ordination (based upon *bodhisattva-śīla*) as the corner-stone of his Mt. Hiei monastery. Mt. Hiei was dedicated to disciplining monks in Mahāyāna ethics — emancipating them from codified *vinaya* and cultivating both secular and spiritual concerns among them — and is, in fact, the womb from which Kamakura Buddhism emerged. Kamakura Buddhism emerged at a time of socio-political upheaval, rebelled against the established schools of Nara-Heian Buddhism, and accommodated the needs of a new breed of men (the *samurai*, peasants, fisherman, etc.) by simplifying doctrine and practice. Simplification does not mean the watering down of the actual contents of Ekayāna principle and practice, but the reformulation of that principle and practice in a way that they can be implemented effectively to cope with the problems of the time. Thus, Kamakura Buddhism does not observe the traditional *śīla-samādhi* path system as disciplinary exercises to realize *prajñā* in a graded succession, but conceives the three implicit in practice: Zen conceives the three in meditation (the discipline underlying all forms of human creativity), Pure Land in faith (the perfect understanding of the nature of Tathāgata, symbolizing wisdom and compassion, as the sole condition for the salvation of mankind), and Nichiren in the Lotus Dharma as he interpreted it (the coming of the Tathāgata to *saṃsāra*, rather than the practitioner aiming to go to the realm of *nirvāṇa*). Zen emphasized the strength of the individual through discipline; Pure Land enabled men to realize the fallibility of mankind and awakened them to realize the strength of the individual through faith and faith alone; and Nichiren promoted Buddhist activism and emphasized the worth of the individual by championing the causes of the underdog. Kamakura Buddhism did not observe the traditional Chinese *pan-chiao* system to establish its doctrinal authority; instead, it advocated the right of selecting scriptures to accommodate actual historical needs. It addressed itself to the masses though, of course, the aristocracy was by no means excluded.

Japan's new religions of the postwar period are an extension of this kind of Buddhist tradition. They identified themselves with the masses and emphasized practice. Their success clearly indicates that when the masses are armed with a unified idea (no matter how irrational that idea may be to an intellectual) and an organization through which they can express themselves (no matter how repulsive that organization may be to an intellectual), they are capable of mustering an enormous strength. Postwar Japan provided conditions favorable for this type of religion to spread among the masses — the spiritual vacuum created by the socio-political upheaval, the masses' indifference to radical left-wing movements and their lack of confidence in the established religions, and the freedom of religion and self-expression guaranteed by the new constitution — because what the masses sought during this period was neither the radical revolution of the Communists nor the intellectual sophistication of Buddhist philosophical thought. They sought a charismatic leader, capable of providing them with a meaning of life in a way comprehensible at their own intellectual level, and a simple teaching which would provide them with a sense of meaning for their own existence. The new religions constitute an integral entity of the Japanese Buddhist historical tradition, which is dedicated to the realization of the spiritual experientially, and to the recreation of a new socio-religious human configuration appropriate to the historical needs of the time as they see it.

10. Conclusion

We have seen that Sōka Gakkai, a representative type of the new religions, came into popularity in postwar Japan, a period marked by socio-political upheavel, and catered to the needs of the masses by identifying itself with the causes of the masses. But the reader will now notice that this paper contains some contradictions. First, it identified Sōka Gakkai as an integral entity of the Japanese Buddhist tradition, representing the bodhisattva doctrine, but at the same time it has criticized Sōka Gakkai. This contradiction is inevitable, for the bodhisattva doctrine is the 'ideal,' not the 'real.' Sōka Gakkai is a historically established religious institution, a *saṅgha*, which like any other Buddhist institution is striving, through improvising skill-in-means, to realize the ideal bodhisattva principle. It is skill-in-means, not the principle underlying that institution, that this paper has criticized.

Second, it has defined skill-in-means as the peak of wisdom, but criticized skill-in-means. Skill-in-means ordinarily involves a series of trials and errors, but what we mean by 'peak' refers to the final perfection of skill-in-means, not a series of trials and errors. It is in this context that the *Mahāvairocana-sūtra* speaks of skill-in-means as the ultimate. The term refers to an insight capable of formulating the most effective method to accomplish the liberation of mankind. But such a method cannot be defined within a fixed conceptual category, since the method we are referring to varies according to historical circumstances, cultural conditioning, and the individual's mental makeup. Third, folk religion was described as the unspiritual, but historically it has been one of the most effective skill-in-means to addressing the masses. Hence the peak of wisdom refers to the utilization, not the elimination, of folk religion as one of the methods to bring about the liberation of mankind.

In historical retrospect, Buddhism would have perished had it not been concerned with the actual problems of the masses. It is not simply a set of philosophical principles to be manipulated by a selected group of intellectuals, but a living institution potentially capable of inspiring the masses and offering ways and means — even incorporating folk religion — to cope with the problems of historical realities. And, inasmuch as it addresses itself to a variety of people, it must exercise extreme tolerance. It is this element of tolerance that marked the transmission of the Dharma from India, through the kingdoms of Central Asia, to East Asia. Buddhism maintains this element of tolerance simply because its doctrine cautions us to avoid the extreme. The doctrine of the absence of the extreme (the middle path doctrine) provides the rational basis to examine our total life and experience in terms of the feedback process between the ideal and the real, *nirvāṇa* and *saṃsāra*, the spiritual and the secular. It is this kind of process which I have referred to as the experiential. A work designed to criticize the new religions merely on the basis of their socio-political response (like Hirotatsu Fujiwara's work on Sōka Gakkai,[24] which Earhart gently refers to as an "audacious treatment"[25]) ignores the historical and doctrinal roots of the new religions. Therefore, this paper has contextualized the new religions within the framework of the Japanese Buddhist historical tradition.

There is one other issue we must face. Does the popularity of the new religions suggest that they might replace the 'old'? No. Although the new religions pose a challenge to the established schools of Buddhism, they do not intend to replace nor are they capable of replacing the old schools, as the schools of Kamakura Buddhism did not and could not replace the schools of Nara-Heian Buddhism. The 'new' and the 'old' will co-exist, as they have in the past. Co-existence is possible because both share a common ideal, the bodhisattva ideal. But what is important to note here is that, inasmuch as the bodhisattva doctrine represents a process philosophy, the tension between the 'new' and the 'old' provides the stimulus for this experiential process. This is important, for any type of religion, inclusive of *bodhisattva-yāna*, is subject to the historical cycle of fossilization and renewal, as historians of religion constantly remind us. Granted these terms are relative, the established schools of Buddhism today represent, relatively speaking, a case of fossilization, while the new religions represent a case of renewal. But, as is now apparent, this renewal is based upon the traditional bodhisattva principle. Regardless of how they may respond socially and politically, the new religions articulate this principle. They attempt to realize the spiritual historically by improvising skill-in-means. It is this skill-in-means which is often criticized by the intellectual and which, from the standpoint of the bodhisattva doctrine, must be viewed with extreme tolerance.

*****

In the preparation of this paper, I wish to acknowledge gratitude to Professor Byron Earhart of Western Michigan University for reading and criticizing the first draft, and to Professor Kazuo Okabe of Komazawa University for providing me with constructive suggestions.

ADDENDUM

At the Conference, two questions were put to me. I wish to respond to these questions in the form of an addendum in this paper, because by doing so it would help clarify the reason why I consider the new religions to be an integral entity of the Japanese Buddhist tradition. The questions revolve around the term Ekayāna. Specifically, a) what is the difference between Ekayāna and Mahāyāna? and b) how is Ekayāna related to the new religions?

First Prince Shōtoku's *Commentary on the Śrīmālādevīsimhanāda-sūtra* (*Shōmangyō-gisho*) claims that there is no difference between Ekayāna and Mahāyāna in their doctrinal contents, but whereas the term Mahāyāna is employed in contrast to Hīnayāna, Ekayāna makes no such distinction. It is an all-encompassing vehicle.

Second, Ekayāna as described in Shōtoku's *Sangyō-gisho* (see notes 2 and 3) articulates a lay *saṅgha* (after all, Vimalakīrti was a layman and Śrīmālādevī was a laywoman, and the central theme of the *Lotus Sūtra* is universal salvation). Hence, because Japanese Buddhism is predominantly a non-monastic *saṅgha*, I feel that the *Sangyō-gisho* laid the foundation of Japanese Buddhism, and that, at least from the post-Nara period, Japanese Buddhism attempted to realize the principle of lay Buddhism in historical succession. But this statement requires some explanation, for Shinran (of the Pure Land School) refers to the term "*hisō-hizoku*," neither monk nor laity, as the ideal image of the Buddhist, and Dōgen (of Sōtō Zen) seemingly preferred the life of a *śramaṇa* in his later years. Actually, though the term "*hisō-hizoku*" makes no distinction between monk and laity inasfar as their potential to realize salvation is concerned, what it points to is a non-monastic *saṅgha* as exemplified in the life of Shinran. A non-monastic *saṅgha* is a lay *saṅgha*. The case of Dōgen poses a more complex problem. For though he had involved himself in what we may refer to as a lay movement in the early days of his missionary career in Kyōto, after his retreat to the Eiheiji Monastery in Fukui (and particularly in his later years at that Monastery), he seemingly preferred monastic discipline. It is precisely for this reason that today the Japanese Sōtō Zen cites two patriarchs, *viz.*, Dōgen, who is referred to as the "*kōso*," and Keizan, who is referred to as the "*taiso*." Both terms mean the original patriarch, that is, the founder of Japanese Sōtō Zen tradition. Keizan is considered the "*taiso*" simply because, unlike Dōgen, he incorporated elements of folk religion to spread the Sōtō tradition. The popularity of Sōtō Zen today owes much to the manner in which that tradition was spread among the masses — who preferred a non-monastic *saṅgha* — by Keizan. The popularity of Rinsai Zen too is due to Yōsai's willingness to incorporate elements of folk religion. The two major schools of Heian Buddhism — Shingon and Tendai — aggressively incorporated elements of folk religion. Thus, in the light of what I have stated above, it can be established that one of the consistent historical themes in Japanese Buddhism is the development of a lay *saṅgha*, by incorporating elements of folk religion. The new religions, incorporating elements of folk religion, seemingly have succeeded in developing a lay *saṅgha*, which previously existed only in principle. Ekayāna bodhisattvayāna is an all-encompassing school, willingly incorporating elements of folk religion as skill-in-means to spread the Dharma.

FOOTNOTES

1 For a comprehensive definition of the term 'new religions,' see Byron Earhart, "The Interpretation of the New Religions of Japan as New Religious Movements," *Religious Ferment in Asia.* Robert J. Miller (ed.) (Lawrence, Manhattan, Wichita: The University Press of Kansas, 1974) pp. 171-173.

2 *Sangyo-gishō.* See Takakusu Junjirō, *et al*, *Taishō shinshū daizōkyō* (The Taishō Edition of the Tripitaka in Chinese) hereafter abbreviated as *T.* (Tokyo: The Taishō issaikyō kankokai, 1924) vol. 56, pp. 2185-7.

3 Shinshō Hanayama holds that Prince Shōtoku composed the *Sangyō-gisho*, but many Japanese Buddhologists and historians assume that the text was written by a ghost writer, not by Shōtoku, sometime during the reign of Emperor Temmu (673-686), the period when the forces which brought about the Taika Reform were overthrown. The power of the Temmu government was derived from men who catered to the Buddhism of the Asuka area. It is speculated therefore that Shōtoku was idolized and utilized as an instrument of unification and credited as the composer of the text by the new government. In his *Shōtoku taishi gyōsei hokke gisho no kenkyū* (Tokyo: Iwanami shoten, 1944), Hanayama claims Shōtoku as the author of the *Sangyō-gisho.* His view, however, is criticized by Kōjun Fukui and others. See Fukui's "*Sangyō-gisho* no seiritsu o utagau" [Doubts on Shōtoku as the author of the *Sangyō-gisho*] in the *Journal of Indian and Buddhist Studies.* (Tokyo: Japanese Association of Indian and Buddhist Studies, March 1956) Vol. IV, No. 2, pp. 308-20. Hanayama's defense of his original thesis follows in *ibid.*, pp. 321-30. He further defends his thesis in "Nihon bukkyō-shijō ni okeru Shōtoku taishi no ichi" [Prince Shōtoku's position in the history of Japanese Buddhism] *ibid.* March 1957. Vol. V, No. 2, pp. 539-44. See also Saburō Ienaga, "Jōgū shōtoku hō-ō tei-setsu" [Theories concerning the composition of the *Sangyō-gisho*] in *Shōtoku Taishi shū* in Nihon shisō taikei series (Tokyo: Iwanami shoten, 1975) vol. 2, pp. 545-54. Though Hanayama's view is being criticized extensively, it must be admitted that no decisive conclusion has been arrived at on the authorship of the *Sangyō-gisho.* However, the discovery of a Tun-huang manuscript seemingly supports the view that at least the *Śrīmālādevī-simhanāda* commentary was modeled upon a Chinese work of the Northern Dynasties. See Akira Fujieda, "The Manuscripts of the *Sheng-man ching* from the Northern Dynasties: A Study of Variant Commentaries," The *Tōhō Gakuhō.* (Kyoto: Jimbunka-gaku kenkyūjō, March 1969) No. 40, pp. 325-49.

4 Shigeyoshi Murakami. *Kindai minshu shūkyō-shi no kenkyū* (Studies on the People's Religion in Modern Japanese History. Kyoto: Hozokan, new edition, 1963).

5 Takagi Horoo. *Nihon no shinkō shūkyō* (Japan's New Religions). (Tokyo: Iwanami shinsho, No. 365 , 4th printing, 1961).

6 Although Byron Earhart does not make specific reference to the Japanese Buddhist tradition, he does deal extensively and perceptively with methodological issues in interpreting the new religions

of postwar Japan. See Byron Earhart, "The Interpretation of the New Religions of Japan." *op. cit.*, pp. 169-88. But since my paper limits the discussion to Buddhist-derived new religions of postwar Japan, Earhart's approach and mine are different. Furthermore, Earhart deals with the new religions from the perspective of the phenomenology of religion. In this paper, I am attempting to contextualize the Buddhist-derived new religions within the framework of the Japanese Buddhist tradition and examine the new religions within the limits of that framework — on the supposition that Japanese Buddhism maintains a model for renewal within its own tradition. In examining Sōka Gakkai, however, the reader is invited to examine Byron Earhart, "Recent Western Publications on Sōka Gakkai" in *History of Religions.* Mircea Eliade, Joseph M. Kitagawa, Charles H. Long eds. (Chicago: The University of Chicago Press, Vol. 15, No. 3, Feb. 1976) pp. 264-88. Here, Earhart, with his usual perceptive analysis reviews one translation (Horotatsu Fujiwara. *I Denounce Sōka Gakkai.* Worth C. Grant (tr.) (Tokyo: Nishin Hōdo Co., 1970)) and two works (Carl H. Gross. *Sōkagakkai and Education.* Institute for International Studies, 1970; and Dayle M. Bethel, *Makiguchi: The Value Creator, Revolutionary Japanese Educator and Founder of Sōka Gakkai.* New York: John Weatherhill, 1973).

7 For a full translation of the *Imperial Rescript on Education*, see Wm. Theodore de Bary (ed.) *Sources of Japanese Tradition* (New York & London: Columbia University Press, 1967, 3rd printing) vol. II, pp. 139-40.

8 For details, see *Shutaisei ronsō* (Discussions on Shutaisei Theory). Shin'ichi Mashita, comp. (Tokyo: Kakuyōshō, 1948).

9 Studies based upon this survey are found in the *Shūkyō binran* (Handbook on Religion). Shūkyō renmei, comp. (Tokyo: Shūkyō renmei, 1948).

10 Murakami, *op. cit.* pp. 3, 14, 24, 43, etc.

11 The *1965 Yearbook on Religion.* The Japanese Ministry of Education, comp. (Tokyo: Aoki Press, 1966) pp. 132-33.

12 The *Asahi* enumerates 14,446,855 Nichiren shōshū believers. The Nichiren shōshū is a Nichiren sub-school with which the Sōka Gakkai maintains legal and ecclesiastic affiliation. Within the 14,446,855 Nichiren shōshū believers, the *Asahi* enumerates 11,904,729 as Sōka Gakkai believers. See the *1965 Asahi Yearbook.* The Asahi Press, comp. (Tokyo: The Asahi Press, 1966) p. 495 (n. 1).

13 The *1965 Yearbook on Religion*, pp. 148-51.

14 The *1969 Asahi Yearbook*, p. 292b. This statement was already articulated in the summer of 1965 at an interview I had with the Sōka Gakkai executive members. See note below.

15 This statement is from an interview I had with a group of Sōka Gakkai executive members, the identity of which I was requested to withhold, at Taiseki-ji in the summer of 1965.

[16] Cited in Shūken Suzuki. "Sengo henkaku to bukkyō kyōdan" (Postwar Changes and Buddhist Institutions), *Kōza: Kindai Bukkyō* (Modern: Buddhism), Vol. VI. Editorial Committee of Hozōkan, comp. (Kyoto: Hozōkan, 1961) p. 184.

[17] *loc. cit.*

[18] *loc. cit.*

[19] *Toshi ji-in no shakai-teki kinō* (The Social Functions of Urban Temples). Laymen's Association, comp. Vol. I. (Kyoto: Heirakuji shoten, 1959) p. 143.

[20] *Ibid.* p. 142.

[21] *T.* 18.848, p. 1c.

[22] *T.* 26.1524, p. 233a.

[23] Shinran, "Kyōgyōshinshō," *Shin-shu seikyō zensho, Vol. II.* Shin-shū seikyō zenshó hensan-jō, comp. 1941, 3rd printing, p. 2.

[24] See Hirotatsu Fujiwara, *I Denounce Sōka Gakkai.* Worth C. Grant (tr.). (Tokyo: Nishin Hōdo Co., 1970). For the original in Japanese, see Hirotatsu Fujiwara, *Sōka Gakkai o kiru* (Tokyo: Nishin Hōdo, 1970, 8th printing).

[25] Byron Earhart, "Recent Western Publications on Sōka Gakkai," *op. cit.* p. 265.

THE MYŌKŌNIN
JAPAN'S REPRESENTATION OF THE BODHISATTVA

Leslie S. Kawamura

The *myōkōnin*, i.e., an outstandingly faithful adherent of the Buddha-dharma, has become known to the Western world mainly through the wroks of D.T. Suzuki, who can be credited for having made the *myōkōnin* a viable topic for scholarly research.[1] In this paper, I shall attempt to show how the *myōkōnin* represents the Bodhisattva ideal in Japan. I shall develop this paper by discussing three topics:

I. The compilation of the *Myōkōninden*,

II. The textual basis for the term "myōkōnin," and

III. The *myōkōnin*, Seikuro, as a Bodhisattva.

I. The compilation of the Myōkōninden

The practice of recording the biographies of faithful followers of the Buddha-dharma was not something which began with the writing of the *Myōkōninden*. In the history of Japanese Buddhism, it began with the writing of the *Ōjōden*[2] during the Heian Period (794-1185). The writing of these biographies reflected the assimilation of Buddhism into the common milieu and the gradual loss of status that was showered upon the monks previously.

In Sōken Suzuki's view, the *Ōjōden* was written by righteous monks who protested against a number of other monks who not only sought worldly fame, economic gains and political power, but who were contributing also to the degenerating condition of Buddhism in a *mappō* (degenerating) era of Buddhism during the Heian period. In contrast, but still somewhat similar in the manner in which it came into play, the *Myōkōninden* was composed as a reply to uneasy feelings and demands that the common people had and also as a protest against the old established religions — a protest that resulted from a gradually changing Japanese society.[3]

The biographies found in the *Myōkōninden* relate the lives of the *myōkōnin* from all walks of life and from various quarters of Japan.[4] We find the biographies of female as well as male Buddhist adherents; of farmers, business men, retainers and samurais; of priests and nuns, officers and village heads; of doctors, fishermen, packhorse drivers, and *shamisen* (a three stringed instrument) players; of calligraphers, artists, Japanese *sumo* wrestlers; of firemen, transport carriers, beggars, housewives, children and prostitutes. This variety of kind has one thing in common — the people are all outstandingly faithful *nembutsu* practitioners.

In a strict or limited sense, the term *myōkōninden* refers to a particular body of literature first composed by Gōsei (1721-1794) towards the end of the Tokugawa regime in Edo Japan (1600-1867). This particular body of literature gradually developed into a text of five chapters and a sequel (*Myōkōninden-zokuhen*) that constitute the present-day edition of the *Myōkōninden*. In recent years, however, texts bearing the same title have appeared; but these texts must be distinguished from the original composition in that they add modern day *myōkōnin* who do not appear in the original body of literature begun by Gōsei. In this paper, the *Myōkōninden* refers to that body of literature begun by Gōsei and which gradually developed into a text constituted of five chapters and a sequel.

As pointed out above, Gōsei began this movement by composing a text called the *Myōkōninden*. In 1818, Gōsei's disciple, Seigai (1753-), wrote an *Introduction* to his eacher's work and in it, he expressed a desire to have the ork published. His *Introduction* also informs us that ōsei's successor, Rizen (1753-1819), made editorial changes o Gōsei's texts.[5] It was not, however, until almost a alf a century after Gōsei's death that, in 1842, his composition was actually put into print by Sōjun (1791-1872), ho made additional editorial changes and added a chapter f his own.[6] Thus, the *Myōkōninden* that introduced the iographies of the *myōkōnin* to the Japanese public and by hich the Japanese became familiar with the term *myōkōnin* rior to Sōjun's actual printed text, must have been Gōsei's omposition with Rizen's editorial changes.

Aside from adding a chapter of his own to Gōsei's composition, Sōjun, later and gradually, over a sixteen years' period, from 1842-1858,[7] composed and edited other biographies into *Myōkōninden* which finally became additional chapters constituting the version that comes down to us. It is also known that Zō-ō (dates unknown) published a sequel to the *Myōkōninden* that he called the *Myōkōninden Zokuhen*.

The chronological order in which the various editions (chapters) were actually composed has been outlined by Rinsei Sasaki as follows:[8]

Chapter One	Gōsei	1818 (Rizen's changes)
		1842 (Sojun's changes)
Chapter Two	Sōjun	1843
Chapter Three	Sōjun	1847
Myōkōninden Zokuhen	Zō-ō	1850[9]
Chapter Four	Sōjun	1856
Chapter Five	Sōjun	1858

From the information given above, we see that the *Myōkōninden Zokuhen* was compiled before Sōjun wrote chapters four and five. This is peculiar in view of the fact that the edition handed down to us as one version of the *Myōkōninden* puts Zō-ō's sequel after chapters four and five and makes it chapter six. This indicates that the version of the *Myōkōninden* that has been passed down to us in a printed book form was compiled by bringing together various editions (chapters) and the *Myōkōninden Zokuhen* into a single volume consisting of six chapters with twelve divisions.[10]

However, how are we to account for the pecularity of having Zō-ō's sequel published before chapters four and five? One scholar, Sasaki, suggests that there must have been two editions of the *Myōkōninden*, one consisting of Gōsei's composition, Seigai's *Introduction*, and Zō-ō's *Myōkōninden Zokuhen*; the other one was made up of Gōsei's composition to which Sōjun added his corrections and his other chapters.[11] Another scholar, Fukuma, is of the opinion that Sōjun planned to end his *Myōkōninden* with the completion of chapter three, and therefore, the *Myōkōninden Zokuhen* follows it.[12] Both of these theses seem tenable, and just what the actual situation was when the various editions (chapters) of the

Myōkōninden were being published during the Edo Period is still a problem.

In dealing with materials concerning the *Myōkōninden*, the order in which the various editions were published is not the only problem that one confronts. There are many others, but owing to the fact that a discussion of them would warrant writing a book on the subject, I shall merely mention one more in passing. It should be noted that a close examination of the earlier manuscripts of the *Myōkōninden* reveals discrepancies between the various manuscripts and between the manuscripts and the printed texts.[13] This suggests not only the need to study the *Myōkōninden's* development historically in order to ascertain the *myōkōnin's* personality within a certain cultural-historical context, but also the need to produce a reliable edition of the biographies that clearly indicates the idiosyncracies of the compiler and the editor of those texts within a cultural-historical framework.

Finally, we must discuss how certain people were selected for inclusion in the *Myōkōninden*. The most obvious reason lies in the fact that the greatest number of *myōkōnin* found in Gōsei's composition and in Sōjun's chapters were people who lived in areas surrounding Kyoto and Nara. This suggests that these people were selected by Gōsei and Sōjun because such *myōkōnin* were the ones with whom they had their closest ties.

In contrast, the later versions of the *Myōkōninden*, that is in the versions in which the title is used in a wider sense and which were composed after the Meiji Period (1868-1913), a greater number of *myōkōnin* come from the Hiroshima area.[14] This seems to indicate that the concentration of *nembutsu* adherents, especially those of the *myōkōnin* type, shifted from the Kansai area to areas surrounding Hiroshima sometime between the Heian and Meiji periods. This also indicates the movement of Buddhism from the mountain centres, such as Hiei and Koya, that were monk oriented, to the plain areas where Buddhism was assimilated into the populous.

II. The textual basis for the term "*myōkōnin*"

The term "*myōkōnin*" (*Miao hao jen*) was probably used for the first time by Shan-tao (613-681) in commenting on the term *puṇḍarīka* found in the *Meditation Sutra*. Near the end of this sutra, Buddha addresses Ānanda with the following words:

> Know that a person who practices the *nembutsu* is a *puṇḍarīka* among men. Bodhisattva Avalokiteśvara and Mahāsthāmaprāpta become his intimate friends. He will sit at the place of enlightenment (*bodhimaṇḍa*) and will be born into the Buddha family.[15]

Shan-tao comments at length on this passage as follows:

> The passage beginning with the phrase, "a person who practices the *nembutsu*" and ending with the phrase, "born into the Buddha-family," means that the merits [derived from] concentrating on the *nembutsu* is supreme, and indeed, cannot be compared with [the merits derived from] other sundry practices. Furthermore, the passage elucidates the following five points:
>
> 1. One should be continually mindful of Amitābha's name.
> 2. One should praise a person who recites [Amitābha's name].
> 3. One who habituates himself in the *nembutsu* practice is an exceedingly rare person and is without compare; therefore the *Sūtra* metaphorically describes him as a *puṇḍarīka*. A *puṇḍarīka* is the name of a beautiful and rare flower among men. It is the name of a supreme flower among men. It is a name of a wonderful flower among men. Here [in China] we call it a *Ts'ai-hua* (a divine-tortoise flower). "A person who practices the *nembutsu*" is a beautiful person among men; he is a wonderfully likeable person (*miao hao jen* = *myōkōnin*) among men; he is the most superior among men; he is a rare person among men; and he is an excellent person among men.
> 4. If one continually recites Amitābha's name Bodhisattva Avalokiteśvara and Mahāsthāmaprāpta will always follow him like a close friend.
> 5. Even in this life, he obtains such benefits and after death, he will enter the Buddha family, which is the Pure Realm. Having arrived there, he will listen to the dharma for a long time and will visit other Buddha Lands in order to perform *pūja* to the Buddhas; thereby, the cause for enlightenment is fulfilled and the effect matures.

> How could the place of enlightenment (*bodhi-maṇḍa*) be far away.[16]

It is point 3 that is of interest to us here. Point 3 indicates that a *myōkōnin* is analogous to a *puṇḍarīka*, a very beautiful and rare flower. The commentary informs us further that a *myōkōnin* is a practitioner of the *nembutsu* and is a superior, rare, and excellent person among men. This wonderful person is bestowed with the merits of having Avalokiteśvara and Mahāsthāmaprāpta as close friends and of sitting at the place of Enlightenment.

In his text called *Senjakushū*, Honen (1133-1212) comments on the term *miao* (*myō* - wonderful) as follows:

> [Shan-tao's] phrase, 'wonderful person among men,' means that a *nembutsu* practitioner is beautiful even though inferior and 'wonderfully likeable person among men,' means that a *nembutsu* practioner is to be praised even though bad.[17]

That the phrase, 'even though inferior and bad' does not mean an evil person in contrast to a good person, but a person who is beyond the limits of good or evil, can be seen in Shinran's (1173-1262) *Shōshin Ge*:

> All common men, whether they be good or evil,
> If they hear and believe in the Tathāgatha's
> Universal Vow,
> Will be praised by the Buddha as "men of great
> and superior understanding."
> Such a person is also called '*Puṇḍarīka*.'[18]

Thus the *myōkōnin* is a wonderful person who is not limited to the boundaries of good and evil, who believes in the Tathāgata's Universal Vow, who gains various benefits in this life,[19] and who, as we shall see later, is praised as a man of great and superior understanding.

It was on the basis of such textual evidences that Gōsei chose the term *myōkōnin* to describe the outstanding *nembutsu* practitioners discussed in his *Myōkōninden*.

III. The myōkōnin, Seikura, as a Bodhisattva

In his book, *Nihon no Kindai-ka to On no Shiso* (Japan's Modernization and the Feeling of Indebtedness), Sōken Suzuki has classified the *myōkōnin* in accordance with the society of their time. These *myōkōnin* supported the government orders, were content with their present life situation, practiced filial piety, were honest and compassionate, and were given recognition by the feudal lords for their good conduct. Suzuki's classification consists of the following four categories:[20]

1. The *myōkōnin* within the Tokugawa Shogunate system (1603-1868),
2. The *myōkōnin* in the period of Meiji Restoration (1868-1913),
3. The *myōkōnin* within the system of Imperial Absolutism (1930-), and
4. The *myōkōnin* within the modern democratic society (1945-).

"These distinctions represent an attempt to see the *myōkōnin* in relation to their progressive or conservative ethical orientation resulting from their religious views."[21]

The religious views of the *myōkōnin* were characterized by a feeling of joy (*yorokobi*), of gratitude (*arigatai*), of unworthiness (*mottainai*), and of indebtedness (*katajikenai*). These characteristics[22] that characterize a sincere practitioner of the *nembutsu* are found in Seikuro of Yamoto, a *myōkōnin* within the Tokugawa Shogunate system.

According to Gōsei's *Myōkōninden*, Seikuro lived in Hakotate Village, Yoshino District, Yamoto Prefecture (present day Nara). He was endowed with a dull disposition from birth and was unable to read even his name printed[23] on his umbrella. However, with regard to matters of filial piety, he was without compare. Owing to the poverty stricken circumstances of his family and an untimely death of his father, Seikuro had to wander from job to job in order to support his aging mother. He respected the Buddha-dharma from very early in his life and continually repeated the *nembutsu* while walking, standing, sitting, or reclining.

Seikuro was married, but lost his wife early; consequently, he was saddled with the responsibility of bringing up his daughter, Koman. When she became of age, he adopted Kyuroku, a gambler and fighter, for her husband and for his heir. He spent the remaining portion of his life in retirement, until the winter of 1749 when he contracted paralysis. In spite of his illness, Seikuro continued to appreciate the *nembutsu* without dreading the coming of his death.

Finally, at the age of 73, Seikuro passed away on August 4, 1750.[24]

From this brief description one can infer Seikuro's deep respect of the Universal Vow and his life of joy, of gratitude, of unworthiness, and of indebtedness. Seikuro's deep trust in the Universal Vow enabled him to appreciate whatever took place in the manner that it did; therefore, both good events and bad events in his life were accepted as human conditions. This acceptance of reality-as-it-is has been expressed by D.T. Suzuki with the Pure Land notion of *kono-mama* (I am that I am) that refers to a state of spiritual contentment:

> ... RELIGIOUS consciousness is awakened when we encounter a network of great contradictions running through our human life. When this consciousness comes to itself we feel as if our being were on the verge of total collapse. ...
>
> "What is the meaning of life?" ... demands not an abstract solution but comes upon one as a concrete personal challenge. The solution must be in terms of experience. We then abandon all the contradictions that appear on the plane of intellection, for we must feel in a practical way contented with life.[25]

In strict Pure Land orthodoxy, one cannot equate a *myōkōnin* to a bodhisattva or vice-versa; however, it seems feasible to discuss the characteristics of a *myōkōnin* in the light of a bodhisattva's characteristics and uncover similarities found in both a *myōkōnin* and a bodhisattva.

What then characterizes a bodhisattva? Although this question finds no simple solution, in brief, the following characteristics, pointed out by M. Igarashi, can be noted:

1. A bodhisattva pursues the Buddhist path single heartedly.
2. A bodhisattva has the mind to benefit himself as well as others.
3. A bodhisattva practices the six or ten perfections (*pāramitā*) that are at the basis of the Mahāyāna path.
4. A bodhisattva takes the vow to practice in such a manner that his practice will benefit all beings.[26]

Of those four basic characteristics, a *myōkōnin* is similar to a bodhisattva in his pursuit of a Buddhist path single heartedly. A *myōkōnin* differs from the bodhisattva on this point in that his thrust or drive to pursue the path comes from his deep and sincere faith that the Vow of Amida has been fulfilled. In Seikuro's life, we read of the following incident:

> Once, the feudal lord's mother summoned Seikuro and asked, "When did you obtain Faith?"
>
> Seikuro replied, "I believe it was when I was about 42 that I realized that I should aspire for the Pure Land. In those days, I had several doubts about the path to liberation. Somewhere along the way, all my doubts dispersed. Now, I look forward to birth in the Pure Land and enjoy repeating the *nembutsu* to repay my indebtedness to the Buddha. All this I take gratefully as the working of the Other Power.[27]

Secondly, a *myōkōnin* is similar to a bodhisattva in his attempt to benefit himself as well as others. Again, the *myōkōnin* differs from a bodhisattva on this point in that, unlike a bodhisattva who habituates himself in these benefits because this practice is his ethical impulse, a *myōkōnin's* activities happen to benefit others simply from his constant feelings of joy, gratitude, unworthiness, and indebtedness in Amida's Compassion. In Seikuro's life, we find the following incident:

> ... While Seikuro was at a service, a thief entered his dwelling by breaking down a wall. Seven ounces of silver money that Seikuro had left under a straw mat had been taken. Upon hearing about this, people would say, "I am sorry to hear about the theft."
>
> Seikuro replied, "A man who commits theft must be, indeed, short of money. But alas, he broke into my house where there is nothing to steal. It was certainly a pity. However, he was able to take seven ounces of silver money. This was the change I had left over from 15 ounces of silver money that I had earned from selling rape seeds. The other 8 ounces had been spent to pay for the laundry bill owing from spring. On any other occasion, I would not have had even 7 ounces of silver money. How joyful I am that the thief came at the right time. He took great pains to break in and did not leave empty-handed! It was only a small amount, but I am grateful that it was there for him."
>
> When people heard his reply, they were put out. "What nonsense is this?" they asked. "Joyful after having been robbed!"

> Seikuro replied, "Why ought I not to be happy? I, the victim of the theft, am likewise an unenlightened fool by nature, quite capable of committing theft; but fortunately, owing to the Buddha's compassion, the mind to steal does not arise in me. On the contrary, isn't it wonderful that I can be the one from whom someone can steal! If this Seikuro had a reputation for stealing something belonging to someone else, even if it were 5 or 10 ounces of money, then I would bring disgrace not only upon myself but upon all my fellow believers. I would then not be able to continue my association with my fellow *Nembutsu* practitioners. To have a thief enter my home is indeed imprudent of me, but this incident brought no disgrace to me nor to my fellow *Nembutsu* practitioners. What could be more joyful?"[28]

Thirdly, with regard to the bodhisattva's practice of the six or ten *pāramitās*, a *nembutsu* practitioner realizes that not only does he not have the capacity to practice the *pāramitās* but whatever good he may do is always rooted in his selfishness. The Vow of Amida was established for the sole purpose of leading such a person to Enlightenment. The *nembutsu* practitioner comes to the awareness that the practice of the *pāramitā* which has been completed by Dharmākara in becoming Amida Buddha is transferred to him as the *nembutsu* and a sincere mind. Therefore, when the *nembutsu* practitioner repeats the *nembutsu* with a diamond-like faith, he is on the same level as a bodhisattva who has completed the practice of goodness and the fulfillment of the vow. In view of this fact, the *nembutsu* practitioner reaps all the benefits of the bodhisattva who practices the perfections. Therefore, although it is difficult to pinpoint a *myōkōnin's* various activities as reflecting either the perfections of giving, of ethical behavior, of patience, of endeavour, of concentration, or of wisdom in particular, the incidents in his life reflect the operation of all of those perfections. For example, the following incident illustrates both the perfection of giving and the perfection of endeavour.

> At one time in his life, Seikuro used to visit the Honganji Temple 6 or 7 times a year and on each occasion, he would carry fire wood on his back. He adhered to the pattern

of washing the wood, drying them, and when on the road, of not putting them down on an unclean spot. Because this act was done so often and with such sincerity, the Honganji Temple set his fire wood aside to be used only for cooking the rice that was to be put before the altar.[29]

Fourthly, with regard to a bodhisattva's vow, unlike a bodhisattva who establishes and fulfills his vow, a *nembutsu* practitioner senses a feeling of unworthiness and indebtedness to Dharmākara's Vow. Thus, whenever he sees the woes of others, that result from their karmic ensnarement, he simply sympathizes with them and acts in the manner of "I am that I am." A *myōkōnin* does not pass judgment on any human situation. Gōsei writes:

The following summer — the summer of 1749 — I ran into Seikuro on Kyoto. I said, "Last year when you visited Etchu Province, you surely met many admirable *nembutsu* practitioners didn't you?"

To that Seikuro replied, "I was impressed by the fact that Shinshu teachings flourished everywhere. I cannot speak for the *nembutsu* practitioners there, but I can say that, more than they, I appreciated being there."

His reply is indeed impressive. We rejoice only in finding sincere faith in others. Seldom do we take the time to reflect upon our own spiritual situation. Seikuro constantly reflected upon his own situation without trying to find glory in someone else's treasures. To rejoice in the assurance of one's birth in the Pure Land is indeed an admirable thing.[30]

In view of these similarities, one can conclude that a *myōkōnin* is Japan's representation of the bodhisattva; however, one may ask whether this conclusion can be documented with Jōdo Shinshu texts. As I have mentioned before, one cannot equate the *myōkōnin* to a bodhisattva directly, but within the Pure Land texts, there seem to be statements that can be used to substantiate my claim. For example, in Shinran's *Kyō-gyō-shin-shō*, we find the following statement:

Singleness of mind is the true cause for birth into the Pure Land. One who attains this true diamond-like faith leaps crosswise from the turbidities of the five lower existences and the eight obstacles to happiness. Without a doubt, he will be endowed with ten benefits in this life. What are the ten?

1. He will be protected by unseen heavenly beings,
2. He will be endowed with the utmost virtues,
3. He will be able to turn evil situations into good,
4. He will be protected by the Buddhas,
5. He will always be praised by the Buddhas,
6. He will always be protected by Amitābha's spiritual light,
7. He will be joyful,
8. He will realize the feeling of indebtedness and repay it,
9. He will always act out of great compassion, and
10. He will go in the rightly established group.[31]

This means in effect that a *nembutsu* practitioner gains benefits in this life that are similar to the benefits gained by a bodhisattva.

Moreover, in the *Mattosho*, we read that a *myōkōnin* is a person equal in status to Maitreya, (i.e., he will become an Enlightened One in his next birth):

> A man of faith is a true disciple of the Buddha. He is one who recollects properly. He is embraced and not forsaken; therefore, he is called, "One with a diamond-like faith." He is called, "An excellent person, a wonderful person (*myōkōnin*), a superior person, and a rare person." Know that he is a person in the rightly established group; therefore, he is called, "One equal to Maitreya-buddha."[32]

FOOTNOTES

1 That D.T. Suzuki introduced a history of *Myōkōnin* studies in Japan is attested to by Y. Kashiwabara, *Kinsei Shomin Bukkyo no Kenkyu*(Kyoto: Hozokan, 1971) p. 144. For D.T. Suzuki's introduction of the term *Myōkōnin* into the English see *Mysticism Christian and Buddhist* (London: George Allen & Unwin Ltd., 1957) p. 174; also D.T. Suzuki, *Shin Buddhism* (New York, Evanston, and London: Harper & Row, 1970) p. 75-92. For D.T. Suzuki's earliest study of the Myōkōnin, see his *Myōkōnin* (Kyoto: Hozokan, 1976 second edition. First printing in 1945).

2 The practice of compiling the biographies of *Nembutsu* practitioners as exemplifying the ideal human example was believed to have begun in the Heian period with the compilations of the *Ōjōden*. There are various editions of the *Ōjōden* written by such people as Yasutone, Oe, Miyoshi and others, but, on the whole, these *Nembutsu* practitioners adhered to the Tendai and Jōdō *nembutsu* practices. See S. Suzuki, *Nihon no Kindaika to 'on' no Shiso* (Kyoto: Horitsu Bunka-sha, 1964) p. 112.

3 *Ibid*. p. 113-121. S. Suzuki points out three differences regarding the development of the *Ōjōden* and *Myōkōninden*:

1. Historical context — i.e. the *Ōjōden* was compiled during that time constituting the historical movement from Ancient times of National Stature to the Medieval Feudalism and the *Myōkōninden* from a Modern Feudalism to Modern Capitalism.
2. The difference in social status of the people involved.
3. The purpose or objective for writing the biographies differs.

4 See Y. Kashiwabara, *op. cit*. p. 10. Y. Kashiwabara has charted the 157 biographies found in the six volumes of the *Myōkōninden* according to (1) their occupation, (2) their historical era, and (3) the biographies having distinct features.

5 See Nagata Bunshōdō Edition, *Myokoninden* (Kyoto: Nagata Bunshōdō, 1958) p. 2. See also Rinsei Sasaki, "*Myōkōninden* to sono Sakusha tachi" in *Studies in Buddhist Culture* (Kyoto: Hozokan, 1964) vol. 2, p. 283.

6 Rinsei Sasaki, *Ibid*, p. 283.

7 *Ibid*. p. 283. Kashiwabara, *op. cit*. p. 9 gives the dates 1843-1858.

8 R. Sasaki, *Ibid*. p. 284.

9 S. Suzuki, *op. cit*. p. 111 gives the date 1859.

10 This edition has been published by Nagata Bunshōdō and has been referred to as the Nagata Bunshōdō Edition (see note 5 above).

11 R. Sasaki, *op. cit*. p. 285. See also Y. Fujikawa, *Shin-sen Myōkōninden* (Tokyo: Daizō Shuppan Kabushiki-kaisha, 1966) p. 2.

12 K. Fukuma, "Shoki Myokoninden Hensan no Rekishi-teki Haikei ni tsuite" in *Shinshū-shi Kenkyu* (Kyoto: Nagata Bunshōdō, 1966) p. 483, note 2.

13 For a study on the various discrepancies see J. Doi, "Gōsei sen *Myokoninden-ko*"in *Kokubun gaku Ronsō* (Kyoto: Ryukoku University, 1978) vol. 23, p. 14-21 and J. Doi, "Gōsei sen *Myōkōninden* (sho)" in *Shugakuin Ronshū* (Kyoto: Shūgakuin, 1977) vol. 47, p. 115-132. See also Z. Asaeda, "Shohen *Myōkōnin* no ichi Kōsatsu" in *Bukkyo-shi Gaku Kenkyu* (Kyoto: Ryukoku University, 1978) vol. 20, no. 2, p. 52-74.

14 Here the term Hiroshima area includes the Hiroshima, Fukuoka, and Yamaguchi prefectures. See M. Igarashi, *Hogan-riki no Sekai* (Tokyo: Yayoi Shobō, 1977) p. 27.

15 See J. Takakusu and K. Watanabe (ed.) *Taisho Shinshu Daizokyo* (Tokyo: Society for the Publication of the Taisho Tripataka, 1922-33). Hereafter *T*. See *Kuan wu liang ch'ou fu ching* vol. 12, no. 365, p. 346, lines 12-14.

16 *Kuan wu liang ch'ou fu ching cho* in *T*. vol. 37, no. 1753, p. 278a.

17 See *Shinshu Shogyo Zensho* (Kyoto: Kōkyōshoin, 1958). Hereafter *SSZ*. See Honen's *Senjaku-shu* vol. 1, p. 972.

18 *SSZ* vol. 2, p. 44.

19 See p. 233 of this paper.

20 S. Suzuki, *op. cit.* p. 126. Y. Kashiwabara, *op. cit.* p. 130 does not agree totally with Suzuki's divisions, but accepts the first and third divisions as to their contents. The dates given in brackets ( ) are mine.

21 Alfred Bloom, *Shinran's Vision of a New Community* (Kyoto: Shinshū Kenkyūkai: Ryukoku University, 1977) p. 41.

22 I have merely summed up the various characteristics. P.K. Eidmann has dissected the *Myokonin's* personality into forty-one aspects. See his "Pietism in Shin Buddhism: The *Myokonin*", *Occasional Papers* No. IV (Kyoto: Kansai Asiatic Society, 1956) p. 4, note 9.

23 The Japanese language has three components in its written form: the use of Chinese characters (*kanji*); the use of cursive syllabary (*hiragana*); and the use of square syllabary (*katakana*). Seikuro's name was printed in *katakana*, a form which, prior to World War II, any school child knew by grade one or two. Since World War II, the *katakana* has now become restricted to writing out foreign loan words, such as kohi (= coffee), that have become part of the Japanese vocabulary.

24 This is Seikuro's life summarized according to the Nagata Bunshōdō Edition, *Myōkōninden* (Kyoto: Nagata Bunshōdō, 1968. First edition printed in 1958) p. 12-24. My complete translation of Gōsei's account of Seikuro's life will appear in *The Pure Land*, Journal of European Shin Buddhism.

25 D.T. Suzuki, *Mysticism op. cit.* p. 143-144.

[26] M. Igarashi, *op. cit.* p. 15.

[27] See Nagata Bunshōdō Edition, *Myōkōninden*, p. 17.

[28] *Ibid.* p. 21-22.

[29] *Ibid.* p. 16.

[30] *Ibid.* p. 20-21.

[31] *SSZ.* vol. 2, p. 72.

[32] *SSZ.* vol. 2, p. 660.

INDEX

abhāva, 73
Abhidhamma Piṭaka, 21
abhidharma, 159
Abhidharmajñānaprasthāna-śāstra, 163
Abhidharmahṛdayaśāstra, 163
abhipreta, 69
Abhiras, 58
Abhisamayālaṃkāra, 68
Abhisamayālaṃkārālokā, 101
abhisaṃbodhi, 67
abolishment of impurities, 113
absolute, 213; monarchy, 195; revelation of the, 173
Ācārya [Haribhadra], 101
accumulations, two, 102
Achaemenid, domination, 44; empire, 38
act, know how to, 128
acting Buddha, 183
action, Bodhisattva's vows and, 134; disciplinary code of, 197; filial, 131; for realizing enlightenment, 97; philosophy of, 146; ten, 134
activities, 158; altruisitic, 182; of a Bodhisattva, 73; supernormal, 157
addiction, 117
adhimukticaryābhūmi, 69
adhiṣṭhāna, 179
adult education classes, 198
advaya, 66; *vṛttiḥ*, 67
affirmation, 117
afflictions, 139
Afghanistan, 43
agony of the intellect, 211
Ahura, 40; Mazdāh, 41, 58
aim, ultimate, 71
Ajīvikism, 53
Akahata, 199
Akṛtajñā, 127
akṣara, 54
ālayavijñāna, 106
all, encompassing school, 219; pervasive energy, 112, pervasively present, 113
Allied Occupation, 199
Altan Khan, 89
altar, 233
altruism, 20, 23
altruistic, activities, 182; motivation, 95; nirvāṇa, 63
amaca, 35
Amaravati, 46
amātya, 35
American, jazz, 196; way of life, 195
Amesha Spentas, 40-41
Amida, 7; Buddha, 232; Vow of, 231-232; Compassion of, 231
Amitābha, 7, 31, 34, 156, 165; heavenly, 7; one with, 181; Path of the Original Vow, 175; protected by the spiritual light of, 234
Amitābha's, Mind transferred, 181; name, 175, 227; Pure Land, 181; salvation, 167; vow of salvation, 169; vow, salvation through, 181; vow, power, 181
Amoghavajra, 156, 162
An Shih-kao, 157; translation bureau of, 153
Ānanda, 227
ancestral worship, 147
ancient, Buddhas, 135; China, 144; Chinese deities classified into three categories, 147; Chinese leaders, 145; Chinese sages, perfection in the moral path, 145; times of National Statute, 235
Āndhra, 58
anger, 141; free from, 139; three fires of attachment, delusion, and, 129
animal, 141; reborn as an, 145
animate being, 114
animistic religion, 81
anjin, 177
antaḥpura, 34
antecessor, 90
anthropomorphic images, 117
Antioch, St. Ignatius of, 158
anxiety, 203, 198; human, 213
apocalyptic, description, 28; visions, 13
appreciative discrimination, 114
apratiṣṭha-śamāviṣṭa(-jñāna), 67
apratiṣṭhatā, 62; *nirvāṇa*, 63, 65, 67; *saṃsāra*, 65; *saṃsāra-nirvāṇa*, 63; *nirvāne niviṣṭaṃ*, 64
apratiṣṭhitā, 66
archon, 154
arhat, 20, 32-33, 35, 61; highest goal for, 62

arhatship, 61
arigatai, 229
aristocracy, 214
army of converters, 204
art, 156
artists, 224
Ārya Vimuktisena, 105
āryamārga, first stage of, 98
aśaikṣa-mārga, 98
asaṃkhya kalpa, 175
asaṃkleśa, 70
asaṃskṛta, the uncompounded, 67
Asaṅga, 73, 104
ascending of wisdom, 74
ascent, motivating power of, 72; of wisdom, 71
ascetic, 54; discipline, 91; mysticism, 84
Asha, 40
Asia, Central, 32, 43, 153, 216; East, 155-56, 216; Western, 154
Asian Continent, 171
Aśoka, 19, 24-25, 33, 44, 55; conversion to Buddhism, 27; Dhamma, 55; pillars, 25; rock-inscriptions, 44
aspiration, 114, 206; wishful, 97
Aspiring Attitude, 97; Bodhicitta of, 99
āśraya-parāvṛtti, 66
assembly, Vulture Peak, 143
Association of Democratic Scientists, 197
Aṣṭasāhasrikāprajñāpāramitāsūtra, 153, 162
Asuka area, 220
atano ca nirvāṇa saṃpati, 37
attachment, 129; free from, 139; three levels of, 64; *see*, three fires
attain, bodhi, 95-96
attainability, spirit of, 132
attaining Buddhahood, 175
attainment, confidence of, 137; of Buddhahood, 176, 183; of Buddhahood in the present life, 176; ten kinds of, 66
attitude, aspiring, 97; Bodhicitta of Realizing, 99; docetistic, 160; ethical, 98; mental, 204; of aspiration, 100; three kinds, 65
attributes of the Bodhisattva, 158
atom, 112
audience, 155; Bodhisattvas, 155
Aurṇikas, 58
auspicious birth, 158
austerity, 70
avabodhi, 114
Avalokiteśvara, 8, 20, 31-32, 41, 73, 84, 139, 154, 227; Legendary, 48
Avataṁsaka, 134; sect, 172
avatāra, 45
Avesta, 40, 42
avinivartaṇa, 66
avinivartanīya, 176
avoid the extremes, 216
avyākṛta, 106
awaken the Bodhi Mind, 180
awareness, 232; ethical, 121; mental, 102
ayāya saṃbodhiṃ, 26
Aztec war-god Huitzilopochtli, 48

baby, 130, 160
Bacon, Francis, 111
Bactrian Greeks, 46
bad events, 230
bagā, 74
Bahalia, 35
bahu-jana-hitāya, 34
Bala, 29, 33, 36
Balambat in Swat, 44
baptism by fire, 157
Baranasi, 127
barbarians, 153; impure, 46
bastard Sanskrit, 53
Bdag-nyid chen-po Bzang-po-dpal, 86
bde, 122
bde-ba chen-po byang-chub-kyi rmad-du byung-ba'i le'u, 112
bder-gshegs syying-po, 122
Be-ri, King of, 90
beautiful, children, 139; person, 227
becoming a Buddha, in the present body, 177
beggar, 160, 224
begging bowl, 168
beginner, 182
behavior, Japanese religious, 209, 210; socio-religious, 211; patterns, 120
Being, affinity with, 115; expanse of, 116-17; intrinsic meaning of, 117; mystery of, 112; open and unsubstantial, 99; openness of, 116; perfected, 144; playfulness of, 113
Beings, benefits of, 160; salvation of all, 172; vow to save, 155
belief, firm, 184; right practice of, 184; structure, 160; system, 115

believers, in the established schools, 201; Nichiren-shōshū, 221; number of, 201; Sōka-Gakkai, 201
bell of Nikolai Cathedral, 210
belonging, sense of, 205
Benares, 5
benefit(s), 233; giving to sentient beings, 168; of all sentient beings, 95; of beings, 160; of the bodhisattva, 232; of others, 68, 158, 230; own, 98; secular, 210; ten, 233
Besnagar column, 45
beyond the limits of good or evil, 228
Bhabra (Bairat) Edict, 54
Bhadanta Vimuktisena, 105
bhadraghata, 6
Bhagavad Gītā, 37, 44
Bhagavān, 40
Bhāgavata sect, 45
Bhagavataḥ Śākyamuneh pratimā, 30
bhakti, 54, 57
Bhāratavarsa, holy land of, 46
Bharhut, 24-25, 46; Jātaka reliefs of, 54; stūpa, 22
bhāvanā-mārga, 98
bhavopapatti, 68
bhūmi(s), eleven, 70; first, 69, 98; second, 70; seventh, 70, 100; sixth, 70; ten, 72
Bible, New English, 57
Bibliographique Nationale, 143
biographies, 223, 235; of faithful followers, 223
biology, 118
birth, a miraculous, 68; absence of, 117; auspicious, 158; causes of, 69; in Pure Land, 166, 169; of the Buddha, 187; paradoxical, 68; place of, 69; stories, 145; true cause for, 233; series of deaths and, 153
birthday of Śākyamuni, 159
Bka'-brgyud-pa, 86
Bkra-shis lhun-po, 88
bla, 84
Black-hat Karma-pa, 87
black hole, 116, 118, 123; Kerr, 123; Reissner-Nordstrom, 123; Schwarzchild, 123
bliss, 122, 190; expanse of ineffable ultimate, 117; great, 177
blissful ignorance, 111
Bloch, Jules, 26-27
bloody demand of human flesh, 128
bō (of land), 208
Bodh Gayā, 26, 67
Bodhi, 22, 35, 55, 117, 175, 178; for the benefit of all sentient beings, 95; thought of, 95; to embark upon the journey toward, 96; tree, 25, 55; wish to attain, 95-96
Bodhicaryāvatara, 5
bodhicitta, 95, 103, 114; as *citta* and *caitta*, 96; created by the power of meditation, 102; elicited by sign, 102; essence of, 104; of Aspiring, 99; of Realizing Attitude, 99; of ultimate truth, 102; phenomenology of, 95; practice of, 98; twenty-two steps of, 98, 100; two steps with regard to, 96 various aspects of, 96; vow, 99
bodhicittotpāda, 103
bodhimaṇḍa, 227, 228
Bodhi Mind, 169, 181; awakening of, 180; first awakening of, 178; Great, 182
bodhipraṇidhicitta, 96
bodhiprasthānacitta, 96
bodhisatta, Pali, 20; pre-natal existence as a, 53
Bodhisattva, 1, 14, 19, 21-22, 35, 61, 84, 119, 125, 132, 153, 177; appellation for, 155; as a Buddha-to-be, 73; as an infallible shepherd, 82; as represented in the birth-stories, 145; aspires for enlightenment, 96; attributes of, 158; benefits of, 232; Buddha identity, 183; career of, 157; celestial, 154; chapel, 29; concept, 153; controversy about, 158; firmness of, 70; *gṛha*, 35; highest stage of, 160; husband, 6; idea, 125; idea in China, 126; ideal, 158, 160, 165; ideal principle, 215; idealism, 165; image of, 142; Iranian influence, 57; in the Pure Land, 181;

king, 128; light of the, 53; literature, 125; *mārga*, 72; Meditation, 158; myōkōnin as a, 223; names, directory of, 155; of Mahāyāna, 20; of wisdom, 11; ordinary career, 177; path, 74, 165, 170-171, 184; practices of, 169, 212; precepts, 170; propitious phenomena of, 106; realizes equanimity and nonduality of saṃsāra and nirvāṇa, 67; Śākyamuni as, 160; *śīla*, 213; soterological role of, 81; spirits, 6; stages, 178; Ten Positions of, 133; three typologies of in China, 144; variations, 157; vow, 132, 168; vows for perfect and quick enlightenment, 168; worship, 142; wrathful, 156
Bodhisattvabhūmi, 69, 104
Bodhisattvabuddhānusmṛti-samādhisūtra, 162
Bodhisattva Doctrine, 90, 215; a process philosophy, 217; Ekayāna, 193; esoteric system of, 165; secularized the saṅgha, 194; spiritualized the laity, 194
Bodhisattva does not turn back from either saṃsāra or nirvāṇa, 67
Bodhisattva enters saṃsāric life, 68
Bodhisattvahood, 126
Bodhisattva Jōgyō, 170; incarnation of, 184
bodhisattvayāna, 217
Bodhisattvayāna-Ekayāna, 219
Bodhisattva-Vajragarbha, 135-136
Bodhisattva's, birth, four kinds of causes, 69; career, causal stages of, 180; characteristics, 230; original vow, 5; personality, 107; process of perfecting wisdom, 212; rebirth, 69; resolution, 64; role as savior, 144; turbidities, 62; Vow, 5, 20, 233; vows and actions, 134
Bodhisattvas, as transcendent beings, 160; as saviors, 138; cult of, 29; cult of the heavenly, 31; cult of the Mahāyāna, 41; cultivation of, 134; heavenly, 29, 31, 34, 37, 48, 154; living, 157-158; living people as, 157; names of, 155; of the Space Age, 49; ordination platform for, 165; Original Actions of, 133; past, 135; phantasma, 155-156, 158; ten clevernesses of, 133; ten concentrations of the, 133; ten flying methods of, 133; ten seals of, 133; ten towns of, 133; vows of, 135, 157; works of, 136; worship of, 127, 142
Bodhisattvas' holy places, 139; vows, 133
Bodhisatvo chatrayasti pratiṣṭhapito (sic), 29
body, becoming a Buddha in the present, 177; Buddha, 8, 62; fleshy, 159; ghostly, 131; king of beautiful, 128; noumenal, 179
bodies, three, 176, 179
bondon-ichijō, 189
Book of Rites, 146
Bosisatva-gaha (sic), 29
boundaries of good and evil, 228
Bounteous Immortals, 42
brda'-las byung-ba, 102
Brahmā, 70
Brahma's Net Sūtra, 168
brahmins, 128
branch-heads, 205
'Bras-spungs, 88
bsam-ldan, 98-99
Bsam-yas debate, 81
bsgom-stobs-kyis byung-ba, 102
Buber, Martin, 12
Buddha, 178, 227; ancient, 135; aspect of the practitioner, 178; becoming in the present body, 177; birth of, 187; Body, 8, 62; Cosmic, 176; dharma, 229; Dīpaṅkara, 25, 27; disciple of, 170; family, 227; future, 7, 28; Gautama, 127; Gotama, 21, 25; *honmon*, 190; Kāśyapa, 131; Konāgamana, 24-25; land, 133, purification of, 66; Mahāvairocana, 176; manifestations of a, 154; Mind, 174, 181; nature, 8, 173, 181; nature, man possessed, 177; nature, primordial element of, 98; One equal to Maitreya, 234; original state, 175, 190; originally

enlightened, 179; past lives of, 126; portrait of, 127; temporal, 190; to-be, 73;; Śākyamuni, 183; wisdom, 62
Buddhabhadra, 134-136
Buddhabhūmisūtra, 67
buddhahood, 19, 98, 173, 178, 183; attainment of, 183; in the next life, 176; innate, 179; instantaneous attainment of, 176; quick attainment of, 175-176; shortcut to, 176; transparency and lucency, 119; ways of attaining, 175
buddhaiḍuka, 59
Buddhaṃ saraṇaṃ gacchāmi, 45
Buddhamitrā, 29
Buddha's, birth, 25; birthday, 158; death, 25; efforts, 231; enlightenment, 25, 183; first preaching, 25; glory, 178; Parinirvāṇa, 167, 169; power, 179; Self-Enjoyment Samādhi, 183; skill in communication, 4; teachings, 232
Buddhas, cult of the early, 24; forms of, 31; future, 27-28, 73; Mathura, 30; pacceka, 35; praised by the, 234; protected by the, 234; sons of, 136; supernatural powers of the, 136; worlds of, 136
Buddhavaṃsa, 54
Buddhism, 122; a living institution, 216; assimilated into the populous, 226; assimilation of, 223; Chinese, 126; Chinese converted to, 145; degenerating condition of, 223; family in, 2; Heian, 165; heretical teaching of, 148; historical themes in Japanese, 219; Indian, 177; introduction to the Tibetan court, 82; Japanese, 165, 223; Kamakura, 169, 214, 217; lay, 193; 213; Mahāyāna in the context of Japanese, 171; Meditational, 81; Nara-Heian, 214, 217; "New", 159; persecution of, 82, 167; popular, 22, 31; primitive, 19, 43; renaissance of, 83; scholars of, 194; schools of Heian, 219; splits within, 153; Tibetan, 118; transmission of, 187; transmitted to Japan, 167; Vajrayāna, 83
Buddhist, activism, 214; Canon, Chinese, 153; catalogue *K'ai-yüan lu*, 125; Chinese, 137; church, 24; democracy, 206; derived new religions, 221; Dharma, 169; East Asian, 157; hagiographic accounts of missionaries and teachers, 157; ideal image of, 218; institution, 215; inscriptions of the Western Decan, 37; Japanese, 48; Japanese historical tradition, 215; Japanese tradition, 194, 218, 221; meditation, 156; monks, 61; notion of wisdom, 211-212; path, 230; philosophical thought, 215; philosophy, 103; saṅgha, 195; Sanskrit, 20, 22, 38; societies, 81; stories, 3; temples, 210; tradition, 159; texts, Chinese, 161; vows, 83
Buddhologists, 194; Japanese, 220
Buddhology, 24-25; of Theravāda, 45
buppō minshu shugi, 206
Burma, 10, 33
business enterprises, 203
business men, 224
busshin-ichijō, 174
butchering of cattle, 41
byang, 113, 116
byang-ba, 112
byang-chub, 22, 114, 116; *kyi sems*, 112, 115-116; *sems-dpa'*, 22, 112, 116-119; *sems-dpa'* level, 120; *sems-dpa'i theg-pa*, 119

caitta, 106; *bodhicitta* as, 96
cakkavatti, 28
Cakkavatti-sīhanāda Sutta, 28
cakravartī kings, 31
Cakravartī-rāja, 70
calamities, 184; three, 183
calligraphers, 224
calligraphy, 209
camps, 160
caṇḍāla, 69
canonical, translation of texts, 82
capacity, cognitive, 113; different, 177; mental, 213; to practice, 232
capitalistic societies, 197

capricious gods, 84
career of the Bodhisattva, 157
categories of the mind, 111
cattle, butchering of, 41
causal, philosophy, 146; practices, 183; stages of a Bodhisattva's career, 180
cause, and effect, 178; for birth, 233; for enlightenment, 227; four kinds, for Bodhisattva's birth, 69
causes of birth, 69
cavalry, 89
celestial beings, 127
"Celestial" Bodhisattvas, 154
Central Asia, 32, 43, 153, 216; invaders from, 46;
central Tibet, 83, 86
centres for pilgrims, 139
ceremonial manual, 146
ceremonies, 157
cetanā, 104
chain of dependent causation, 24
Ch'an, 81; masters, 82
Chang Yen, 140
charisma, diminution of, 88; of office, 88; of person, 88
charismatic, leader, 215; personalities of Sōka Gakkai, 204
charnel house, 142
Che-tao ching, 142
chemistry, 118
Chen Cheng-to, 143
Chên wei shih lun, 62
Ch'eng-chü kuang-ming ting-i ching, 139
ch'eng-fo sheng-tao, 150
Ch'eng-kuan, 138
chiai yu tz'u che'eng, 150
Chien-pei yi-ch'ieh chih-te ching, 134, 137
ch'ih (to hold), 138
Chih-ch'ien, 127, 133, 149
Chih-lu-chia-ch'en, 133
Chih-yao, 139
child, inseparability of mother and, 117; reincarnation, 91
children, 224; beautiful, 139; school, 198
Ch'in Kung, 162
Chin-sha-t'an, 143
China, 37, 47, 81, 155, 167; a Mahāyāna stronghold, 159; ancient, 144; Bodhisattva idea in, 126; development of Mahāyāna Buddhism, 138; introduction of Mahāyāna Buddhism in, 138; missionaries coming into, 160; socio-political situation in, 139; spread of Küan-yin worship in, 140;
Chinese, 31; Buddhism, 126; Buddhists, 137; Buddhist Canon, 153; Buddhist texts, 161; civilization, 126; commentaries on the *Vajracchedikā*, 64; converted to Buddhism, 145; deities, 147; early translations, 133; history, personal deity, 147; illiterate, 146; leaders, 145; masses, 139; monk, Mahāyāna, 81; opera, 148; pro Buddhist tradition, 144; religious traditions, 144; sages, 145; scholars, 137; three typologies of Bodhisattva literature in, 144; tradition, 132; Zen, 169
Chinggis Khan, 85
Chiu-hua, 139
choice, 42
chorus-singing, 199
choruses, Union-affiliated, 197
chos-'byung, 83
chos-lugs, 101
Chos-rgyal, 84
Christ, as a phantom being, 159; Jesus as, 159
Christian, Church, 210; eastern, 39
Christology, Gnostic, 154, 158, 160
Chronicle of Japan, 167
Chu Fa-hu, 134
Chu Fa-tu, 158
Ch'u-san-tsang chi-chi, 149, 157
chub, 112, 116
chub-pa, 112
Chui-yü, 148, 152
Church, 89; Buddhist, 24; Christian, 210; and state, 91
cintāmaṇi, 6
circumambulating, 189
citta, 103; bodhicitta as, 96; motionless, 107
Cittamātra, 120
cittopāda, 95, 103, 105
civil, service, 209; war, 89
civilization, Chinese, 126
"clean" politics, 207
cleansing, 116
clear sky, 114
clergy, 209

close friend, 227
co-existence, 217
code of ethics, 205
codified *vinaya*, 214
cognition, 105; super-normal, 98
cognitive capacity, 113
cognitiveness, pristine, 112, 115-116
cognitivenesses, five, 117
collapse, 116, 230
collective political action, 197
column, Besnagar, 45
coming-hither, 72
Commandments, Five, 130
commentarial literature, 133
Commentary of Hua-yen Ching, 138
commitment, 6
common, men, 228; milieu, 223; people, 223
Communist, 196; leaders, 198; organizations, 197; Party, Japanese, 196; teachers' unions, 198
community activities, 209
communities, rural, 207
companionship, 198
comparative studies of religion, 161
compassion, 5, 65, 102, 114, 132, 211-212; descending of, 74; descent of, 71; great, 98, 119, 127; wisdom and, 211
compassionate, 229
complete enlightenment, 24
compounded, 67
comrades, 197
concentration, 232
concentrations, ten, 133-134
conceptual, category, 216; thematization, 116
condition, without, 146
conduct, good, 229; rules of, 169
confessing, ten methods of, 133
confession, 204-205
confidence of attainment, 137
conflict, source of, 211
Confucian, doctrine, 146; program for personal cultivation, 146; scholars, 131
conscience, 211; moral, 145
consciousness, 105, 176, 230; crisis, 169; Japanese religious, 199; religious, 230; five kinds of sensory, 106
Conservatives, 197
consummate perspicacity, 113, 119
consummateness, 116
Contemplation, Path of, 98
contentment, spiritual, 230
control, government, 201
conventional, aspect, 102; truth, 212
conversion of all citizens, 206
converters, army of, 204
Conze, E., 64
corps leaders, 205
Cosmic, Buddha, 176; unity, 179
cosmos, 48
counsels of Theravāda, 42
courage, 113
creation, magical, 69; new, 42
creativity, 113, 121
crescent moon, 98
crisis, consciousness, 169; Dharma, 166; socio-political, 193, 200
critics, 203
crystal, 112
Cukhsa, Satrap of, 34
cult of, bodhisattvas, 29; earlier Buddhas, 24; heavenly Bodhisattvas, 31; Mahāyāna Bodhisattvas, 41
cultivation, of Bodhisattvas, 134; of wisdom, 184; sets of, 134; spiritual, 125-126, 132
cultural, conditioning, 216; revolution, 152
Cundīdevīdhāraṇīsūtra, 162
cyclic time, 43

Daimoku, 170, 204
Dalai Lama, 90; fifth, 87; first, 88
Daḷhanemi (King), 28
danger of the *hongaku* view, 182
dangerous sojourn, 141
Ḍani, 44
danka, 195
darśāna-mārga, 98
daśa, 133
daśabhūmi, 135
daśabhūmika, 133
Dayal, Dr. Har, 21-22, 33
Dbus, 89
de (direction), 122
de-bzhin gshegs-pa'i snying-po, 122
deMallmann, Dr. Marie Thérèse, 21
dead, God is, 48

death, 45, 141, 158, 182, 227, 229; absence of, 117; Lord of, 10; series of births and, 153
debate of Bsam-yas, 81
Decadent Dharma period, 167
defilements, guarding of, 70; obstacle of, 71, of desire, 70; of the saṃsāric world, 70; saṃsāric, 71
degenerating condition of Buddhism, 223
deities, 174; personal in Chinese history, 147-148
delusion, free from, 139; of three fires, 129
democratic government, 195, 206
democracy, 206
demons, 31; and spirits, 139; malicious, 84
Dependent Causation, 24
dependent co-origination, 70
Descartes, René, 111
descent of compassion, 71
descriptive, imagery, 118; term, 117
desire, 113; defilements of, 70; man's will and, 96
despicable passions, 232
despondency, 166
depression, 203
detachment, three levels of, 64
deva, 36
Devadatta, 128
Devānaṃpiya Piyadassi-King, 25
developing, process, 193; the six *pāramitās*, 97
development, industrial, 203; Japan's industrial, 208; moral, 6; of Mahāyāna Buddhism in China, 138; of mind, 103
devotion, 98
Dga' ldan, 88
Dge-'dun grub-pa, 88
Dge-lugs-pa, 88, 96
dhamma, 25; lipi, 33; trips, 25
Dhammavijaya, 28
dharma, 8, 34, 40, 102, 155, 227; crisis, 166; in its genuine form, 167; in its imitative form, 167; Lotus, 214; period of decadent, 167; post-Imitative period, 167; right, 167, 170; Supremacy of the Lotus, 202; three periods of, 166; transmission of, 216; true efficacy of the, 84
Dharmākara, 7, 232
Dharmakāya, 36, 62, 125; Buddha, 173; Four virtues of, 190
Dharmarāja, 84
Dharmarakṣa, 31, 135, 137, 139, 154, 159, 162
dharmas, realm of, 135-136; ten, 133
Dharmayaśas, 158
Dharmodgata, 153
Dharmottara, 163
Dhauli, 26
dhṛti, 70
dhyāna, 72, 159
diagrams, geometric, 118
dialectic materialism, 196
diamond-like faith, 232-234
dichotomy, 212
different, capacities, 177; versions of scriptures, 138
dignitary beings, 70
dignity of man, 206
diminishing attraction to the established schools of Buddhism, 208
diminution of charisma, 88
Dīpaṅkara Buddha, 25, 27
Dīpavaṃsa, 55
direction(s), 122; ten, 132-133, 135
directories of Bodhisattva names, 155
disciplinary, code of action, 197; vows, 88
Discipline, ascetic, 90-91; individual through, 214; monastic, 219; Zen, 196
disciple, of the Buddha, 170; true, 234
discrimination, 213
disgrace, 232
disgust, 70
dissatisfaction, 198
Divākara, 156, 162
divergent schools, 153
divination, 203
divine, beings, 28; relation between the mundane and, 160; tortoise flower, 227
divinity of the emperor, 195
Divyāvadāna, 54
docetic, groups, 159; notions, 158; tendencies, 154; traditions, 154
docetism, 160
docetistic attitudes, 160

doctors, 224
doctrinal, authority, 214; major shifts, 154
doctrine, *ekayāna* bodhisattva, 193; esoteric system of bodhisattva, 165; bodhisattva, 90, 194, 215, 217; Kuan-yin, 139; of transfer of merits, 32, 35-38, 48; perverted, 203; philosophical, 32; simplifying practice and, 214; ten, 173
dog, 69
Dōgen, 164, 170, 218
dogma, 195; sectarian, 195
dogmatism, 111
doubt, 233; net of, 135
dowry, 129
dpa', 115, 117
dragon, 10, 176; King, 9
drought, 144
Druj, 40
Drumakinararājaparipṛcchā, 162
duality, 116; evolving of, 66-67
dull disposition, 229
'dun-pa, 98
duṣkaracaryā, 70
duty of historian, 47
dvayā vṛttiḥ, 66
dwelling, 138; Ten, 138
dynamic view, 119
dynamics, of experience qua experience, 115; of reality, 118

Earhart, Byron, 221
early, Chinese translations, 133; period of occupation, 196
earnest resolve, 43
earth, 98, 138, 176; Kuan yin descends to, 144
East Asia, 155-156, 216
East Asian Buddhists, 157
Eastern, Christian, 39; Isles of the Blessed, 10; Mongols, 85
ecclesiastic, affiliation, 221; landlords, 208; law, 206
economic, gains, 223; oppression, 196; security, 197; theory, 196
ecstasy, 122
edict, 167
editions of the *Myōkōninden*, 225
Edo, Japan, 224; Period, 226
education, government directives on, 198; Imperial Rescript on, 195, 197, 199
edūka, 47, 58-59
effect, 178, 227; cause and, 178
effort, self, 7
Ego and the Id, 12
egocentricity, 14
egoists, intellectual, 196
eight, obstacles to happiness, 233; thematizing operations (of the 'mind'), 116; types of behavior patterns, 120
eighteenth vow, 7
Eighth Rock Edict, 25, 54
Eiheiji Monastery, 219
Einstein-Rosen 'wormhole' diagram, 118
Eisai, 165
ekarasa, 67
Ekayāna, 165, 213; and Mahāyāna, 171; bodhisattva doctrine, 193; bodhisattvayāna, 219; Buddha-Mind, 174; differs from Mahāyāna, 171; difference between Mahāyāna, 218; directly expounded, 172; Esoteric, 173-174; ideal, 166, 170-171, 181; ideal, Pure Land, 174; Kegon, 174; Mantra, 174; of the *Saddharmapuṇḍarīka sūtra*, 172; Original Vow, 175; precepts, 168; principle and practice, 214; Vajra, 174
elderly, reverence to, 132
electorate, 206
electromagnetism, 118
elementary school, 198
elephants, 128
eleven *bhūmis*, 70
eleventh level of 'light everywhere', 119
elixirs, 146
embraced and not forsaken, 234
emotion, human, 210; impurity of, 112
Emperor, 147, 167; divinity of, 195; renounce the dogma of his divinity, 199; Shun, 144; Temmu, 220; Yao, 144
empiricism, 111
employment possibilities, 208
emptiness, 211; doctrine of, 126; insight into, 212
empty, and eternal space, 137; space, 135-136; words, 141
en'yū, 173

endeavour, 232
endon, 175; *bosatsu-kai*, 168; precepts, 188
energy, 122; all pervasive, 112; spiritual, 121
enjoyable life, 231
enjoyment, supreme, 70
Enlightened One, 1
enlightened, self, 179
enlightening presence, 5
enlightenment, 21, 27, 202, 213, 232; apart from practice, 182; Bodhisattva aspires for, 96; Bodhisattva vows for perfect and quick, 168; cause for, 227; complete, 24; final, 154; full, 166; germ of, 98; identity, 183; in this world, 169; instant, 180; instant method of, 81; leading others to Ultimate, 98; Mahāyānistic way towards, 97; original, 182; personal, 159; place of, 227-228; practice identity, 183; realize aspiration for, 97; sincere wish for, 97; state of, 84, 158; ultimate, 172, 183
ensnarement, karmic, 233
entourage, mental factors as, 107
eons, 128; of time, 158
Epic, 57
equality, human, 213
Equality Wisdom, 67
erh-shih-ssu-hsiao, 149
errors, trials and, 216
esoteric, 173; Ekayāna, 173-174; side, 180; system of Bodhisattva doctrine, 165; teaching, 173; viewpoint, 168
essay-writing, 198-199; as a vehicle of indoctrination, 198; groups, 197
essence, noumenal, 180; of bodhicitta, 104; of the precepts, 169
essential difference between *praṇidhicitta* and *prasthānacitta*, 99
established school, believers of, 201; diminishing attraction to, 208; of Buddhism, 201, 217; of religion, 200
established temple, 209
eternalistic extremes, 116
eternity, land of, 184; Pure Land of, 183
ethic, 195
ethical, attitude, 98; awareness, 121; behavior, 232; considerations, 120; concepts, 195; impulse, 231; orientation, 229
ethicists, 6
ethics, code of, 205; individual, 121; Mahāyāna, 20; of whole systems, 121
etymology, 22
Euclidean geometry, 111
event, bad, 230
events, good, 230; Sakyamuni two, 67
ever-lastingness, 190
everything, ground of, 112
evil, 117, 135, 228; beyond the limits of, 228; boundaries of, 228; abstaining from doing, 168; passions, 175; person, 228; situations, 234
evildoers, 175
evolution of basis, 66
evolutionary, force, 121; process, 119, 121
evolving of, duality, 66-67; non-duality, 67
excellent person, 227
execution, 139, 141-142
executives, 205
exist entitatively, 113
existence, five lower, 233; five ways of, 132; pattern, 154
exoteric teachings, 169, 173
expanse, of Being, 116-117; of ineffable ultimate bliss, 117
experience(s), 115, 212, 230; and life, 212; dynamics of, 115; five, 117; mystic, 157; personal, 204; qua experience, 113; religious, 126; spiritual, 210; thematizations in, 113; total life and, 213
experiential, philosophy, 193; process, 213
expertise, 119
expression, freedom of, 208; self, 195, 215
extinction, 68
extreme, 216; avoidance of, 216; externalistic, 116

fables, 24
fabricated scriptures, 141
faith, 32, 181-182, 203, 214; diamond-like, 232-234; firm, 176, 181; healing, 203;

faith, individual through, 214; man of, 234; one thought of, 189
faithful followers, biographies of, 223
faithful practitioner of the *nembutsu*, 231
fallibility of mankind, 214
families, hierarchic, 86
family, in Buddhism, 2; income, 209; Khon, 89; Rlangs, 89; ties, 200
Fan wang ching, 168
fanā, 74
fantasy of literary romanticism, 198
farmers, 224
fear, 70
feedback, 212; link, 120; process, 212, 216
feeling of indebtedness, 234
feelings, uneasy, 223
female, 223; novice, 120
festivals and rites, 139
feudal lord, 231
feudalism, Tokugawa, 195
fifth Dalai Lama, 87
filial, action, 131; conduct, 144; piety, 131, 229
final, enlightenment, 154; liberation, 72; nirvāṇa, 64
financial status, 204
fire, 98, 141, 176; baptism by, 157; blazing, 139; three kinds of, 128
firemen, 224
firewood, 232
firm, and unbending intention, 113; belief, 184; faith, 176, 181
firmness, 114; of the Bodhisattva, 70
first, awakening of the Bodhi Mind, 178; awareness of *śūnyatā*, 98; *bhūmi*, 69, 98; class intelligence, 176; Dalai Lama, 88; stage of the *āryamārga*, 98
fish, 130, 143
fisherman, 214
Fisherman's Friend, 10
fishermen, 224
fisherwoman, 143; Precious Scroll of the Kuan-yin, 143
five, characters, 183; characters, *'Myō-hō-ren-ge-kyō'*, 183; Commandments, 130; gestalt experiences, 117; kinds of sensory consciousness, 106; lower existences, 233; omnipresent mental factors, 105; Paths, 97; poisons, 116; pristine cognitivenesses, 117; senses, 116; ways of existence, 132
flames, 141
flesh, 159
fleshy body, 159
flock, 233
flower arrangement, 209
Fo T'u Cheng, 158
folk, literature, 143; religion, 210, 216, 219; tradition, 210
followers, biographies of faithful, 223
for oneself, 121
for others, 121
foreign invasion, 184
form, dharma in its genuine, 167
former lives of Sakyamni, 153
Formless Precepts, 157
forms of Buddhas, 31
forsaken, embraced and not, 234
fortresses, 86
forty-eight minor precepts, 168
fossilization and renewal, 217
founder(s), 203; of the new sects, 184; religious, 148
founderess, 203
founding stratum, 112
four, cosmic periods, 183; kinds of causes for Bodhisattva's birth, 69; Noble Truths, 24; Part Vinaya, 170; Samādhis, 173, 189; Virtues, 179; Virtues of the Dharmakāya, 190; *yugas*, 58
fravashis, 40
free from attachment, anger and delusion, 139
freedom, 121, 190; of expression, 208; of religion, 200-201, 215; of speech, 206; personal, 195; principle of religious, 207; ultimate, 119
Freud, Sigmund, 12
friend, close, 227; intimate, 227
Fukui, 219
Fukuma, 225
fulfillment of the vow, 232
full Enlightenment, 166
funeral rites, 209
future, 134; Buddha, 7, 28, 73; Buddha Maitreya, 43, 47; Buddhas, 27; rebirth, 132

Gandhāra, 29, 44, 46
Gaṅgā, 31
Gaṅgā Valley, 33
gate of exit from nirvāṇa, 211
Gāthās, 40, 42, 58
Gautama, 4; Buddha, 127
Gayā, 25, 55
gazetteer, 142; of the places of pilgrimage, 142
General Douglas MacArthur, 196
generous dowry, 129
Gengibun-shō, 189
gensō-ekō, 213
geographical guides, 142
geometrical diagrams, 118
geo-political power, 90
germ of enlightenment, 98
gestalt, 112; five, 117
Geush Urvan, 58
Ghanavyūhasūtra, 162
ghost, 141; body, 131; of Shinto theocracy, 207; writer, 220
Gifts, Great Lord of, 34
Girnar, 26
giving, 232; benefit to sentient beings, 168
Glang-dar-ma, 82
glaucoma, 115
glory, 233
gnostic, 159; christology, 154, 158, 160; savior, 158
go astray, 116
goal, 119; religious, 148; ten, 134
God, grace of, 45; is dead, 48
goddesses, 128
gods, 128, 144; capricious, 84; Hindu, 31; years of the, 58
going-thither, 72
gold, 98
Gondophares, 35
Good, 117, 228, 232, 234; beyond the limits of, 228; boundaries of, 228; conduct, 229; events, 230
goodness, practice of, 232; vow of, 136
Gōsei, 224, 226
Gotama Buddha, 21, 25
government, control, 201; democratic, 195; directives on education, 198; hierocratic, 85; orders, 228; ordinance, 200; proletarian, 197; Tibetan, 91
grace of God, 45
gradual method, 81
Grand Historian, 144
gratitude, 229
Great, Bliss, 177; Bodhi Mind, 182; compassion, 98, 119, 127; Going Forth, 26; Learning, 146; Lord of Gifts, 34; Practice, 182; Satrap Rajula, 34; vehicle, 119
Greek, Bactrian, 46; Yavana kings, 58
'Grel-ba-don-gsal, 106
ground, 138; of everything, 112; of Wisdom, 135-136
growth, 116, 120
gSang-ba snying-po, 114
gSer-phreng, 96, 99, 104
gsung, 112
gter-ma, 90
Gtsang, 89
guarding of defilements, 70
guideline, 198
guides, geographic, 142
guise of a human being, 72
Gujarat, 46
Gushri Khan, 90
Güyüg Khan, 85
gzhan-don, 121

Hagia Sophia, 39
hagiographic accounts of Buddhist missionaries and teachers, 157
Hakotate Village, 229
happiness, 141; eight obstacles to; 233; worldly, 65
Haribhadra, 105
Hārītī, 130; mother of deity, 130
Heaven, 28, 144; sacrifices to, 147; Tuṣita, 131; Will of, 146
heavenly, Amitābha, 7; beings, 28, 234; Bodhisattvas, 29, 31, 37, 48, 154; Buddhas, 32, 34, 41
hegemons, 83
Heian, Buddhism, 165; period, 165, 213, 223, 226, 235
hells, 69
Hemanta, 30
heresies, 159
heretical teaching of Buddhism, 148
heretics, 47
Hiei, 226
hierarchs, 86
hierarchic families, 86

hierocratic government, 85
highest, goal for an arhat, 62; stage of Bodhisattva, 160; wisdom, 65
Himitsu-ichijō, 172, 174
Hīnayāna precepts, 168
Hīnayānic, nirvāṇa, 62; saints, 65
Hindu gods, 31
Hinduism, 21, 37
Hiroshima, 226
hisō-hizoku, 218
historian, duty of, 47; Grand, 144; lama, 83; of religion, 194
historical, era, 235; needs, 214; possibility, 211, realities, 216; secular, 212; textual angle, 138; themes in Japanese Buddhism, 219
historiography, religious, 83
history, 213; of the T'ang Dynasty, 83; Tibetan political, 81
Hitler, Adolph, 12
Hizōhōyaku, 173
Hobbes, Thomas, 111
Hokke-ichijō, 172
Hokke shūku, 176
holy, land of Bhāratavarṣa, 46; man, 130; men, 132; places, Bodhisattvas', 139
Hōnen, 165, 174, 181, 228; 750th anniversary of, 208
honest, 229
hongaku, 178; theory, 166, 180-181; Kūkai's, 179; Shinran's, 181; view, danger of, 182
Hongan-endon-ichijō, *Honganichijō*, 175
Honganji Temple, 232-233
honmon, 175; Buddha, 190
honorable mother, 231
hope, 166, 206
horse-tail, 130
household, 195
housewives, 199, 224
Hsiang Mountain, Precious Scroll on, 143
Hsiang-shan pao-chüan, 143
Hsieh Fu, 125, 140
hsin, 135
Hsüan Tsang, 32, 62
Hua-yen Ching, 134, 138; commentary of, 138; *shu*, 138
Hui-ssŭ, 167
hui-ti, 135
human, and social life, 118; anxieties, 213; condition, 230; disasters, 139; emotion, 210; equality, 213; individual, 119-120; life, 230; misery, 41; realm of life, 156; sacrifice, 48; situation, 233; tragedy, 202; virtues, 131
human being, 160; guise of, 72; three types, 64
human configuration, recreation of a new socio-religious, 215
human example, ideal, 235
human flesh, bloody demand of, 128
humanistic socialism, 206
Hume, David, 111
Huitzilopochtli, 48
hungry demon, 128
hungry jackal, 131
Huviṣka, 30

I, 120
I am that I am, 230, 233
I and Thou, 12
I Ching, 162
I Geng, 162
iconography, 156
ideal, 213; Bodhisattva, 158; 160; Bodhisattva principle, 215; Ekayāna, 166, 170-171, 181; human example, 235; image of the Buddhist, 218; nirvānic, 72; Pure Land Ekayāna, 174; world of nirvāṇa, 72
idealism, Kantian, 196
ideas, revolutionary, 197; superstitious, 203
ideé fixe, 111
identity, man-Buddha, 178
ideological advances, 210
ideology, 198; left wing, 198
Igarashi, M., 230
ignorance, blissful, 111
Ikeda Daisuke, 204
Ikṣvāku king, 37
illiterate Chinese, 146
illness, 204, 229
image(s), 29-30, 36, 117; of the Bodhisattva, 142
Imitative, Dharma, 167
immanent, principle, 180; reality, 190; theocracy, 206

immeasurable and limitless profits, 143
immortal, 121
Imperial, Absolutism, *myōkōnin* within the system of, 229; Rescript on Education, 195, 197, 199
impermanence, 140
impersonalized governmental institution, 90
imprudent, 232
impure, 213; barbarians, 46
impurities, ultimate abolishment of, 113
impurity of the emotions, 112
incarnation of the Bodhisattva Jōgyō, 184
incarnations, 84
incidental 'pollution', 116
inclination, 114
indebtedness, 229; feeling of, 234
indestructibility, 114
indeterminate, 106
India, 81, 153, 216; post-Mauryan, 53
Indian, Buddhism, 177; masters, 95; works on Kuan-yin, 140
individual, by championing the causes of the underdog, 214; ethics, 121; through discipline, 214; through faith, 214; well-being of the, 206
indoctrination, 197, 199; essay writing as a vehicle of, 198
Indra, 70, 131
Indus Valley, 44
industrial, development, 203; Japan's development, 208; laborers, 196
industrialization, 210
industrialized society, 211
industry, 203
infections, 136
insight, 158, 216; into emptiness, 212
instant, enlightenment, 180; method of enlightenment, 81
instantaneous attainment of Buddhahood, 176
institutionalized religion, 211
intellect, agony of the, 211
intellection, 230
intellectual, acumen, 113-114; egoists, 196; level, 215; Mahāyānists, 48; stimulus, 198
intellectuals, 200; Japanese, 211
intellectualism, psuedo, 203
intelligence, 113, 116, 121; first class, 176; lower, 176; middle, 176
intention, firm and unbending, 113; specific, 98-99; surpassing, 98
interpenetration, 176
intimate friend, 227
intrinsic meaning of Being, 117
introduction, of Buddhism in the Tibetan court, 82; of Mahāyāna Buddhism in China, 138
Intuition, Path of, 98
invaders from Central Asia, 46
invasion, foreign, 184
investiture, 157-158
IQ, 115
Iranian, dualism, 40; influence, 43; influence on the Bodhisattva concept, 57
Isaiah, 38, 57
iye, 195

jackal, 131
jails, 141
Jainism, 21, 53
'Jam dbyangs-bzhad-pa, 100
Jantsch, Erich, 121
Japan, 32, 37, 157; Buddhism transmitted to, 167; Chronicle of, 167; Democratic League, 197; Edo, 224; industrial progress, 210; new religions of postwar, 200; political area of, 206; Socialist Party, 197
Japanese, a twelve year old, 196; Buddhologists, 220; Communist Party, 196; empire, 195; intellectuals, 211; public, 224; religion, 194; religious behavior, 209-210; religious consciousness, 199; social structure, 210; society, 223; Sōtō Zen, 219

Japanese Buddhism, 165, 223; historical themes in, 219; Mahāyāna in the context of, 171
Japanese Buddhist, 48; historical tradition, 215; tradition, 194, 218, 221
Japanese Buddhologists, 220
Japan's, industrial development, 208; military defeat, 193-194; new religions, 200; surrender, 195-196; population, 207
Jātaka, 10, 19, 22-23, 28, 54, 126; Bodhisattvas, 154, 156-157; collection, 54; prose, 54; reliefs of Bharhut, 54; stories, 127; tale, Mahāyāna, 153; tales, 73, 153; verse, 54
Jen-wang ching, 138
Jerusalem, 14
Jesus, 4, 38; as Christ, 159; of the Naassene Psalm, 154
jewels, 118; three, 25, 130
'Jigs-med-gling-pa, 100
Jiji Press, 199
jijuyū-zammai, 183
jikken no ichijō, 172
Jimmin hyōron, 197
jñeya-āvaraṇa, 62
jōbutsu gi, 176
Jōdo, 165, 201, 235; Shin, 201; Shinshu texts, 233
Jōdoshu, 157
Jōgyō, Bodhisattva, 170; incarnation of the Bodhisattva, 184
joy, 229
joyful garden, 70
joys, worldly, 65
judgment, 233
Judaism, post-exilic, 40
'jug sems, 99, 101

K'ai-yüan lu, 125
Kali Yuga, 47, 58
kalpa, 28, 172; *vṛkṣa*, 6
kāma-dhenu, 6
Kamakura period, 165, 174
Kamalaśīla, 81
Kāmbojas, 58
Kang Seng-hui, 127, 149
Kaniṣka, 29-31, 36, 46
Kansai area, 226
Kanṣītakī Upaniṣad, 57
Kant, Immanuel, 111
Kantian idealism, 196
Kao Huo-nien, 150
Kao-wang Kuan-shih yin ching, 141
karma, 33, 37, 45, 157; law of, 82
Karma Bstan-Skyong, 90
Karma-pa, Black hat, 87; Red hat, 89
Karma Pakṣi, 87
karman, 69
karmic ensnarement, 233
karuṇā, 33
Kashiwabara, Y., 235
Kāśyapa-Buddha, 131
katajikenai, 229
Kaṭha Upaniṣad, 57
Kathāvatthu, 21, 53
Kātyāyana, 163
kāya, 62
Kegon, 172; Ekayāna, 174
Keizan, 219
Kenchō, 177
Kerr black hole, 123
Khan, Gushri, 90; Güyüg, 85; Möngke, 85; Mongol, 86
'Khon family, 89
Khoshot Mongols, 90
Khri-gtsug lde-bstan, 82
Khri-srong lde-brtsan, 81
Khubilai, 85
Khuddaka Nikāya, 22
Khuṣaṇa, 35
kindergartens, 209
King(s), Greek (Yavana), 58; Ikṣvāku, 37; of Be-ri, 90; of beautiful body, 128; Prasenajit, 129; Surūpa, 128; turtle, 128; White rabbit, 128
kingship, 132
kisei-shukyō, 193
kleśa, 69, 178; *āvaraṇa*, 62, 71; mind tainted by, 106
Klong-chen rab-'byams-pa, 112, 116, 119
Knife-broken Scripture, 142
knowledge, 32; of the past, 129; required, 128; supernal, 55; ten, 134
Kōjun Fukui, 220
Kokonor, 85, 90
Kokumin bunka kaigi, 199
Koman, 229
Komei Party, 205
Komeitō, 205-206; members, 207
Konāgamana-Buddha, 24-25

Kongo-ichijō, 174
Konko-kyo, 194
Kōnin, 177
kono-mama, 230
Korea, 157
Korean War, 197
Kosai, 174
Kosambī, 29-30
kōso, 219
koṭis, 31, 53
Koya, 226
Kōzen gokokuron, 169
Kṛṣṇa, 37; *avatāra* of Viṣṇu, 47
Kṛta Yuga, 47
Kruskal-Szekeres diagram of the Einstein-Rosen 'wormhole' diagram, 118
Kṣitigarbha, 139, 154-155, 162
Kuan Shih Yin, 9
Kuan-yin, 139; descends to the earth, 144; described in Lotus Sutra, 141; doctrine, 139; Indian works on, 140; popularity of, 141; Precious Scroll of the Fisherwoman, 143; spread of worship in China, 140
Kuang-shih-yin, 139
Kubilai, Prince, 85
Kūkai, 165, 168, 213
Kukai's *hongaku* theory, 179
Kumārajīva, 136-138, 159
Kurozumu-kyō, 194
kuśala-dharma-saṃgrāhaka-śīla, 168
Kuṣāṇa, 29, 36, 43, 45-46
Kusināra, 67
Kwannon, 32
Kwan-yin, 32
Kyōgyōshinshō, 169, 174, 182, 233
Kyōto, 219, 226, 233
Kyuroku, 229

labor unions, 196, 199
laborers, 200; industrial, 196
Lai-t'i, 129
laity, 24, 157, 202, 213; Bodhisattva doctrine spiritualization of, 194; neither monk nor, 218
lam lnga, 97
lama-historians, 83
Lamotte, E., 63
land, *bo* of, 208; loss by landlords, 208; of eternity, 184; of Snows, 81
landlords, ecclesiastic, 208; loss of land by, 208; secular, 208
lanterns, 159
laser beams, 118
laundry bill, 231
law, 31; ecclesiastic, 206; of karma, 82
lay, Buddhism, 193, 213; person, female, 120; male, 120; saṅgha, 193, 203, 218
layman, 218
Layman's Association Study, 209
laywoman, 157, 218
le Nirvāṇa instable, 63
leader(s), charismatic, 215; Chinese, 145; Communist, 198; corps, 205; religious, 145; squad, 205
leading others to ultimate enlightenment, 98
Learning, Great, 146; three, 62; three types of, 184
left-wing, 194, 207; ideology, 198; organizations, 196; writers, 199
legal affiliation, 221
legendary Avalokiteśvara, 48
legends, 24, 38
lèse majesté, 203
letters, 177
lhag-bsam, 98
lhag-mthong, 98
Lhasa, 83
li, 125, 138
Li Chi, 146
Liaka Kusulaka, 34
Liberal Democratic Party, 197
liberation, final, 72; of mankind, 216; path to, 231
lie, 40, 141
life, 212, 227; a way of, 196, 205; after next, 176; and experience, 212, 123; and person of Śākyamuni, 158; enjoyable, 231; force, 84; human and social, 118; meaning of, 215, 230; meaningful way of, 197; next, 176; personal outlook on, 211; realm of human, 156; residue of conditioned, 182; situation, 228; snares of, 159; three worlds of, 112
light everywhere, eleventh level of, 119
light, of the bodhisattva, 53; of the śrāvaka, 53
limpid clearness, 113-114, 119; desiring, 113-114; itself, 114

linguistic limitations, 116
liquid crystals, 118
listening, 112
lists of samādhis, 158
literacy, 142
literature, Bodhisattva, 125; commentarial, 133; folk, 143; prajñāpāramitā, 114; Precious Scroll, 143; propaganda, 204; religious, 142; Tantric, 103; three typologies in Chinese of Bodhisattva, 144; Vedic, 21
literary romanticism, fantasy of, 198
Liu-tu chi-ching, 127
living, Bodhisattvas, 157-158; people as Bodhisattvas, 157; system, 113
Lo-chen Dharmaśrī, 119
Locke, John, 111
loka, 57
Lokakṣema, 31, 133, 157, 162
Lord, 129; of Death, 10
loss of land by landlords, 208
Lotus, Dharma, 202, 214; practitioner, 202
Lotus Sutra, 139, 200, 218; *honmon*, 190; powers of Kuan-yin described in, 141; *shakumon*, 190
love, supernatural, 49; three kinds of attitudes about, 65
loving minds, 65; of Sravakas, 65
lower, five existences, 232; intelligence, 176
Lu Kao, 140
lucency, of Buddhahood, 119
lucid, motionless mind, 107
lung dam-pa, 102
lung ma bstan, 106
Lung-men caves, 140

ma chags, 64
ma-rig-pa, 112
Macedonian conquest, 44
Mādhyamika, 73, 81, 95, 120
Mādyamika-Yogācāra, 84
Māgha, 30
magic worker, 158
magical, creation, 69; transformation, 154
Mahābhārata, 46
Mahābhārata war, 47
Mahābhiniṣkramaṇa, 26
Mahābodhi, 55
mahādānapati, 34
Mahāsannipāta sūtra, 167
Mahāsattvas, 136
Mahāsthāmaprāpta, 31, 41, 227
Mahāsudassana, 54
Mahāvaipulyamahāsamnipātasūtra, 162
Mahāvairocana, Buddha, 176; *sūtra*, 173, 211; Tathāgata, 174
Mahāyāna, 73, 211; and Ekayāna, 171; Bodhisattva of, 20; Chinese monk, 81; difference between Ekayāna and, 218; ethics, 20; in the context of Japanese Buddhism, 171; jātaka tale, 153; mythology, 31; ontological reflections of, 101; path, 230; philosophy, 37; platform of ordination, 213; precepts, 168; *saṃgraha*, 62, 171; stronghold, China, 159; *sūtra-alamkāra*, 104; sutras, 154; tenet of, 66; texts, 159
Mahāyāna Buddhism, development of in China, 138; introduction into China, 138; maturity of, 135
Mahāyānasaṃgraha, 62, 171
Mahāyānic nirvāṇa, 62
Mahāyānistic way towards enlightenment, 97
Mahāyānists, intellectual, 48
Maitreya, 13, 29, 40, 156, 234; future Buddha, 43, 47; one equal to, 234
Maitreyanātha, 98
major, function of the clergy, 209; Rock Edicts, 55
Makhadeva, 54
Makiguchi Tsunesaburo, 203
Makita Tairyo, 140
male, 224; novice, 120
malicious demons, 84
man, 113; Buddha identity, 178; dignity of, 206; of faith, 234; possessed Buddha-nature, 177; religious, 126
Man-ngag lta-ba'i phreng-ba, 113
man's desire and will, 96
Manchu imperial troops, 91
manifestations of a Buddha, 154
manifested forms, 160
Mañjuśrī, 8, 73, 84, 139, 154

mankind, fallibility of, 214; liberation of, 216; salvation of, 214
manovijñāna, 102
mantra, 176
Mantra Ekayāna, 174
manual, ceremonial, 146
manuscript(s), 226; of the *Myōkōninden*, 226; Tun-huang, 220
mappō, 167; crisis, 167; era start, 169, 187; period, 166
Mappō tōmyōki, 167, 169
Māra, 40
Mārkaṇḍeya, 46, 58
Marx-Engels classics, 196
Marxism, 196
Marxists, radical, 196
Maski, 26
mass movement, 193-194
masses, 196; Chinese, 139; welfare of, 206
Master(s), 23, 30; Ch'an, 82; Indian, 95; Yogācāra, 171
material needs, 197
Mathura, 29, 34, 46; Buddhas, 30; inscription, 36; school of sculpture, 30; schools, 46
Mattōsho, 234
maturity of Mahāyāna Buddhism, 135
Mauryan, Empire, 45; regime, 46
Maxwell, James Clark, 118
Māyā, 40, 69
Mazdāh, 40
McArthur, General Douglas, 196
meaning and value which is ultimate, 117
meaning, non dual, 117; of life, 215, 230; of non-cessation, 117; of unorigination, 117
media, 196
Medieval Feudalism, 235
meditation, 132, 168, 214; bodhicitta created by the power of, 102; Bodhisattva, 156, 158; Buddhist, 156; power of, 132; practice of, 183-184; sole practice of, 175; unspecified, 189
Meditation Sutra, 227
Meditational Buddhism, 81
meditative state, 156, 160
meditator, mind of, 156; visualizations of, 156
medium step of the Path of Accumulating Merit, 99
Meiji, 194; Constitution, 195; 201; educational curriculum, 198; Japan, 195; Period, 226; Restoration, 200; Restoration, *myōkōnin* in the period of, 229
memorial services, 209
men, 213; common, 228; holy, 132; of great and superior understanding, 228; rights of, 206
mental, attitude, 204; awareness, 102; capacity, 213; events, 113, 116; makeup, 216; operations, 115; reconstruction, 156; spiritual process, 117
mental factor(s), 106; correlated to the mind, 105; as entourage, 107; five omnipresent, 105
mere sitting, 182
Meridarch Theodoros, 34
merit(s), 20, 27, 32-33, 138, 227; Inferior step of Path of Accumulating, 99; innumerable, 138; making, 154; medium step of the Path of Accumulating, 99; Path of Accumulating, 98; resultant, 183; transfer of, 32, 35, 38, 48, 211; utmost step of the Path of Accumulating, 99
Mesopotamia, 38
Messiah, 4
Messianism, 40
metamorphosis, 117
method, gradual, 81; of conversion, 204
Metteya, 14, 28
mi-gnas-pa, 64
mi-gnas-pa'i mya-ngan-las -'das-pa, 64
Mi-la-ras-pa, 84
Mi-pham, 96
Mi-pham rgya-mtsho, 117
mi-slob-lam, 98
miao, 228
Miao-hao-jen, 227
Miao-se wang yin-yüan ching, 128
Miao Shan, 9
middle, intelligence, 176; Path, 2; doctrine, 216
milieu, common, 223
Milinda-pañha, 39
military, 205; Japan's defeat, 193-194
mind, 103, 113, 116, 178, 213;

a king, 107; a mere perceiving, 106; absence of, 117; categories of, 111; consciousness, 105-106; development of, 103; eight thematizing operations of, 116; having a, 114; keep continuously in, 141; lucid, motionless, 107; mental factors are correlated to, 105; of Wisdom, 125; of the meditator, 156; Rising, 106; settled, 177; sincere, 232; singleness of, 233; tainted by *kleśa*, 106; to steal, 232; troubled, 205; universal, 121
mind-only school, 81
mindful of Amitābha's name, 227
Ming-shan yu-fang chi, 150
ministers, 205
minor, forty-eight precepts, 168
Minshu no hata, 197
Minshushugi kagakusha kyōkai, 197
miracles, 157
miraculous, efficacy, 141; manifestations of Bodhisattvas, 126; stories, 141
misplaced concreteness, 115
missionaries, 154; coming into China, 160; hagiographic accounts of Buddhist, 157
missionary, 219; assault, 204
Mithraism, 40
Mleccha, 58
mnyam-nyid ye-shes,
mo-fa, 167
mock show, 158
model, for religious renewal, 194; for renewal, 221
modern, Capitalism, 235; day *myōkōnin*, 224; Feudalism, 235; institutions, 195; state, 195; technology, 203; urban living, 210
modernity, 210
Moksala, 162
monasteries, 88
monastic, community, 82; discipline, 219; morality, 88; order, 61; saṅgha, 193; system, 23
Möngke Khan, 85
Mongol Khan, 86
Mongolia, 89
Mongols, 85; Eastern, 85; Khoshot, 90
monk(s), 120, 157, 202, 213; Buddhist, 61; neither laity nor, 218; uprighteous, 223
moon, 98; Storage, 167
moral, conscience, 145; defects, cleansing, 114; development, 6; quality, 147; virtues, 127
mother, 117, 229; Goddess, 10; honorable, 231; inseparability of child and, 117; of deity Hārītī, 130
motionless *citta*, 107
motivating power of ascent, 72
motivation, altruistic, 95; to aspire bodhi for the benefit of all sentient beings, 95
mottainai, 229
mounds *(eḍūka)*, 47
Mount Fuji, 205
Mount Vulture, Pure Land on, 190
mountain centres, 226
mṛṣāvāda-parāyaṇāḥ, 58
Mt. Hiei, 165, 213; monastery, 213
mthong-lam, 98
mtshan-gzhi, 105
mudrā, 176
mukti-hitāya, 34, 56
multi-party political system, 206
mundane, 160; relation between the divine and, 160
myō, 228
Myō-hō-ren-ge-kyō, 183; five characters, 183
myōkōnin, 223, 227-228; as a Bodhisattva, 223; in accordance with the society of their time, 228; in the period of Meiji Restoration, 229; modern day, 224; religious views of, 229; textual basis, 223; within the modern democratic society, 229; within the system of Imperial Absolutism, 229; within the Tokugawa Shogunate, 229
Myōkōninden, 224; compilation of, 223; editions of, 225; later versions of, 226; manuscripts of, 226
Myōkōninden-zokuhen, 224
myōkōnin's personality, 226

myriad creatures, 146
mysteries, 118
mystery, of Being, 112
mystic, experiences, 157;
Three Practices, 157; 179;
truth, 179
Mysticism, Ascetic, 84
mythology, 38, 40; of Mahāyāna, 31, 38, 40, 45

Naassene Psalm, Jesus of the, 154
Nādir Shāh, 46
Nāgārjuna, 53, 74
Nagarjunakonda, 37, 45
name, recitation of Amitābha's, 175
names of Bodhisattvas, 155
Namu Amida Butsu, 165
Namu Myōhōrengekyō, 166
Nara, 168, 226, 229; Heian Buddhism, 214, 217
Narendrayaśas, 167
National Statue, 235
nationalism, 195
ñayāsu, 26
needs, historical, 214; material, 197; personal, 199; spiritual, 197
negation, 117; of this world, 73
Nembutsu, 181, 227; adherents, 226; many utterances of, 189; practitioners, 224, 228, 231-233
Neo-Confucian, 148
new, Buddhism, 159; constitution, 215; Creation 42; *English Bible*, 57; Jerusalem, 39; political power, 199
new religions, 193, 215, 219; Buddhist derived, 221; Japan's, 200; of postwar Japan, 200; popularity of, 217; Shinto derived, 194
new religious sects, 209; Nichiren derived, 202
Newton, Isaac, 118
next life, 176
Nibbana, 14
Nichiren, 166, 170, 201, 214; derived new religious sects, 202; doctrine, 202; lexicon, 204; practice, 202; projects, 202; school, 200, 202; as an anti-establishment group, 202; sect, 166; sub-school, 221
Nichiren shōshū, 202; believers, 221
Nidānakatha, 54
Nigliva, 24
Nihon minshushugi bunka renmei, 197
Nihonshoki, 167
Nikāyas, 22, 54
nikkhamisu, 25
Nikolai Cathedral, bell of, 210
nirmāna, 69
nirmāṇakāya, 36, 87, 173
nirupadhiśeṣa-nirvāṇa, 62
Nirvāṇa, 11, 19, 27, 35, 116-117, 178, 213-124; altruistic, 63 *apratiṣṭhita*, 63; final, 64; gate of exit from, 211; Hīnayāna, 62; ideal world of, 72; in which the Bodhisattva does not turn back from either saṃsāra or nirvāṇa, 67; in which the Bodhisattva realizes equanimity and the non-duality of saṃsāra and nirvāṇa, 67; Mahāyānic, 62-63; non-dialectical, 63; not clung to, 64; ultimate, 62; Unstable, 63
nirvānatva, 65
nirvāṇic ideal, 72
Nishida philosophy, 196
niṣkram, 26, 55
no distinction between monk and laity, 218
no-self, 10
Noble Eightfold Path, 24
Noble Ones, Path of the, 98
noesis, 212
noetic principle, 212
non-Buddhist view, 182
non-calculating, 116
non-cessation, meaning of, 117
non-dialectical Nirvāṇa, 63
non-discrimination, 213
non-discursiveness, 116
non-dual meaning and value, 117
non-duality, 67; evolving of, 67; ultimate, 117;
non-dualness, 177
non-enlightenment, 213
non-Mahāyāna schools, 159
non-monastic saṅgha, 218-219
non-ritual facilities, 209
non-thematicness, ultimate, 117
non-turning about, stage of, 66
non-turning back, three stages of, 66

norms, self-evolving, 122
North Wei period, 140
Northern Dynasties, 220
noumenal, 180; Body, 179; essence, 180; reality, 90
novice, female, 120; male, 120
Nunc Dimittis, 39
nuns, 120, 157, 168, 224
nurseries, 209
Nyi-khri rnam-'grel, 106
Nyi-khri-snang-ba, 106

O-mai, 139
Obermiller, E., 63
obfuscation, 113
object for worship, 140
objective, 116; reference, 103
objects, absence of, 117
obscurations, 112
obstacle of defilement, 71
ōbutsu-myōgō, 206
occupation, 235; early period of, 196; policy, 195
office, charisma of, 88
officers, 224
oil, 112
Ōjōden, 223, 235
old, rejection of the, 195
older school, 119
omniscient, 23
one, Buddha Vehicle of the Original Vow, 174; equal to Maitreya-buddha, 234; gold-like, 98; path, 171; Reality, 182; taste *(ekarasa)*, 67; thought of faith, 189; with Amitābha, 181; World Honored, 130
oneness, 177
oneself, 121
ontic sense, 113
ontological reflections of Mahāyāna, 101
opacity of quantification, 113
open and unsubstantial being of all phenomena, 99
openness of the being, 116
opinionatedness, 115, 121
opinions, 115
opponents, 206
optimal operation, 122
Ordeal of Molten Metal, 42
Original Vow, one Buddha Vehicle of the, 174
ordinance, government, 200
ordinary beings, 65; Bodhisattva career, 177; mortal, 84; process of birth and death, 158
ordination, platform for Bodhisattvas, 165; ritual, 157
organic entities, 212
organized religion, 210
Original, Actions of Bodhisattvas, 133-134; Buddha-state, 175; Enlightenment, 182; state of the Buddha, 190; Vow, Ekayāna, 175, Path of Amitabha's, 175
originally enlightened Buddha, 179
organization, 214
orthodoxy, 159
Osaka, 209
ōso-ekō, 213
Other Power, work of the, 231
others, 121; woes of, 233
own, benefit, 98; brand of religion, 206
Ox-soul, 58

pacceka-buddhas, 35
pachinko parlors, 210
packhorse drivers, 224
Padmasambhava, 113, 116
pain, quiescene of, 65
Pakistan, 36, 43
Pāli, 22; bodhisatta, 20; scriptures, 19
pan-chiao, 214
Pañcaviṃśati-sahāsrikālokā, 106
Pañcaviṃśatisahāsrikāprajñāpāramitāsūtra, 162
Panjab, 46
Pao-chüan, 143
paradoxical birth, 68
paralysis, 229
paramārtha-satya, 212
Paramārtha Vehicle, 174
Paramārthadharmavijayasūtra, 162
pāramitā(s), 103, 175, 230; practices, 177; practice of the six, 97
pārarthālambanā, 95
paratantra-svabhāva, 212
paribbājaka, 54
parikalpita-svabhāva, 212
parinirvāṇa, 67, 160
parinispanna-svabhāva, 212
parish, clergy, 209; duties, 209; members, 209; system, 195; temples, 209

parishioners, 208
parliamentary practices, 206
part-time keepers of temples, 209
party guideline, 199
paryavasāna, 211
passions, despicable, 232; evil, 175
past, 134; Bodhisattvas, 135; knowledge of the, 129; lives and deeds, 129; lives of the Buddha, 126
Path, 182; Five, 97; Noble Eightfold, 24; of Accumulating Merit, 98, inferior step of, 99, medium step of, 99, utmost step of, 99; of Amitābha's Original Vow, 175; of Contemplation, 98; of Intuition, 98; of the Noble Ones, 98; of Training, 98-100; one, 171; śīla-samādhi system, 214; to liberation, 23; Ultimate, 98
pathological subjectivism, 122
patience, 232
Patika, 34
Patna, 26
pattern(s), behavioral, 120; of existence, 154
Pausa, 30
peak, 216; of wisdom, 211, 216
peace, world, 206
peasants, 214
pen-ho hsiu-hsing, 150
Pen-yeh, 138
people, common, 223; three types of, 172; Tibetan, 81; wicked, 175
People's, Banner, 197; Cultural Conference, 199; Review, 197
perfect, fusion, 173; wisdom, 55
perfected Being, 144
perfections, 232
performance, low level, 113
performing virtuous deeds, 168
period(s), four cosmic, 183; of Decadent Dharma, 167; theory of three, 167
persecution, 202; of Buddhism, 82, 167
Persepolitan form, 44
person, beautiful, 227; charisma of, 88; evil, 228; excellent, 227; lay, female, 120; male, 120; rare, 227, 234; superior, 234; wonderful, 234; wonderfully likeable, 227
personal, challenge, 230; cravings, 42; deity, 147-148; decision, 42; enlightenment, 159; experience, 204; freedom, 195; needs, 199; outlook on life, 211
perverted doctrines, 203
perversion, 207
Phag-mo-gru, 86; dynasty, 89
'Phags-pa, 85; Lama, 85
phala-jñāna, 62
phala-prahāṇa, 62
Phantasma Bodhisattvas, 155-156, 158
phantom, being, Christ as a, 159; figure, 154
phantomry, 155
phenomena, of the Bodhisattva, 106; open and unsubstantial being of all, 99-100; religious, 194; wholesome, 105; worship of natural, 147
phenomenal, manifestations, 180; plane, 180
phenomenologists, 194
phenomenology, of bodhicitta, 95; of religion, 221
phenomenon, new religions as socio-religious, 194; social, 194, 200
philology, 111
philosophers, Tibetan, 96
philosophical, doctrine of Śūnyatā, 32; positivism, 111; principles, 216; thought, Buddhist, 215; Tibetan texts, 95
philosophy, Buddhist, 103; causal, 146; experiential, 193; Nishida, 196; of action, 146; religious, 126
Phyag-na rdo-rje, 85
physical, forms, 160; life of Śākyamuni, 158; matter, 160
physics, 116, 118
pien-wen, 143
pigeon, 128
pilgrimage, 142; places of, 142
pilgrims, 142; centres for, 139
pillars, Aśoka's, 25
Pingala, 130
pitāmaha, 36
place, of enlightenment, 227-228; of rebirth, 69
plain areas, 226

playfulness of Being, 113
pleasure, 122
poems on scenery, 142
poisons, five, 116; three, 116
polemic, 160
political, action (collective), 197; activist, 196; and social reforms, 91; arena of Japan, 206; corruption, 206; instrument, 207; structure, 207; Tibetan history, 81
political power, 223; new, 199
politics, clean, 207
pollution, incidental, 116
polymer intrusion, 118
popular, Buddhism, 22, 31; imagination, 118
popularity, of Kuan-yin worship, 141; of the new religions, 217
portable radios, 210
portrait of Buddha, 127
positivistic ideologies, 122
post, exilic Judaism, 40; Imitative Dharma period, 167; Mauryan India, 53; Nara period, 218
postwar, constitution, 200; Japan, 200, 215; period, 208
Poṭṭhapādā, 54
Potsdam Declaration, 195
power(s), 27, 32, 139, 158; new political, 199; of Kuan-yin in the Lotus Sutra, 141; of meditation, 132; saving, 31; spiritual, 203; supernatural, 127; 130; 136; work of the Other, 231
practice(s), 211-212; capacity to, 232; causal, 183; Ekayāna principle and, 214; enlightenment apart from, 182; enlightenment identity, 183; Great, 182; Nichiren, 202; of belief, 184; of bodhicitta, 98; of goodness, 232; of meditation, 183-184; of the six pāramitās, 97; of Zen, 183; pāramitā, 177; parliamentary, 206; power, 179; simplifying doctrine and, 214; sundry, 227; Three Mystic, 176, 179; trance, 156; vow to, 230
practitioner, Lotus, 202; of the *nembutsu*, 224, 228, 231-233
praise, 227
praised by the Buddhas, 234
Prajāpati, 36
prajñā, 71, 103, 138, 168, 214
Prajñā-pāramitā, 39, 100, 159; literature, 114; sūtras, 68
Prākrit, 35, 53
prakṛti-viśuddhi, 62
praṇidhāna, 69
praṇidhi, 97
praṇidhicitta, 100; essential difference between *prasthānacitta* and, 99
Prasenajit, King, 129
prasthāna, 97
prasthānacitta, 99-100; essential difference between *praṇidhicitta* and, 99
pratirūpaka, 167
pratiṣṭhā, 64
pratītya-samputpāda, 24, 70
pratyeka-buddhas, 31, 35, 65, 130
prayoga-mārga, 98
pre-Buddhist, Chinese tradition, 144; kingdom, 83
pre-natal existence as a Bodhisatta, 53
precept(s), 157, 168-170; Bodhisattva, 170; Ekayāna, 168; *endon*, 188; essence of the, 169; formless, 157; for spiritual cultivation, 125-126; Hīnayāna, 168; Mahāyāna, 168; religious, 126; ten major, 168, 170; Tendai Mahāyāna, 168; three groups of pure, 168, 170; Three Refuges, 170; violation of, 167
Precious Scroll, literature, 143; on Hsiang Mountain, 143; of the Kuan-yin Fisherwoman, 143
prejudice, 111
present, 134; all-pervasively, 113
present body, becoming a Buddha in the, 177
presence, transfiguring, 14
previous sins, 43
priests, 168, 224
primary, cognitiveness, 121; vow, 211
primitive Buddhism, 19, 43
primordial element of Buddha nature, 98

Prince, Khöden, 85; Kubilai, 85; Shōtoku, 171-172, 193, 218, 220
Princess, Ugly, 129
principle, 125, 138, 180; Ekayāna, 214; noetic, 212; of religious freedom, 207; philosophical, 216; Pure Land, 181
pristine cognitiveness, 112; self existent, 115-116
priya, 36
pro-Buddhist court, 83
process, 118-119; developing, 193; evolutionary, 119, 121; experiental, 213; feedback, 212, 216; mental-spiritual, 117; of Bodhisattva's perfecting wisdom, 212; qualitative, 117; spiritualizing, 213
Prodigal Son, 39
professional status, 204
profits, immeasurable and limitless, 143
proletarian, government, 197; revolution, 196; writers, 196
propaganda literature, 204
prophecy, 46
propitious phenomena of the Bodhisattva, 106
prosperity, 70; of the society, 206
prostitutes, 224
protected by, Amitābha's spiritual light, 234; the Buddhas, 234
provisional teachings, 172, 174
psychological stress, 210
pseudo-intellectualism, 203
P'u-hsien, 139
P'u-sa pen-yeh ching, 133
Pu-sa pen-yüan ching, 127
P'u-sa shih-chu hsing-tao p'in, 134
P'u-t'o-lo-chia shan chuan, 143
P'u-t'o Mountain, 139
puae, 35
public, bathhouses, 210; Japanese, 224; services, 209
pūjā, 34-37, 227
pūjāyai, 35
pūjayiṣyanti, 59
Pulinda, 58
puṇḍarīka, 227-228
puñña, 14
punishment, 132
puṇya, 32, 36-37, 103
puṇyaśālā, 36
pure, 213; three groups of precepts, 168, 170
Pure Land, 4, 37, 214, 230, 233; birth in, 166, 169; Bodhisattva in the, 181; Ekayāna ideal, 174; of Eternity, 183; on Mount Vulture, 190; Principle, 181; School, 218; sects, 165; teachings, 169; texts, 233
Pure Realm, 227, 231
purification of the Buddha land, 66
purity, 190; transparent, 113
pursuit, 119
Pythagoras, 39

qualities, three superior, 102
quantification, opacity of, 113
quarks, 118
quasars, 118
qualitative process, 117
quality, 116; initial transparent, 114
quantifiable entity, 117
quick attainment of Buddahood, 175-176
quiescence, 64; of pain, 65
quintessence, 112

radical Marxists, 196
raids of Tīmūr, 46
rain cloud, 144
Rajula, Great Satrap, 34
Ral-pa-can, 82
rang-byung-gi ye-shes, 115
Rang-byung rdo-rje, 87
rang-don, 121
rape seeds, 231
rare person, 227, 234
rationalism, 111
Ratnagotra-vibhāga, 68
Ratnaketu, 155, 162
rdo-rje, 114
rdo-rje sems-pa, 115
rdzong, 86
real, 213; world of saṃsāra, 72
realities, historical, 216
reality, 115, 178; as-it-is, 230; dynamics of, 118; immanent principle, 190; noumenal, 90 one, 182; saṃsāric, 72

realization of the spiritual, 215
realize aspiration for enlightenment, 97
Realizing Attitude, 97, 100
realm, of dharmas, 135-136; of human life, 156
rebels, 142
rebirth, 69, 87, 210; future, 132; spiritual, 8
reborn, 45; as an animal, 145
recitation of Amitābha's name, 175
reclining, 229
Record on the P'u-t'o lo-chia Mountain, 143
recreation of a new socio-religious human configuration, 215
Red-Hat Karma-pa, 89
Red Purge of 1950, 197
reflect, 233
reformation movement, 88, 91
reformed teachings, 88
reforms, social and political, 91
refuge, three precepts, 170
regent, 86
reincarnation, 87-88; child, 91
Reissner-Nordstrom black hole, 123
Reiyū-kai, 200
rejection of the 'old', 195
rejoice, 233
relation between the divine and mundane, 160
reliable, expertise, 119; impetus, 119
relics, 159
religion(s), 200; animistic, 81; Buddhist derived new, 221; comparative studies of, 161; democratization of, 199; established, 193, 223; folk, 216, 219; freedom of, 200, 215; historians of, 194; institutionalized, 211; Japanese, 194; Japan's new, 200; new, 193-194, 200, 215, 219; organized, 210; own brand of, 206; phenomenology of, 221; popularity of the new, 217; postwar Japan new, 200; shamanic, 83; Shinto, derived new, 194; study of, 159; unspiritual quality of folk, 210
religious, behavior of the Japanese, 209; consciousness, 230, Japanese, 199; culture of Tibet, 91; experience, 126; founder, 148; goal, 148; historiography, 83; leader, 145; literature, 142; man, 126; organization, 200; phenomenon, 194; philosophy, 126; precepts, 126; principle of freedom, 207; renewal, model for, 194; sect, 201, new, 209, Nichiren-derived, 202; slogan, 207; system, 160; thought, socio-psychological implications of, 211; traditions, Chinese, 144; views, 229, of the myokonin, 229
renaissance of Buddhism, 83
renewal, fossilization and, 217; model for, 221
reputation, 232
required knowledge, 128
residue of conditioned life, 182
resolve, 20, 27; earnest, 43
resonance, 115
response, 142; mechanism, 120
responsiveness, 113
resultant merits, 183
retainers, 224
Revelation, 39; of the absolute truth, 173
reverence to the elderly, 132
revolution, 196, 199; proletarian, 196; socio-political, 197; violent, 197
revolutionary ideas, 197
reward, 132
rGyan-snang (*Abhisamaya-alamkāra-āloka*), 101, 106
rift, 135
rig-'dzin level, 120-121
right, Dharma, 167, 170; practice of belief, 184
rightly established group, 234
rights of men, 206
rigs-kyi sems, 115
Rin-spungs lords, 89
Rin-spungs rdzong, 87
Rinzai, 169
Rinzai Zen, 165, 170, 219
rising mind, 106
Rissho kōsei-kai, 200
Rites, Book of, 146; festivals and, 139; funeral, 209
Ritsu, 180
Rizen, 224
Rlangs family, 89
rnam-par rig-pa, 105
rnam-par shes-pa, 105

rNying-ma-pa, 118
robbery, 139, 141
Rock Edict, Eighth, 25;
  Major, 55
Rock inscription, Asoka's,
  44
Rong-zom Chos-kyi bzang-po,
  113
ṛṣi, 46
rtogs, 115
rules of conduct, 169
rural, communities, 207;
  population, 200
Russian songs, 198

Sa-kya Paṇḍita, 85
Sa-skya 'regency', 86, 89;
  sect, 85
sabbaññu, 23
sacrifices to Heaven, 147
ṣad-pāramitā, 135
Sadāprarudita, 153
Saddharmapuṇḍarīka Sūtra, 31,
  39, 42, 72, 165, 170, 193;
  Ekayāna teaching of, 172
sadomasochism, 121
safety, search for, 140
sage, kings, 144
Saha world, 183
Sāhi Huviṣka, 36
Śaichō, 165, 168, 213
Saichō's teaching, 180
ṣaints, Hīnayānic, 65
Ṣaivism, 46
Sakas, 43, 46
Sakastan, 34
Sakro, 131
sakta, 22, 54
Śākya group, 160
Śākyamuni, 72, 153, 173; as
  a Bodhisattva, 160; Buddha,
  183; former lives of, 153;
  life and person of, 158;
  physical life of, 158; two
  events, 67
salvation, of all beings, 172;
  of mankind, 214; through
  Amitābha's vow, 181; universal, 218
śama, 67
samādhi(s), 69, 155, 162, 168;
  four, 173, 189; lists of, 158
Samantabhadrā, 139
Ṣaṃghadevā, 158
samatā-jñāna, 67
śamatha, 172
saṃbhāra-mārga, 98
saṃbhogakāya, 36, 173
saṃbodhi, 20, 24-27
sambodhi-kāmanā-sahagatā, 95
Saṃbuddha, 40
saṃcintya, 68; *bhavapratikāṅkṣī*,
  68, *bhavopapatti*, 68; *upapatti-parigraha*, 68
saṃkleśasyanurakṣaṇā, 70
saṃpatti, 70
saṃsāra, 20, 116-117, 178, 213;
  Bodhisattva realizes equanimity
  and nonduality of, 67; *nirvāṇa-apratiṣṭhatā*, 63; nirvāṇa in
  which the bodhisattva does not
  turn back from, 67; real world
  of, 72
samsaric, defilements, 71;
  entities, 65; life, Bodhisattva
  enters into, 68; reality, 72;
  world, defilements of, 70
saṃsārātyāga, 70
saṃskāra-skandha, 104
saṃskṛta, the compounded, 67
samudāgama, 66
samurai, 214, 224
saṃvara-śīla, 168
saṃvṛtti-satya, 212
samya-saṃbuddha (sic), 36
Sanchi, 46
saṅgha, 215; bodhisattva doctrine
  secularization of, 194; Buddhist,
  195; lay, 193, 203, 218; monastic, 193; non monastic, 218-219
Saṅghadeva, 163
Saṅghilā, 36
Sangyō-gisho, 193, 213, 218;
  Shotoku as author of, 220
sañj, 54
sanjujōkai, 168
sanmitsu, 176
Sanskrit, 22, 26, 35; bastard, 53;
  Buddhist, 20, 22, 38; only, 115;
  Vinaya from, 159
Ṣanta Claus, 48
Ṣāntideva, 5, 101
Śāntiśrī, 37, 57
śaraṇa, 57
Ṣāriputra, 4
Śāriputrābhidharmaśāstra, 163
Sarnath, 29-30
sarva-dukkha-pahānārttham (sic), 36
sarva-loka-hitāya, 33
sarva-satvanaṃ hitā-sukhārtthaṃ
  (sic), 36
sarva-loka-hita-sukhāvaha, 37
sarvasa Sakrastansa puyae, 34
Sarvāstivādin, 34
Satrap of Cukhsa, 34

satta, 22
sattva, 22, 113-114, 117
sattvārtha-krīya-śīla, 168
save, vow to, 155
saving power, 31
savior, 42, 158; Bodhisattva's role as, 144; Gnostic, 158
sbyor-lam, 98
scenery, poems on, 142
scholar(s), Chinese, 137; of Buddhism, 194; Tibetan, 95; Western, 95
school(s), 101; all-encompassing, 219; believers in, 201; children, 198; divergent, 153; elementary, 198; Mathura, 46; newer, 119; Nichirin, 200, 202; non-Mahāyāna, 159; of Heian Buddhism, 219; older, 119; Pure Land, 218; secondary, 198;
Schwarzschild black hole, 123
science, 111
scribes, 159
scripture(s), different versions of, 138; fabricated, 141; on the accumulation of the six Perfections, 127; Pāli, 19; selecting, 214; spurious, 141; translated, 128
sculpture, Mathura school of, 30
Se-ra, 88
sea, *rakṣasa*, 127; trades, 139; treasure, 217, 182
search for safety, 140
second *bhūmi*, 70
secondary school, 198
sect(s), Bhāgavata, 45; founder of the new, 184; new religious, 209; Nichiren, 166, derived, new, 202; Pure Land, 165; religious, 201; Sa-skya, 85; Yellow-hat, 88-89
sectarian, divisions, 153; dogmas, 195
secular, 211-213; benefits, 210; landlords, 208
security, yearning for, 140
seeker, 184
Seigai, 224
Seigan-ichibutsujō, 174
Seikuro, 229
selecting scriptures, 214
self, effort, 7; enlightened, 179; evolving norms, 122; existent pristine cognitiveness, 115-116; expression, 195, 215; independence, 197; repentence, 130
selfishness, 232
selfless generosity, 131
semi-conductor and insulator fields, 118
sems, 112-113, 115-117, 121
sems-byung, 113
sems-can, 114
sems-dpa', 113, 116
sems-las byung-ba, 106
sems-nyid, 113, 115
sems-pa, 104
Senjakushū, 228
sense, impression theory, 111; of belonging, 205; perception, 111
senses, five, 116
sentient being, 115, 129, 132, 135, 178, 182; giving benefit to, 168
separation of state and Shinto, 199
series of births and deaths, 153
serious diseases, 141
sesame seed, 112
sets of cultivation, 134
settled mind, 177
Seven days of the Sword, 28
700th anniversary of Shinran, 208
750th anniversary of Honen, 208
seventh *bhūmi*, 70, 100
sgom-lam, 98
Shahbazgarhi, 26
Shakai hyōron, 197
shaku-buku, 204
shamanic religion, 83
shamanism, 91
shamisen, 224
Shan-tao, 167, 227
Shanghai Yüeh Company, 152
Shaoshyant, 40, 42
sheer lucency, 113
Shen, 149
Shen-mo chia, 131
Sheng-man ching, 220
shepherd, Bodhisattva as an infallible, 82
shes, 121
Shes-rab-kyi pha-rol-tu-phyin-pa, 114
Shigatse, 88
shih, 137
Shih-chu ching, 138
shih huo-hsiang, 134
shih ming, 134
Shih-ti ching, 133, 135
Shih-ti p'in, 138

shih-ting, 134
shikaku, 178
shikan-tada, 175, 182
Shin-sen Myōkōninden, 235
Shingon, 165, 168, 201, 219
Shingon-ichijō, 174
shinkō-shukyō, 193
Shinran, 7, 165, 181, 218; *hongaku* theory, 181; 700th anniversary of, 208
Shinshu teachings, 233
Shinto, derived new religions, 194; ghost of, 207; separation of state and, 199; shrine, 210
Shō gonjutsu kyō, 171
Shōbōgenzō, 182
Shōmangyō-gisho, 218
shopkeepers, 199-200
shortcut to Buddhahood, 176
Shōshin Ge, 228
Shōtoku, as the author of the *Sangyo-gisho*, 220, Prince, 171-172, 193, 218, 220
Shraosha, 42
Shugo kokkai shō, 172
Shutaisei, group, 196; theory, 197
side-jobs, 209
Siddhārtha Gautama, 26, 30
Siddhattha Gotama, 19, 25
sign, *bodhicitta* that is elicited by, 102
signs, 102
śikṣā, 62
Sikṣānanda, 136
śīla, 72
śīla-samādhi path system, 214
Śīladharma, 136
silver money, 231
simplifying doctrine and practice, 214
sincere, mind, 232; wish for enlightenment, 97
singleness of mind, 233
Sircar, D.C., 34
Sister Irma, 1
sitting, 229
Śiva, 45; beneficient aspects of, 47
Śivi, 128
Six, Dynasties, 140; *gatis*, 69; elements, 176; pāramitās, 72, 184, developing of, 97, practice of, 97; perfections, 135, 230, Scripture on the accumulation of, 127
sixth, *bhūmi*, 70; Rock Edict, 33
skill-in-means, 211, 215-216
skillful means, 72
sku, 112
sky, 119; clear, 114
smon-sems, 99, 101
sNang-srid kha-sbyor bdud-rtsi bcud-thigs 'khor-ba thog-mtha' gcod-pa'i rgyud phyi-ma, 116
snares of life, 159
Snows, Land of, 81
so-sor thar-pa level, 120
social, and political reforms, 91; injustice, 202; phenomenon, 194, 200; responsibility, 119, 121; *Review*, 197; status, 235; strata, 193; stratum, 210; structure, Japanese, 210
socialism, humanistic, 206
Socialists, 196-197
societies, Buddhist, 81; capitalistic, 197
society, industrialized, 211; Japanese, 223; *myōkōnin* in accordance with, 228; *myōkōnin* within the democratic, 229; prosperity of the, 206
socio-political, changes, 199; crisis, 193, 200; revolution, 197; situation in China, 139
socio-psychological implication of religious thought, 211
socio-religious, behavior, 211; phenomenon, new religions as, 194; recreation of a new human configuration, 215
Śōdasa, 34
Sojun, 224
Sōka Gakkai, 193, 199-200, 202-203, 221; believers, 201; charismatic personalities of, 204; mecca, 205; political federation, 205; seiji remmei, 205
Soka Kyoiku Gakkai, 203
sokushin jōbutsu, 91, 176, 177, 213
solid-state field, 118
song(s), 90; of Simeon, 39; Russian, 198
son(s), of the Buddhas, 136; of the clan, 135; of the Most Victorious, 135
sopadhiśeṣa-nirvāṇa, 62
Sopara, 26
sorcery, 203

soteriological, angle, 138; role of the Bodhisattva, 81; significance, 126
Sōto Paper, 208
Sōtō Zen, 165, 218-219
source of conflict, 211
South, Bihar 26; India, 129
sovereignty, 177
space, 176; empty, 135-136; empty and eternal, 137
Space Age, Bodhisattvas of the, 49
specific, characteristics, 116; intention, 98-99
speech, freedom of, 206
Speyer, J., 63
spheres, three world, 112; transcendent, 156
Sphuṭārtha, 106
spirit of attainability, 132
spirits, Bodhisattva, 6; demons and, 139
spiritual, 210-213; and temporal head of Tibet, 90; contentment, 230; cultivation, 125-126, 132; energy, 121; experience, 210; is trans-historical, 212; journey, 26; light, protected by Amitābha's, 234; map, 145, 148; needs, 197; operations, 116; organization, 119; power, 203; realization of the, 215; rebirth, 8; situation, 233; vacuum, 195, 215
spirituality, 115
spiritualization, 194, 211, 213
spiritualizing process, 213
splits within Buddhism, 153
spontaneously present, 113
Spooner, D.B., 44
spread of Kuan-yin worship in China, 140
sprul-sku, 87, 90
sprul-pa, 84
spurious scriptures, 141
squad leaders, 205
śramaṇa, 218
śrāvaka, 21, 31; light of the, 53; loving minds of, 65; turbidities, 62
śrāvakayāna, 171
Śrāvastī, 29
Sri Lanka, 10, 33, 54
Śrīmāladevī, 218
Śrīmālādevīsiṃhanāda-sūtra, 193, 220
Śrīmālāsiṃhanāda-sūtra, 171, 174
srog, 84
St. Ignatius of Antioch, 158
St. Josaphat, 39
St. Luke's Gospel, 39
stage(s), 119; of non-turning about, 66; tenth, 125
state, 89, 184; church and, 91; separation of Shinto and, 199
Shinto, 199, 203
state(s), of meditative trance, 155; of non-retrogression, 176; trance, 158
statistics, 194
Stcherbatsky, Th., 63
steal, mind to, 232
Sthiramati, 66
stone-carving, 44
stories, Buddhist, 3
story-telling, 23
straw mat, 231
stress, 203; psychological, 210
Strīvivartavyākaraṇasūtra, 163
students, 200
study, academic, 88; of religion, 159
stupa, 34, 59; Bharhut, 22
sub-schools, 201
subjective, 116; reference, 103
subjectivism, pathological, 122
sublime wisdom, 68
substance, 116
succession, 214
Sudaṣa, 34
śūdras, 37, 45, 58
suffering, 132, 140
Suffering Servant, 38
Sufism, 74
Sukhāvatī, 31, 72, 166
Sukhāvatīvyūha, 31, 37
Sukhāvatīvyūhôpadeśa, 211
Sumati, 54
Sumedha, 25, 27, 54
sumo wrestlers, 224
sun, 144
sundry practices, 227
Śuṅga, 23; kings, 45
śūnya, 48
śūnyatā, 32, 68, 73, 102, 126; first awareness of, 98
Śūnyavāda, 48
superhuman emanator, 90
superior, 227; person, 234; three qualities, 102
supermen, 49

supernal knowledge, 55
supernatural, love, 49; power of of the Buddhas, 136; powers, 127, 130
supernormal, activities, 157; thorough and intrinsic cognition, 98
superstitious ideas, 203
supremacy of the Lotus Dharma, 202
supreme, and consummate virtues, 182; body, 70; enjoyment, 70; truth, 212; Wisdom, 128
Śūraṅgamasamādhisūtra, 160
surpassing intention, 98
Surūpa, King, 128
sūtra, 227
sutta, 28
Sutta Piṭaka, 21-22
Suvarṇaprabhāsa (uttamarāja) sūtra, 162
Suvikrāntavikramiparipṛcchaprajñāpāramitāsūtra, 162
Suzuki, D.T., 223, 235
svabhāva dharmakāya, 174
svabhāva, three, 212
Śvetāśvatara Upaniṣad, 44, 55
Swat, 36; Balambat, 44; relic casket, 34
sword, 141; Seven days of the, 28
Śyāmaka, 131-132, 149
symbiotic theocracy, 91

Ta'i Si-tu, 86
tadbhāva form, 57
Taika Reform 220
Taiseki-ji, 205
taiso, 219
Takht-i-Bahi, 35
taking a vow, 160
T'an ching, 157
T'an luan, 72
T'ang Dynasty, 82, 143, 157, 162; history of, 83
tantra, 156
Tantric, literature, 103; materials, 156; texts, 88
Tao, ten places of, 133
Tao-cho, 167
tapestry, 122
target subject, 204
Tathāgata, 63, 137, 181, 214; of Unhindered Light, 182; Universal Vow, 228
tax, 82
Taxila, 29, 34; copper plate, 34; silver scroll, 29, 35
tea ceremony, 209
teachable concept, 102
teachers, 160, 198; hagiographic accounts of Buddhist, 157
teachers' unions, Communist, 198
teaching(s), 209; Buddha's, 232; Ekayāna of the *Saddharmapuṇḍarīka-sūtra*, 172; esoteric, 173; exoteric, 169, 173; provisional, 172, 174; Pure Land, 169; Saicho's, 180; Shinshu, 233; temporary, 171-172; true, 171
technology, 203
teenagers, 210
telos, 119
temmu government, 220
Temple(s), 208; Buddhist, 210; Honganji, 232-233; part-time keepers of, 209; parish, 209; Tōdaiji, 168; village parish, 208
temporal Buddha, 190
temporary teachings, 171-172
Ten, actions, 134; benefits, 233; *bhūmis*, 72; clevernesses of Bodhisattvas, 133; concentrations, concentrations of the Bodhisattvas, 133; dharmas, 133; directions,132-133, 135; doctrines, 173; Dwellings, 134; 138; endurances, 134; flying methods of Bodhisattvas, 133; goals, 134; kinds of attainment of fruit, 66; knowledges, 134; major precepts, 168, 170; methods of confessing, 133; perfections, 230; places of Bodhisattvas' vows, 133; places of Tao, 133; positions, 134; positions of the Bodhisattva, 133; seals of Bodhisattvas, 133; towns of Bodhisattvas, 133
tenant-farmers, 196, 208
Tendai, 165, 180, 201, 235; Mahāyāna precepts, 168; priest, 169
tendencies, 112
tenet of Mahāyāna, 66
Tenri-kyō, 194
tension, 213

Tenth Stage, 125
territories, 205
testimony, 197
Thailand, 10, 33
the cross, 159
theg-pa, 119
thematicness, ultimate non-, 117
thematization(s), 117; host of, 113; in experience, 113
theocracy, 85, 87; ghost of Shinto, 207; immanent, 206; symbiotic, 91
theoretician, 196
Theravāda, Buddhology of, 45; counsels of, 42
Theravādins, 48
Theüdora, 34
theif, 231
Thirteenth Rock Edict, 27
Thou, 120
thought, momentary, 180; of bodhi, 95
Thusness, true, 182
three, aspects of time, 112; Bodies, 179; calamities, 183; fires of attachment, anger, and delusion, 129; groups of pure precepts, 168, 170; Jewels, 25, 130; kinds of attitudes about love, 65; kinds of fire, 128; Learnings, 62; levels of attachment and detachment, 64; life worlds, 112; Mystic Practices, 176, 179; periods of Dharma, 166; period theory, 167; poisons, 116; Refuges, 170; stages of non-turning back, 66; superior qualities, 102; *svabhāva* theory, 212; types of human beings, 64; types of learning, 184; types of people, 172; typologies of Bodhisattva literature in Chinese, 144; vehicles, 171; world spheres, 112; world system, 132; worlds, 116
thugs, 112
ti, 138
Ti-tsang, 139
Tibet, 81, 156; Central, 83, 86; religious culture of, 91; spiritual and temporal head of, 90
Tibetan, 22; Buddhism, 118; Court, introduction of Buddhism to, 82; empire, 83; government, 91; people, 81; philosophers, 96; philosophical texts, 95; political history, 81; scholar, 95
tiger, 10
time, cyclic, 43; eons of, 158; three aspects of, 112
Timur, raids of, 46
tisraḥ śikṣāh, 168
Toda Jōsei, 203
Tōdaiji Temple, 168
Tokuda, 196
Tokugawa, 194; feudalism, 195; regime, 224
Tokugawa Shogunate, *myōkōnin* within the, 229
Tokyo, 209; Boogie-woogie, 196
tolerance, 216
total life and experience, 213
tou-sa, 133
Tou-sa ching, 133
Toyama, 233
tradition(s), Chinese religious, 144; docetic, 154; folk, 210; Japanese Buddhist, 194, 218, 221; Japanese Buddhist historical, 215; pre-Buddhist Chinese, 144
Training, Path of, 98-100
trance, practices, 156; states, 158; states of meditative, 155
transcendent, 159-160; being, bodhisattvas as a, 160; spheres, 156
transfer, merits, 211; of merit, 32, 35-38, 48
transfiguring presence, 14
transformation, 155; magical, 154
transhistorical, spiritual, 212
translated scriptures, 128
translation bureau of An Shih-kao, 153
translation, mechanical, 111; of canonical texts, 82; techniques of, 133
transmigration, 117
transmission, of Buddhism, 187; of the Dharma, 216
transparency and lucency of Buddhahood, 119
transparent purity, 113
transport carriers, 224
treasure(s), 145, 233; from the sea, 127; sea, 183; text, 90
trials and errors, 216
trichilocosm, 112
trikāya, 36
Triṃśikā, 62
triratna, 25, 34
troubled mind, 205

troubles, 198
true, cause for birth, 233; disciple, 234; nature, 169; teachings, 171; Thusness, 182
trust, 32, 230
truth(s), Four Noble, 24; revelation of the absolute, 173; supreme, 212
Tsa Pao-tsang ching, 128
Ts'ai-hua, 227
tshogs-gnyis, 102
tshogs-lam, 98; *'bring*, 99; *chen-po*, 99; *chung-ngu*, 99-100
Tsong-kha-pa, 88, 96, 104
Tsukamoto Zenryu, 140
Tun-huang cave, 143, manuscript, 220
turbidities, of the Bodhisattva, 62; of the five lower existences, 233; Śrāvaka's, 62
turbulent waters, 139
Tuṣita heaven, 53, 131
twenty-two steps of bodhicitta, 98, 100
two, accumulations, 102; steps with regard to bodhicitta, 96; vehicles, 171
typological schemes, 160
typologies, of Bodhisattva literature in Chinese, 144
typology, 126

U-dum-bstan, 82
ubhaya-kula, 57
ubhaya-loka, 57
ubhaya-loka-hita-sukhāvaha, 37
udyāna-yātrā, 69
Ugly Princess, 129
ultimate, abolishment of impurities, 113; aim, 71; aspect, 102; Enlightenment, 183, leading others to, 98, of the Buddha, 172; freedom, 119; indivisibility, 116; liberation, 84; meaning and value, 117, nirvāṇa, 62; non-duality, 117; non-thematicness, 117; Path, 98; truth, bodhicitta of, 102
umbrella, 229
unchanging, 117
unchangingness, 116-117
underdog, championing the causes of the, 214
underdogs, 202
understanding, 115; men of great and superior, 228
Underworld, 84
uneasy feelings, 223
Union, affiliated choruses, 197
United States, 195
unity, 205; of the evolutionary force, 121
universal, mind, 121; salvation, 218; support, 127; Vow, 228, 230
unorigination, meaning of, 117
unspecified meditation, 189
unspiritual, 216; qualities of folk religion, 210
Unstable Nirvana, 63
unworthiness, 229
Upaśūnya, 162
upāya, 72, 102
upāya-kauśalya-pāramitā, 48
Upper House, 199; of the Diet, 205
uprighteous monks, 223
utpāda, 105
utmost step of the Path of Accumulating Merit, 99
utter the name of Tathagata of Unhindered Light, 182, 189

Vairocana, 112
Vaiśālī, 3
Vaiṣṇavism, 46
Vajra, 114, 174
Vajracchedikā, 64; Chinese commentaries on, 64
Vajra Ekayāna, 174
Vajragarbha Bodhisattva, 135-136
Vajrapāṇi, 84, 156, 158
Vajraśekharasūtra, 173
Vajrayāna Buddhism, 83
valour, 114
value, 120, Creating Education Association, 203; non-dual, 117; ultimate meaning and, 117
varjayiṣyanti, 59
Varnasi, 36, 46
various aspects of bodhicitta, 96
Vasubandhu, 62, 67, 104, 171
Vedic, 22; literature, 21
Vehicle(s), Great, 119; of the Original Vow, 174; Paramartha, 174; three, 171; two, 171
venerable country, 101

vibhutva, 69
Vidyutprabhā, 155, 162
vihārayāttā, 25
vijñāna, 105-106
Vijñānavāda, 171
vijñapti, 105
Vijñaptimātratāsiddhi, 62
village, heads, 224; parish-temples, 208
Vimalakīrti, 218
Vimalakīrti Nirdeśa Sūtra, 3, 68, 193
vimuktikāya, 62
vinaya, 159; ceremony, 157; codified, 214; Four-Part, 170; from Sanskrit, 159; *Piṭaka*, 21, 23
violation of precepts, 167
violent revolution, 197
vipaśyanā, 98, 172
Vīrapuruṣaddatta, 37
virtues, 132; four, 179; four of the dharmakāya, 190; human, 131; moral, 127; of Wisdom, 134; supreme and consummate, 182
visions, apocalyptic, 13
Viśiṣṭacāritra, 170, 184
Viṣṇu, 45
visualizations, 118, 156, 158; of the meditator, 156
vllcanic plasmas, 118
vow(s), 20, 25, 27, 71, 158; and Actions, 134; as works, 137; bodhicitta, 99; bodhisattva, 5, 20, 132, 233; disciplinary, 88; eighteenth one, 7; fulfillment of the, 232; of Amida, 231-232; of Bodhisattvas, 135, 157; of goodness, 136; one Buddha Vehicle of the Original, 174; Path of Amitabha's Original, 175; primary, 211; taking a, 160; to practice, 230; to save beings, 155; Universal, 228, 230
Vulture Peak Assembly, 143

walking, 229
wang-ku lai chin, 150
Wasan, 175, 181
water, 176; turbulent, 139; Wisdom, 128-129
way(s), 119; of attaining Buddhahood, 175; of life, 196, 205
wealth, 145
wedding night, 143
welfare of the masses, 206
well-being of the individual, 206
Wen-shu, 139
Western, Asia, 154; Caves, 45; Decan, Buddhist inscriptions of, 37; Kingdom, 83; scholar, 95
White rabbit king, 128
Whitehead, A.N., 115
wholesome phenomena, 105
wicked people, 175
will, 104; man's desire and, 96; of Heaven, 146
wind, 176
wine, 90
wisdom, 5, 23, 27, 71, 102, 132, 168, 184, 211-212, 232; and compassion, 211; ascending of, 74; ascent of, 71; Bodhisattva of, 11; Buddhist notion of, 212; cultivation of, 184; Equality, 67; Ground, 135-136; highest, 65; Mind of, 125; peak of, 211, 216; perfect, 55; process of Bodhisattva's perfecting, 212; sublime, 68; supreme, 128, virtues of, 134, water, 128-129
wish, for enlightenment, 97; to attain bodhi, 95-96
wishful aspiration, 97
without cause and condition, 146
woes of others, 233
womb, 214
women, 90, 213
Wonder-Women, 49
wonderful, 228; person, 234
wonderfully likeable person, 227
work of the Other Power, 231
working class, 197, 199
works, of Bodhisattvas, 136; vows as, 137
world(s), affirmation of, 73; enlightenment in this, 169; Honored One, 130; meaningful, 121, negation of, 73; of Buddhas, 136; peace, 206; Saha, 183, three, 116; three life, 112; three spheres, 112; three systems, 132
worldlings, 154
worldly, fame, 223; happiness, 65; joys, 65
worship, 34-35; object for, 140; of natural phenomena, 147; of the Bodhisattvas, 127, 142; popularity of Kuan-yin, 141

"Wrathful" aspect, 156; Bodhisattva, 156
writer(s), ghost, 220; proletarian, 196
Wu-t'ai Mountain, 139

Yakśa, 128
Yamoto Prefecture, 229
yāna, 119
yang-srid, 87
Yangs-pa-can, 89
yānikas, 65
Yar-lung, region, 90; valley, 83
Yasna, 58
Yast section, 42
ye, 121
ye-shes, 121
yearning for security, 140
years of the gods, 58
Yellow-hat sect, 88-89
Ying-yen chi, 140
Yogācāra, 73, 81; -Mādhyamika, 84; masters, 171
yojanas, 31, 53
yorokobi, 229
Yoshino District, 229
youth, 199; organizations, 198
yü-ch'iu-fo che, 150
yü-lan Kuan-yin pao-chüan, 143
yu shih-ti chu, 150
Yüan Wei dynasty, 142
Yudhisṭhira, 58
yuga, 47, 58

Zarathushtra, 40
Zen, 201, 214; Chinese, 169; discipline, 196; Japanese Sōtō, 219; practice of, 183; Rinsai, 165, 170, 219; Sōtō, 165, 218-219
Zō-ō, 225
Zoroastrianism, 40
Zurvanism, 40